The Human Nature Debate

The Human Nature Debate
Social Theory, Social Policy and the Caring Professions

Harry Cowen

Pluto Press

LONDON · BOULDER, COLORADO

In memory of my mother Sybil Cowen

First published 1994 by Pluto Press
345 Archway Road, London N6 5AA
and 5500 Central Avenue
Boulder, Colorado 80301, USA

97 96 95 94
6 5 4 3 2 1

British Library Cataloguing in Publication Data
A catalogue record for this book is available from the British
Library

Library of Congress Cataloging in Publication Data
Cowen, Harry, 1942–
    The human nature debate: social theory, social policy and the
caring professions / Harry Cowen.
    210p. 21cm.
    Includes bibliographical references and index.
    ISBN 0-7453-0904-6
    1. Man. 2. Philosophical anthropology. 3. Nature and nurture.
4. Man—Animal nature. I. Title.
BD450.C654   1994
128—dc20   94–25613
                                                      CIP

ISBN 0 7453 0904 6 hardback

Designed and produced for Pluto Press by
Chase Production Services, Chipping Norton, OX7 5QR
Typeset from the author's disk by
Stanford DTP Services, Milton Keynes
Printed in Finland by WSOY

Contents

Preface

The initial idea for this book was first mooted in the 1970s when I was was living in Manchester; it was to be part of a series on 'ideas' for workers and was to be published by Pluto Press. It was to be of handbook format; the topic and structure of the book was angled so that it could be used as a political tool in argument, basically for demonstrating conclusively that there was no such thing as human nature. At the time the political climate was ebullient, change from below was still regularly discussed, the Labour government had been in office a number of years. Although unemployment had risen, collectivist organisations were nevertheless strong. Rampant individualism was a frame of mind one associated with American capitalism rather than with British society. I 'shelved' the project, however, in the wake of new directions in my life.

During subsequent years I would keep returning to the topic, frequently sifting through new material on human nature, making jottings, thinking about the subject, but never mustering the time actually to write the book, although I was researching and writing in other academic areas. 'Human nature' figured at various junctures in my teaching, such as philosophies of planning, although less so in the area of social policy; but I carried around the topic in my head. Fortuitously, as it happened, I came across Roger van Zwanenberg of Pluto Press in 1992 during a publisher's reception at the annual conference of the British Sociological Association held at the University of Kent, Canterbury, retold the tale, and so started again, on this occasion for real. Only this time round, some 17 years later, the world is a different place; here in Britain, individualism since 1979 has constituted an icon for anticollectivist policies and self-directed concerns. The 'balance' between east and west world views has clearly tilted towards western capitalist values; mass unemployment grips many parts of society here and in Europe, and pessimism and cynicism are familiar stances. Hence, the reference points and mode of language for discussion have shifted. Ironically, such is the currently available surfeit of titles on postmodernism, I had intended to make no reference to it. This was easier said than done. Postmodernism *is* part of the intellectual sea change, and thus cannot be avoided. A related personal change was the shift in my focus towards how human nature functions as *theory*, which has become a major theme of the book.

The fascination of the human nature debate for me is the way it illustrates that theory need not be sterile or boring. Analysing the assumptions made by any explanation brings one down to basics, showing in what sense an argument or position is ideological or reflects an identifiable world view. Whilst theory may so easily slide into abstraction and seemingly become nothing to do with us, the focus on how we are being portrayed anchors the discussion. Beneath the surface of debates in social theory, a deeper debate is taking place concerning our human nature. Alternatively, the debate may well be conducted overtly, steeped in acrimony.

What has also drawn me consistently to the topic is that it knows no artificial academic disciplinary boundaries. I feel that philosophy, an often exciting subject which by definition must engage with discourse on those features that make us human, exercises no 'natural' monopoly over the topic, despite its classics in the field. But because understanding the nature of human nature is not an abstract undertaking, its concerns intermesh with other cognate disciplines, not least social theory. This is what I have concentrated upon in this book, albeit selectively. Thus there is more extensive discussion of social and psychological theories than of anthropological or linguistic theories. Travelling full circle, however, theory is meaningless unless it connects at some point with practical action. This is why I have chosen to analyse policy issues as juxtaposed to human nature theory, since they illuminate each other. Selection also provides *some* circumscribing boundaries for a topic potentially without limits. I have framed the contents primarily as an introduction to the subject for undergraduates on social science courses, as well as for students doing applied social studies or professional courses. But hopefully it will be of interest to a wider audience. Finally, in the course of producing this book I have received valuable assistance, encouragement and comments on the manuscript from Tony Rosie (always an unstinting source of support) and Mike Sullivan – any errors are clearly my own; thanks also for advice on particular topics to Dee Carter and Mike Littledyke, to Ian Jones for ever ready references and to participants of the stimulating 'caf tutorials' on the state of the nation. Thanks are due to Cheltenham and Gloucester HE college, especially the Department of Community and Social Studies, for making that teaching load a little bit lighter, and to the Pluto Press team for seeing the project through to its conclusion.

December 1993

1

The Human Nature Debate

Introduction

Human nature is a concept with which we are all familiar. As if following Hamlet's advice to his players, the phrases come trippingly on the tongue. Recently, during a British radio interview an ex-champion boxer from the 1930s explained the traditional weekend fights in his Welsh mining valley as 'just human nature'. Statements like 'people are basically greedy' or 'you can't change human nature' are frequently summoned to clinch an argument. From this position, the invocation of 'human nature' appears to express not so much a casual observation as a total perspective, nonetheless powerful for its brevity.

A theory of human nature expresses relationships and underlying assumptions about the world. Indeed, it suggests what it is to be human by providing explanations about human behaviour, events and attitudes. It offers the basis of beliefs about a whole range of human responses and social action. Discussion about human nature has spanned the humanities and the sciences. All great literature from Shakespeare and Goethe to the modern dramas of Ibsen and Becket illuminate the human condition. Stephen Hawking's *Brief History of Time* has opened yet a further explosive chapter questioning accepted views of the cosmos, the certainties of science and the concept of God. Before looking at social sciences it may be useful briefly to present some examples of cognate approaches to explaining human nature – philosophy, anthropology and sociobiology.

Quite clearly, the human nature debate is one of perennial interest to philosophers, who have engaged with the topic through such concepts as personal identity, causality and ethics, striving to answer questions such as 'what are we?', 'where do we come from?', 'what should we do?', and 'where are we going?'. This has led to the study of relationships between language and consciousness, intentionality and purpose, cognition and understanding. Most philosophical debate divides into materialistic philosophies on the one hand and idealistic philosophies on the other, essentially disputes as to whether we are able to transcend ourselves or whether we are bound by the material world. Materialism in philosophy means that whatever exists is matter, or is entirely dependent on matter for its existence. Idealism refers to the notion that what is usually referred to as 'the external world' is created in some way by the mind. Furthermore major intellectual endeavours in other humanistic disciplines have had recourse to philosophy because 'their thinking went to the very root of human existence' (Trigg, 1988, p. 3). The limitation of the philosophical approach *per se* is its traditional mode of rational discourse which relies upon abstract reasoning and analysis.

Anthropology places the emphasis upon the aspects of life that humans create for themselves, namely culture, which is then transmitted to other generations in a social way. It is concerned with the elements of culture that have made humans distinguishable from other species: features such as the making of tools, the creation of language, the regulating of sexual relations through a family system, rites of belief system, and artistic expression. Geertz, a major cultural anthropologist, has neatly summarised the anthropological approach to human nature (Geertz, in Platt, 1965, p. 116):

> Man is to be defined neither by his innate capacities alone, as the enlightenment sought to do, nor by his actual behaviours alone, as much of contemporary social science seeks to do, but rather by the link between them, by the way in which the first is transformed into the second, his generic potentialities focused into his specific performances.

Human nature and culture cannot be separated (Geertz, 1972, p. 35); but the approach assumes that human behaviour is highly plastic.

Sociobiology, another contemporary example of an approach towards defining human nature, claims to represent a scientific 'evolutionary' perspective whilst incorporating insights from anthropology. Its predominant argument relates to the effects of our genetic make-up on our behaviour, deploying the mechanism of Darwinist evolution. Ethologists studying patterns of animal behaviour (Ardrey, 1967; Lorenz, 1967; Morris, 1968) have basically contended that human beings' biological heritage and 'killer instincts' lie at the heart of all wars. In effect, innate aggression explains modern warfare. Sociobiologists offer a broader account of humans which is meant to break down the opposition between heredity and learning. 'Mankind viewed over many generations shares a single human nature within which relatively minor heredity influences recycle through ever changing patterns between the sexes and across families and entire populations' states Wilson (1978, p. 50). The methodology is clearly reductionist, in its reducing of human nature to genetic features, and thus it is ideological (meaning that it suggests ideas and norms which are directed towards particular political or social forms of action).

As will be discussed later (Chapter 5), the approach has met with severe criticism in the light of its revived social Darwinism and racist and sexist ideology. Nonetheless there has been a renewed programmatic turn in social sciences to forge non-reductionist ways of understanding the interconnections between biological and social mechanisms and processes (Benton, 1991, pp. 1–29; Dickens, 1992). This book is especially concerned with the types of answer given by the social sciences to the 'human nature question', the way they underpin theories and how they are applied to social policy and professional practice. But they are answers which remain informed by the philosophical, the anthropological or the scientific. Although the idea of human nature is ostensibly philosophical, its manifestations are socially and politically grounded. The following section looks at how these connections have been made historically.

So far we have discussed the general relevance of human nature concepts, and their importance in formulating theory. Further, we have looked at theoretical approaches in modern social science which have informed contemporary practical policy areas. Yet where do we proceed in understanding precisely how theories of human nature relate to broader social ideas and events? What is the nature of the linkages between social theory and human nature theory? To provide an answer, we must situate ideas about our nature in their historical context. Ideas of human nature and human possibilities have constantly changed. One needs to comprehend the interconnections between the historical, the social, the philosophical and the political. Thinkers' ideas must be located against the backcloth of their particular society, material conditions and current intellectual traditions, since thinkers are circumscribed by what is called the paradigm of their epoch (that is, the universally accepted explanation or theory of the time; Einstein's theory of relativity is one modern example).

The dominant metaphor of any age acts as a landmark in locating the societal pressures and influences fashioning historical concepts of self. The nineteenth century's overarching metaphor of the biological organism offers a cogent example. On the other hand, certain theories and ideas about human nature have endured through the centuries. The same idea may reappear at different periods in history in a range of guises and with diverse consequences. In effect, no simple linear or cumulative process occurs in the life of a concept, despite the nineteenth-century hegemonic notion of progress. A brief survey of the major theories of human nature, through a process of simplified classification, may assist in heightening our awareness of the historical basis of the key ideas. At the same time it serves as an entrée into major modern debates and themes of concern to students of the social sciences and the caring professions.

Models of Human Nature

For clearer exposition the discussion of the theories will be best executed by grouping them under a series of models. Models of what it is to be human, or models of woman (usually couched in the generic sense of 'man'), have been stylistically presented in forms varying from subtle gradations (Nash, 1968; Berry, 1986) to the sharp dichotomy (Hollis, 1977). Whilst a model represents a pattern, it is essentially a sustained and systematic metaphor (McFague, 1982, p. 71). Models in political theory and political science have always employed metaphors. For example, in history one encounters the metaphor of the machine, powerful in the seventeenth and eighteenth centuries; or the metaphor of the organism, predominant in the later years of the nineteenth century, corresponding to the emergence of evolutionary thought, and its re-emergence with increasing ecological concerns during the twentieth century.

Given the significance of metaphor for the human and social sciences in the historical context, the purpose here is to discuss a series of models characterising the prime elements of major theories of human nature, different conceptions of being human which may be identified as recurrent in more recent times. The models adopted here are as follows:

(a) the rational model of human nature;
(b) the spiritual model of human nature;
(c) the mechanical model of human nature;
(d) the organic model of human nature;
(e) the environmentally determined model of human nature;
(f) the existential model of human nature;
(g) the social model of human nature.

It is to these particular models that we now turn.

The Rational Model of Human Nature

The Ancient Greeks Plato and Aristotle produced some of the most durable portrayals of human existence in history. But their concerns for rational thought sprang out of the immediate context. Questions were posed for the first time, because of the emancipation of the individual from the group in the Iron and Coin Age, the historical upheavals and the breakdown of a stable, hierarchical society. All manner of changes had opened the way for political reflection. Groups like the Sophists had thrown down the gauntlet to the notion that the natural world was harnessed to the social world, and in so doing encouraged an atmosphere of antisocial individualism. Plato (429–347 BC) was the supreme advocate of humans as rational beings who live the life of reason derived from knowledge of ultimate reality

(Trigg, 1988, p. 15). It was this ability that distinguished humans from animals. At the same time humans are seen to be distinct moral beings in that they create their own values. But significantly the authority of humans possessing identifiable personality characteristics figures substantially in the Platonic model.

In Plato's *Republic* the schema of rational society corresponds to the three parts of the soul: the rational (head), the spiritual (heart) and the appetitive (stomach). Hierarchy in society then becomes analogous to the human organ, and inequalities are viewed as rational and natural. Interestingly, the *Republic* was radical in its view of women, with Plato's abandonment of property and the family, which entailed the abolition of woman's traditional sphere within the guardian class (Okin, 1980, p. 27).

Plato's thought may be detected in the nineteenth-century organic concepts of humans, whilst the conceptual split between mind and body has been perpetuated through the philosophy of Rene Descartes until the present. As we shall see (Chapter 8) Platonic rationalism has exerted substantial influence on modern western medicine. Justification of the idea of natural inequalities constitutes a key issue in the contemporary debates over social policy. Aristotle (422–384 BC), the other major Greek rationalist and Plato's pupil, also believed the power of reason, a moral as well as an intellectual faculty, to be the distinguishing factor between animal and human. He sees all human and natural life as being teleological, that is possessing an end goal (*telos*). The human's end is achieved through rational choice.

Biology certainly plays an important part in Aristotle's model. The human soul incorporates the nature of the plant and also the soul of animals. But the power to think is the decisive factor. Aristotle's writings convey early depictions of the social nature of humans, particularly the importance of political characteristics. Humans are viewed as political in essence, and Aristotle's *Politics* assumes political association as integral to the definition of being human. Embodied within this notion is the idea that humans need to co-operate with each other, and that co-operation adds to the common good. Nevertheless, Aristotle's own teleology demonstrates hierarchy and structure in the universe, and inequality between master and slave is considered natural. The rationalism of Plato and Aristotle still fails to penetrate the assumptions regarding what is natural in humans. Class differences are rationalised, as indeed are gender differences. Okin (1980) points to Aristotle's belief in the natural superiority of men over women, and notes that modern scholars have implicitly accepted this, while being critical of Aristotle's master–slave hierarchy. On the other hand, Saxenhouse (1991, p. 51) argues that 'in Aristotle's writing there is no hatred of women; rather, there is the attempt, from the perspective of the male, to understand the origins of the female and her role in the male city'. Aristotle's understanding of the female in the political world leads to a vision of hierarchy, but not submission on all levels.

The Spiritual Model of Human Nature

Spiritual conceptions of human nature clearly influence philosophical ideas and beliefs about the world. In the western context, Judaeo-Christian beliefs have exerted a substantial bearing upon attitudes towards caring for the poor, and upon value structures prominent in social work. Eastern religions have embodied a particular view of humans as inner-directed, far more inclined to the external world *per se* than with social interactions. Hence, religious definitions of human nature have advanced a variety of answers regarding their engagement with the material world, ranging from inner-directedness and other-worldliness to opposition against social and political oppression (as found in the writings of contemporary liberation theologians, for example Illich or Freire).

Judaeo-Christianity's main tenets in characterising humans' nature may be described in the following way. First, humans are made in the image of God, and possess a self-consciousness enabling the ability to love freely; second is the belief in life after death; third, the notion of spiritual freedom (given by God); and fourth, man's fall from grace, the idea of original sin, intimating 'a flawedness in man, an inability to reach his true potential'. For Christians, there is also the idea of the regeneration of 'man' through turning to the Church and Jesus ... the restored relationship of humankind with God through the life, death and resurrection of Christ (Philpot, 1986, p. 144). Sixth, Christianity teaches, too, that unless man works with God in the world, then his efforts will be foredoomed to failure (Philpot, 1986, p. 147).

Within Christianity itself coexist various perspectives regarding human nature. Catholicism, largely through the writings of St Augustine and St Thomas Aquinas, accepts the conception of the human as being in the universe. Aquinas stressed that the distinctiveness of humans from animals resides in the realm of the former's *free choice*. Human nature is essentially good in spite of sin's impact. But in the event of a clash between the earthly and heavenly orders, human laws and social standards must be subordinated to the higher natural law. Suppositions of universal order, natural hierarchy and harmony dominate so that the individual is recognised as an integral part of an organic whole led by heavenly virtues. Protestantism, however, most trenchantly in the works of Luther and Calvin, presents a highly individualistic conception of being human, its attention trained upon the earth, bringing religion into the world but not of the world nor for the world (Marcuse, 1972).

As counterpoint to the Catholic ideas, Luther and Calvin were anti-rationalistic, emphasising the depravity of human nature resulting from the Fall, and with salvation deriving from faith alone and Jesus's teaching to do good works on earth and to follow the New Testament. These ideas appeared in the context of crucial economic changes, whereby capitalist processes gave rise to bourgeois individualism and the notion of the free labourer.

Interpretations placed on the nature of the relationships between this particular model of human nature and the economic structures of the period have been consequential for the ongoing agency–structure debate in sociology, such as Weber's *The Protestant Ethic and Spirit of Capitalism* (1958) and also for social work principles which stress both respect for the individual and the work ethic. Spiritual beliefs regarding the nature of human life, death, religion and God, suggesting the wholeness (holistic) of human beings, constituted major traditional explanations of health and sickness before the onset of the modern biomedical model founded on the Cartesian split between the human body and the mind (Turner, 1987). With regard to eastern philosophies and mysticism, Hinduism offers a picture of human as inner-directed, denying the world as having value due to its lack of permanence. It is argued that the only reality is one disclosed through intense discipline and meditation. Contemplation aimed at the ultimate state of nirvana holds the physical passions in check. A key development in health approaches in the west (Chapter 8) has been a return to holistic medicines with a strong underpinning of Zen Buddhism. In social work, too (Chapter 9), eastern mysticism has influenced client-centred approaches dealing with the achievement of personal insight.

The Mechanical Model of Human Nature

By the seventeenth century one encounters the growing ascendancy of capitalism accompanied by the creed of individualism. Although mediaeval thought and the spiritual coda persists, intellectual thought becomes increasingly materialistic. The human as a machine serves as the leading metaphor. New modes of rational deduction and the establishment of science as the new paradigm regarding the place of human beings in the scheme of existence herald the beginnings of the desacrilisation process and overt challenge to the Christian theologies. Ideas flourished in mathematics, astronomy, medicine and physics, as well as mechanics. Many of these advances were driven by the rapid economic developments of the period, and the requirements of more accurate measurement in industry.

Politically, the century witnessed in Europe the emergence of the nation state and absolutism. Events of the English revolution, a situation of conflict between warring factions over the issue of the natural right of kingship, served as a backcloth to the writings of Thomas Hobbes (1588–1679), most typifying the deployment of the mechanical metaphor in the portrayal of human nature. Hobbes's central idea is that human actions are wholly determined, and basically motivated by self-preservation. Human traits are personified as aggressive, selfish, competitive, diffident, and seeking after glory. However, Macpherson (1962) argues that in fact these were traits that Hobbes confronted in seventeenth-century capitalist England. Basically the political philosopher was 'reading back' current social practices into a snapshot of human nature.

The Hobbesian methodological framework for analysing the human personality was the precursor of modern psychological techniques. Hobbes thinks that psychological explanations are similar to physical and geometrical ones. In particular, he advances physiological postulates, and applies the techniques of mathematics and physics in his representation of humans as cosmic atoms in constant collision with each other. Where humans exist in a state of nature, unconstrained by sets of laws, claims Hobbes, then they have to survive as best as they may. His analogy between human life and battle anticipates the ethological school's reliance upon aggressive instincts as explanations for war and violence.

Hobbes uses his theory of human nature politically. The mental portrait of humans in nature becomes a political appeal to human beings in society. All citizens, he reasons, must hand over their personal power out of self-interest into the care of a sovereign power: Leviathan. Individual rights and freedoms are denied. Here, then, is one of the most potent models of human nature based upon the most pessimistic assessment of what it means to be human, employed as an expostulation favouring absolutist government as a means of achieving social and political stability. Its problem is that it gives undue weight to the individual as an isolated entity divorced from socially conceived processes, a precursor of methodological individualism in sociology (Chapter 4). The diagnosis of social problems based on such a model would also seem to imply authoritarian and undemocratic solutions and policies, issues taken up in Chapter 7. As we shall see in the next section, this accentuation of biological factors and instinct in accounts of human nature strengthened during the nineteenth century. Its echo through modern debates over Freudianism, culture, race and gender is discussed in Chapters 2, 3, 5 and 6.

The Biological (Organic) Model of Human Nature
The nineteenth century was an epoch of unparalleled wealth in western capitalism. Natural progress as a concept was the icon for human affairs into the early twentieth century. Biological notions of human existence became synonymous with evolutionary change,

constituting the paradigmatic science of the century. Unlike the Hobbesian mechanical personification it was imbued with the spirit of optimism. Charles Darwin (1809–82) stands with Marx as a seminal theorist of the age. Trained in the study of biological nature, his scientific approach held immense implications for our conceptualisation of what we are as humans. His theory of evolution contributed crucially to consolidating the image of a world in which all situations in human life can be reduced to biological situations (Kolakowski, 1968). Darwinism focused on the idea of individual species bereft of any fixed nature but changing in the struggle for existence; hence the thrust towards change. Human characteristics were to be explained in terms of evolution through natural selection (Chapter 3).

The second half of the century was predominantly a Darwinian age. Social explanations used biology as their metaphor. Social theory itself was infused with the organic metaphor essential to the writings of Auguste Comte and Herbert Spencer, founders of the new discipline of sociology. But the extent of change envisaged was circumscribed. Evolution becomes a way of describing an attitude to social change (Williams, 1974). To comprehend how the scientific entails the ideological, one must note that the predominant organic social theories to an extent *preceded* Darwin's theory. Williams (1974, pp. 114–15) recalls that Darwin's reading of Malthus had influenced him in developing his notion of the preservation and destruction of species. In neither the natural nor the social sciences was extended or prolonged consideration given in early Darwinism to the relationships between species struggling for survival on the one hand and the natural environment on the other (Dickens, 1992, p. 21). Further, the development of genetics by Sir Francis Galton and of eugenics by Mendel, underpinned by the principle of the survival of the fittest, was an additional element in the social application of biology which wrought destructive consequences in terms of the dissemination of racist and sexist world views, and the propagation of mass slaughter.

This has constituted the basis of imperialist racist ideology in the twentieth century as well as reflecting it. Spencer's theory of the organic evolution of society synthesised biology and social theory, and in so doing justified the conflict of individuals and acquisitiveness in capitalist society, and the prevailing ideologies of imperialism. Steven J. Gould (1991, p. 28) demonstrates how the nineteenth-century iconography (visual representation) of evolution is overwhelmingly directed, sometimes crudely, sometimes subtly, towards reinforcing a comfortable view of human inevitability and superiority. It is a view which is inevitably racist, and owes its pedigree to a much earlier version of a chain of being or ladder of linear progress, described by Gould as 'a motley sequence ... from birds to crocodiles to dogs and monkeys, and then up the conventional ladder of human groups' (1991, p. 29) finishing with the white European's 'nobly arched head'. The implications of this theory of human nature for the contemporary controversies over social inequalities constitute the main thrust of Chapter 5, which considers racism and sociobiology, while Chapter 6 analyses the rationalisation of gender inequalities. In the next section we turn to a model which eschews the pessimistic determination of biology and leans more towards the external environment's power to shape human beings' moral capacities.

The Environmentally Determined Model of Human Nature

The model of human beings as determined by their environment is often associated with Jean-Jacques Rousseau (1712–78) whose picture of natural human goodness and the potential of human beings offers in the spirit of the Enlightenment an optimistic antidote to the Hobbesian and social Darwinist portrayal. The main feature of Rousseau's theory of human nature is that a human being's nature is pliable instead of fixed. Human characteristics are seen as formed by the social environment. Unlike Hobbes's analysis of presocial beings in a state of nature, fundamentally in conflict, Rousseau's posits one of harmony with nature, compassion and basic goodness. The misery suffered by human beings has been created by the society, principally with respect to the creation of inequalities between humans. Their natural virtue has been depraved by civilisation. Rousseau's *Social Contract* charts how the new frameworks of social organisation converged with the institution of property and the growth of wealth, leading to self-interest, theft and crime.

Rousseau's portrayal of the common nature of mankind may be contrasted with Plato's conception of innate inequalities. The distinction between these two concepts is significant, in that the former allows for the recasting of an individual's attributes and fostering all manner of possibilities and potential in *all* while the latter calls for the reproduction of an unchanging, universal essence and denies innovation among human kind. Yet an evil human-made environment may nevertheless be unmade. Institutions may be replaced by better ones; inequality may be replaced by equality; selfish goals may be replaced by communal ideals and practices. Rousseau affirms education to be crucial for the nurture of potential in all humans (not merely for a few) and the unfolding of the individual's intrinsic capacities for self-realisation. This anticipates the existentialist and humanistic psychology of Abraham Maslow (1968) whose scheme for a hierarchy of needs points to the ultimate human need for self-actualisation, and whose model is discussed in Chapters 8 and 9 *vis-à-vis* approaches in nursing and social work.

However, just in case we acclaim Rousseau's theory as truly emancipatory for all humans, his idea of equality is clearly selective. Indeed, his mode of discourse for attributing to nature passive female characteristics is viewed as archetypal by Moller Okin (1980, p. 106). His definition of the natural, so that it is replicated in society, provides the support for his segregationist educational policies which aim to make women appealing sexual objects and submissive wives.

Also clearly in the line of environmental determinists was Robert Owen (1771–1858), a nineteenth-century utopian socialist, who argued that human beings' nature is made for them, rather than by them (Owen, 1813). Generally, environmental conditions (geographical, social and political) make humans' nature. Owen's particular significance here lies in his interventionism as a paternalistic employer. For Owen, too, private property was the root cause of exploitation and greed under capitalism. Owen believes that behaviour can be altered by changing the environment, and that human beings could be made more co-operative. His social engineering experimentation at New Lanark, Scotland, was aimed at moulding the workers' character, by provision of improved working conditions, decent homes and a better town environment.

Owen's endeavours were part of a socialist movement drawing attention to the centrality of material conditions in people's lives. However, the whole focus on controlling and transforming the individual's environment soon becomes manipulation of 'pliable' human beings, which is the antithesis of the self-activity and empowerment envisaged by a truly social model of human nature. Such manipulation became the hallmark not only of the behaviourist techniques of experimentalist psychology, discussed in Chapters 2 and 5, but of crude Stalinist social engineering (Chapter 2).

The Existential Model of Human Nature

The nineteenth century saw an unprecedented growth of socialist and collectivist movements. Existentialist concepts of human nature may be understood as antithetical to these collective phenomena. Three main concerns characterise existentialism: focus on the individual human being and her/his uniqueness; interest in the meaning or purpose of human lives, and the primacy of *inner* or *subjective* experience; and concern with the *freedom* of individuals, which is seen as their most vital and distinctively *human* characteristic (Stevenson, 1987, p. 89). Existentialists, then, convey belief in the abilities of each individual being to choose authentically for herself her own attitudes, purpose, values and way of life. Religious existentialism is best represented by the writings of the Danish theologian Soren Kierkegaard (1813–55), generally accepted to be the first modern existentialist and a key influence on Jean-Paul Sartre, the prime exponent of twentieth-century existentialism (discussed in Chapter 2). Kierkegaard distinguishes three main ways of life: the aesthetic, the ethical and the religious, but considers the religious, Christian way to be the highest, viewing the individual as an ultimate category, understanding the real existence of the individual as being what the individual is before God (MacIntyre, 1966, p. 217). To quote: 'It is useless for a man to determine first of all the outside and afterworld fundamentals. One must know oneself before knowing anything else' (Kierkegaard, *Journals*, 1835, 1951, cited in Fromm and Xirau, 1968, p. 225).

Atheistic existentialism is best characterised by the German philosopher Friedrich Nietzsche (1844–1900). Nietzsche's notion of alienated or unanchored existence emerges through his statement 'God is dead' (suggesting that as we have now seen through the illusions created by religion, then it is necessary for humans to rethink the whole foundations of their lives). No universal human nature exists for Nietzsche. Humans must find their meaning and purpose in human terms alone, not in religion or spirituality. Humans are in a vacuum, faced with the prospect of meaninglessness and nihilism. Yet it is up to human beings to act and to change. Nietzsche emphasises freedom of humans to alter their whole value base.

A new secular 'Superman' is invoked as carrier of the will to power. Proclaims Nietzsche: 'I love him who lives for knowledge and who wants knowledge that one day the Superman may live. And thus he will his own downfall' (Nietszche, *Thus Spoke Zarathustra*, cited in Fromm and Xirau, 1968, p. 232). Yet deep down, in spite of his call for the higher realms of individual action away from the sameness of the 'herd', Nietzsche held the pessimistic option of humans that they were anyway past redemption.

It is this mood of nihilism that has been transported into the twentieth century. The century's existential anxiety is a subject for exploration in Chapter 2. The human search for ontological security and self-identity as a theme within social science theory is pursued in Chapter 4, whilst the pathological implications for the caring professions of 'angst' and the fragmentations of identity are investigated in Chapters 8 and 9. But the problem of theories of human nature that conceptually sever the individual from the material world is how to produce individual solutions to problems that are intrinsically part of the material and social world. In this respect, a model which roots the dynamic thrust of individual purpose *socially* (as opposed to passively) is particularly appropriate.

The Social/Communal Model of Human Nature

Anarchist and Marxist ideas have both contributed to the debate on human nature. Petr Kropotkin (1842–1921) argues that it is human co-operation that is natural rather than competition or conflict. Why, indeed, must we assume that conflict instead of co-operation is our nature? Humans are communal beings, and the commune is the chief social form to correspond with human beings' nature, but government is the antithesis of human freedom. Any kind of central political authority always distorts and destroys the spontaneity and harmony of the relationships human beings establish in society (Kropotkin, 1902). As such, we may understand why the abolition of the state figures so highly in anarchist thought.

The response of Karl Marx (1818–83) to the unsettling forces of industrial capitalism was truly revolutionary in terms of its impact upon the direction of human history, but Marx's grafting of his model of human potential and 'becoming' to the material world of production shattered erstwhile visions of human and social change. He focuses on the significance of labour and production in human activity and the necessity to transform nature in defiance of the whole idea of an unchanging nature. His *Sixth Thesis on Feuerbach* (Easton and Guddat, 1967, p. 402) states: 'Feuerbach resolves the essence of religion into the essence of man. But the essence of man is no abstraction inherent in each single individual. In its reality it is the ensemble of the social relations.'

Hence the potential of men and women changes as societies change, especially the driving forces of production seen as a social activity. Although Marx argues that there is no real unchanging human nature, he does identify continuing common properties universally shared by human beings. Such properties help explain why it is that human societies develop and why in the process they transform the beliefs, abilities and desires of their inhabitants. Marx's most significant work in this direction was *Economic and Philosophical Manuscripts of 1844*, where one encounters the genesis of the concept of 'species-being'. Here he adopts the material emphasis of *labour* as the essence of humans. Through labour, that is working upon the objective world: 'man proves himself to be a *species-being*. This production is man's active species-life. Through this production, nature appears as *his* work and his reality.' Marx distinguishes human beings from animals, by dint of their self-conscious life activity, as opposed to animal life activity. Human beings can reflect, change things, improve, erect goals and plan for the future. Hence the importance of history when studying humanity. However, this consciousness remains inseparable from productive activity. The Marxian theory of the intrinsic connection between bodily labour and ideas of the head clearly runs counter to the dualism of earlier rationalists like Aristotle and Descartes, a dualism which has wielded intellectual hegemony over perspectives in health and sickness.

Erich Fromm (1961, p. 13) encapsulates the parameters of the debate as to the validity of a Marxist view of human nature: 'Marx's "materialistic" or "economic" interpretation of history has nothing whatsoever to do with an alleged "materialistic" or "economic" striving as the most fundamental human drive.' It is the understanding of history based on the fact that human beings are the authors *and* actors of their history. In Chapter 2 we discuss the full implications of the respective Marxist interpretations in the twentieth century.

The Marxian approach became a major stream of sociology from the 1960s and influenced new critical approaches in social policy. The extent to which the social model of human nature may be seen as shifting the emphasis in medicine and health towards non-physical diagnoses and solutions, and the effectiveness of radical social work theory, are assessed in Chapters 8 and 9. Certainly, the tendency of Marxists to fetishise the import of economic structures has proved a major stumbling block to its acceptance by humanists, whilst Marx's blindness to gender differentiation is no less than other theorists in the masculinity of his theory which 'promotes a view of nature as the (feminised) passive substratum of (hu)manly efforts' (Stefano, 1991, p. 159).

Into the Twentieth Century

The debates and contending models have re-emerged, informing discourse in theory, policies and practice across the twentieth century. For example, Hobbesian atomism underlies the individualism of late twentieth-century capitalism, now most generally expressed in the idea of an enterprise culture. Biological theory and social Darwinism have played a key part in racism, fascism and Nazism, whereas the life of the instincts and the unconscious played a rather different emancipatory role in Freudism psychoanalysis. Shifting social and economic conditions, and the mercurial power exercised by the Soviet Union bureaucracy paralleled a constricting social engineering version of Marxism. Humans were to be changed through transformation of the totality of economic and social conditions. The policies of the Stalin era were intellectually justified by rigid Marxist-Leninist 'scientific' laws of dialectical materialism. At the same time, however, as we shall see in the next chapter, their crude determinism did elicit challenge from critical theory and Marxist humanism.

The images of human nature and burgeoning meaninglessness suggested by Kierkegaard and Nietzsche in the nineteenth century presage Sartre's focus on the authentic individual in the twentieth century. This century has been one of great affluence as well as mass destruction and warfare; a century in which the logic of rationality has been stretched to the limits, where bureaucracy and planning have operated at a massive scale, where technology and management have taken over from pure science as paradigm. The computer and artificial intelligence have been adopted as metaphor for human behaviour and the human mind (Gentner and Stevens, 1983). Giant transnational corporations *and* market forces increasingly shape the strategies and economic policies of national states. The 1990s are in the midst of a major restructuring of the institutions and organisations through which health, education and social services are delivered at the community level. Managerialism's new individualistic language reflects fresh issues as to how far human nature is driving or being driven by powerful economic imperatives, as discussed in Chapter 7.

Human Nature, Theory and the Caring Professions

Finally, what *sort* of connections obtain between theories of human nature, social theory and applied areas? Basically, theories are concerned with making sense of reality and the world we live in. Theory is of prime importance both to individuals *and* to the societies we inhabit. Our conceptions of ourselves ('human nature') derive from the assumptions we make about reality and experience. To this extent, our conceptions of nature will generate theory. By accepting a picture of humans as determined by instincts or physical environment, we are more likely to interpret social action, behaviour, events and problems as determined. Similarly, characterisations of humans as essentially individualistic will produce elucidation of, for example, criminality, in terms of an individual's personal disposition. These characterisations structure our expectations of what is possible, and hence how we set about diagnosis and cure of social ills. Rubington and Weinberg (1989, p. 57) suggest that the range of sociological explanations of social problems *call* for action by the manner in which they are defined as problems in the first place. But these perspectives are tied to concepts of human beings held by particular interests at particular times. Platt (1989, p. 27) traces the route of the social pathology approach to crime to the idea of the criminal as less than a fully-fledged human being, borrowing social pathology's pessimistic orientation about the inelasticity of human nature and the working classes' moral vacuity from social Darwinist thought, and its metaphors from the medical professions' 'imagery of pathology, infection, immunisation, and treatment'.

George Steiner (1971) delineates the period from 1850 onwards as representing the replacement of optimism with pessimism, which became a social icon in the wake of the Jewish Holocaust experience. A social theorist has produced a volume entitled *Pessimism* (Bailey,

1988, p. viii) out of the belief that it is a powerful form of social consciousness in the midst of the risks of nuclear war, increasing hunger and gross environmental pollution, which may be overcome by better understanding.

Yet theorising meets resistance; applied professions tend to prefer a hard-headed practical approach, whilst notions of 'common sense' and the language of facts are substituted for explanation. However, the whole galaxy of facts is open to interpretation in that what we perceive as practical topics suitable for investigation are steered by our conscious or unconscious theories based upon our purposes and our prognoses of what is possible. A necessary inter-relationship exists between theory and practice, for instance state interventionism. Theories may be used as a critical tool, but also as a resource for intervention and the steering of policy making (Bailey, 1980, p. 115). Models and theory guide practice in the health professions, for example in the definition of health and sickness in the treatment of patients or in strategic planning for ageing. Within the fields of social work and social care, the value one places upon clients will influence the definition and diagnosis of problems, the adoption of particular forms of therapy or coun-selling, the implications for anti-discriminatory practice, and resource allocation decisions.

It is revealing to note the spheres of explanation most favoured to date in the caring professions. The scientifically derived con-structions of the self have been to the fore in psychological theories, and the latter have proved popular with the caring professions. The health professions have utilised insights from a number of theories. In the first place, they have turned to social learning theory, an applied form of behaviourism. Secondly, they have adopted theories of perception and social cognition, whereby the person's percep-tions are situated centre stage. This has provided the foundation for the strong individualistic orientation of traditional health education strategies (Naidoo, 1986). The third mode of explana-tion has been in exploration of ideas regarding health and sickness in their historical development. Scientific methods in conceptual-ising human ideas, feelings and action have been vigorously applied in all these areas, but debate surrounds the issue of whether such approaches really do provide a fuller understanding of human beings' health needs (Stanton Rogers, 1971, p. 70). These issues are explored in depth in Chapter 8.

Social sciences have come to play an increasing part in the intel-lectual anchoring of social work, although the profession has been more deprecating than other professions of social theory, preferring the more individualistic casework or the readily controlled use of behavioural science. Social work has traditionally emphasised the centrality of practice which may seem eminently sensible.

Nevertheless, theory informs practice and, indeed, to cite Howe (1987, p. 22), 'different theories offer contrasting views of human nature and ultimately the purpose of social work itself'.

As with the adoption of particular modes of explanation in health, social work has looked to psychology rather than to other disciplines for accounts of human behaviour proving more amenable to practical application, albeit lacking in the human dimension. The turn to scientific-oriented psychology, it has been argued, is due to the perceived need for certainty, given the grossly uneven character of the social workers' caseloads, and an alleged compulsion for social work to prove its professional competence in handling and 'curing' difficult social problems, for example juvenile delinquency (Clark and Asquith, 1985).

A number of theories may be identified, each driven by a singular conception of human nature as having influenced approaches in social work. To begin with, the Freudian approach of psychoanalytic theory has been important, yet more so in the United States than in Britain. Human behaviour is interpreted through humans' efforts to satisfy basic, innate needs, presaging a pessimistic perspective on human nature. Secondly, social learning theory has fitted into social work practice. The third grouping of functionalist-type explanations includes social systems theory and behavioural theories. The humanistic-existential theories have suggested an open-ended characterisation of human potential. Finally, radical theories of the Marxist and feminist varieties have placed the stress upon socially constructed forms of oppression and exploitation, suggesting the precedence of social being over human consciousness.

Themes and Organisation of the Book

The remainder of this book deals thematically with the constant tension between proactive and deterministic or reductionist models of human nature. It engages with major twentieth-century theories before investigating in detail how certain models, in harness with key social and political developments, have personified racism, sexism, human exploitation and oppression, whilst others have attempted to steer theory and practice towards co-operation. The chapters probe the use of specific models in social theory, their practical policy ramifications and discrete applications in health, social work and social work education.

Chapter 2 considers dominant theories of the twentieth century, the Freudian, behaviourist, existentialist and Marxist theories of human nature. They are discussed in the context of mass-scale horror and profound economic, technological and political change. The chapter analyses the ways in which humans conceive of themselves in the face of such transformations. It juxtaposes radical Freudian and Jungian accounts of the unconscious with the scientistic behaviourist perspective of the externally manipulated human. Sartre's substitution of the committed authentic individual for a generalised human nature is expounded. It articulates the urgency of the debate between materialist Marxist conceptions and those of critical theory and socialist humanism.

Chapter 3 examines the series of debates which counterpose the biological to the cultural. It explores the 'animal nature' and 'human nature' assumptions that underscore theories of ethological and sociobiological theories, and discusses the pertinence of cultural difference through contending models of human nature in the work of social and cultural anthropologists.

Chapter 4 focuses on sociology and social theory, probing the ways in which particular models of human nature bolster, implicitly or explicitly, theoretical approaches in sociology. It enquires into why certain models have dominated within the disciplines, assessing issues of self, social construction, agency and structure in sociological and social theory.

Chapter 5 focuses on the central contemporary discourse regarding the relevance of the biological metaphor in explaining class gender and racial inequalities. Assessment is made of the use of intelligence tests, issues of racism, sexism and ethnocentricism, and the social and political implications of writings by ethologists and sociobiologists. It examines how far any theories may offer adequate explanations of antisemitism and the Holocaust.

Chapter 6 traces the ways in which social theory and theorising on the nature of human nature has tended to exclude or marginalise women, and discusses how feminist thinkers have disputed received male-oriented theories of human nature, an assessment of the importance of feminist portrayals of human nature for policy and the caring professions, and the specific nature of the debate concerning sexuality, sexual preference and biology.

Chapter 7 provides an analysis and evaluation of the prominent social philosophies and models of human nature reinforcing social policies and policy making, examining the polarities of optimistic and pessimistic views of human nature in the modern context, the impacts of determinism and voluntarism, the relevance of prognoses of basic needs for government strategies, and the incidence of racism, sexism and ageism in social policy.

In Chapter 8 the methods used in the health professions are scrutinised in the light of theories of human nature, through analysis and evaluation of models and theories underpinning education and practice in health care, the implications of the use of particular diagnostic models such as the medical and holistic models, the tendencies towards ethnocentricism in western medicine's concept of 'body' and of concepts of mental health and illness.

Chapter 9 identifies and differentiates approaches in social work according to the underpinning models of human nature, through detailed investigation into the theories and models of human nature that have influenced perspectives in social work theory, method and practice. It investigates applications of Skinner's behaviourism in the treatment of clients, the viability of humanistic psychology and the client-centred therapies of Freud, Maslow and Rogers, the specific role that spiritual models play in caring, and the influence of Marxism on radical social work.

Further Reading

General Surveys

Christopher J. Berry, *Human Nature* (Macmillan, 1986). Focuses more on debates in political philosophy.

Erich Fromm and Ramon Xirau (eds.), *The Nature of Man* (Ungar, 1968). Readings from different cultural perspectives.

Alisdair MacIntyre, *A Short History of Ethics* (Macmillan; RKP, 1966).

Brian Morris, *Western Conceptions of the Individual* (Berg, 1992). Covers theories of the human subject in philosophy, psychology, anthropology and sociology in a highly readable style.

Susan Moller Okin, *Women in Western Political Thought* (Princeton University Press, 1979; Virago, 1980).

Raymond Plant, *Modern Political Thought* (Blackwell, 1991). Chapter devoted to historical survey of human nature concepts in political theory.

S. Radhakrishnan and P.T. Raju, *The Concept of Man* 2nd edn. (Allen and Unwin, 1966). Includes Islamic, Chinese and Jewish human nature theories.

Leslie Stevenson, *Seven Theories of Human Nature* 2nd edn. (Oxford University Press, 1987). A concise exposition of 'human nature' in Christianity, Freud, Lorenz, Marx, Sartre, Skinner and Plato.

Leslie Stevenson (ed.), *The Study of Human Nature: A Reader* (Oxford University Press, 1981). Extracts from classical writings, Islamic, Chinese and Jewish theories, Skinner, Chomsky and others.

Roger Trigg, *The Idea of Human Nature* (Blackwell, 1988). Focuses on the Greeks, Aquinas, Hobbes, Hume, Darwin, Marx, Nietzsche, Freud and Wittgenstein.

Selected Classic Models of Human Nature

Plato, *The Republic* (Penguin, 1955).

Thomas Hobbes, *Leviathan*, 1651 (Penguin).

David Hume, *A Treatise of Human Nature* (ed.) L.A. Selby-Bigge (Oxford University Press, 1978).

2

Human Nature Theory and the Twentieth Century

History, as we observed in Chapter 1, is witness to an impressive range of human nature theories. Four powerful theories of human nature in particular have underpinned the ideas and social thought of this century: Freudianism, behaviourism, existentialism and Marxism. On the surface they convey sharp distinctions in: prognosis for change, focus on the individual or upon external social and environmental factors; the weight accorded to scientific methodology or humanistic analysis; and the emphasis placed on the biological or the socially constructed.

All, with the possible exception of the existentialist model of human nature – an unerringly philosophically inclined perspective – have expressed themselves through the scientific metaphor. Freudian psychoanalytical insights and behaviouristic ideas have related to the dominant social science of the epoch, psychology, deemed a 'science' of the human personality. Sartrean existentialism has engaged with the meaning of the psychic *life* in the twentieth century. None of the theories, however, has remained autonomous and unaffected by any of the others. Each may be characterised by *internal* conflicts in interpretation *vis-à-vis* its scientific status. All entail political ramifications, although the extent to which this is openly recognised tends to vary.

The chapter investigates these theories in the context of economic catastrophe, war, and rapid technological developments. It traces their intellectual roots in nineteenth-century thought, and analyses their particular insights as they relate to human beings' self-portrayal, veering between the free agent of change and the determined being; between the committed Marxist revolutionary and the human driven by irrational unconscious forces as portrayed by Freud and Jung. The chapter concludes with discussion of the theories' significance for the development of social science and their policy ramifications. Although the organic biological metaphor and its specific social applications have also proved to be profoundly important during the twentieth century, detailed discussion of the perspective and its relationship to racism is postponed until Chapters 3 and 5.

Psychoanalytical Freudianism

Sigmund Freud's (1856–1939) psychoanalytic picture of human nature is oriented towards the inner person's basically biologically derived motivations. In this sense, the intellectual pedigree of the Freudian model of human nature, stressing instincts, may be located in the Darwinian biological science of the nineteenth century – an emphasis which laid Freud open to the attack of naively reducing everything to bodily instinct. For Freud, as for Darwin, humans are largely biologically contructed individuals comprising a bundle of biological drives and instincts operating beyond their control. Freud's work aims to create a Darwinism of the mind.

But whilst the theory aligned itself with this nineteenth-century 'scientific' pedigree, the very centrality of uncontrollable *sexual* biological urges or instincts represented a direct affront to the nineteenth-century Victorian morality that found the ugly side of life rather distasteful. It also challenged the nineteenth-century aura of optimism with his explanation of mass aggressiveness (May, 1992; Biddiss, 1977, p. 59).

Europe had plunged into a war which led to deaths on an untold scale and of unparalleled carnage, shattering the illusions about rational decisions and progress. The very scale of mass destruction provided the setting for Freud's concept of the destructive urge embedded deep down in the human being, an enormous problem for civilisation to solve. The grand nineteenth-century ideals of liberalism and freedom faded with the 'Great War', to be replaced by the growth of pessimism and the spirit of despair. This mood was exacerbated as the economic depression overwhelmed Europe and the United States, leaving millions jobless.

Freud postulates that the nature of the human lies in the basic inner drives which are preconscious or unconscious. The human personality is constructed from a series of identifiable layers – the unconscious, the preconscious and the conscious. *Ego and the Id* (1923) treats the layers of personality in terms of an id, an ego and a superego. These represent: the instinctual drives (id); the awareness of the external environment (ego); and the moral element of humankind (superego). At the level of the id resides the human instincts, representing on the one hand *life*, the thrust towards love (Eros), and on the other the *death* instinct or wish to die. Human beings, then, are born with a bundle of energies. Human nature constitutes this battle of energies between the life and death instincts (Freud, 1920) and between the sexual drive and the aggressive drive. Within the Freudian framework humans possess unconscious desires which may determine their personality and behaviour.

A further component of the Freudian picture of human nature does in effect modify the stress on biology *per se* by pointing to the significance of early childhood experience, so that traumatic experiences are capable of affecting a person's mental disposition. Human *development* is dependent upon sexuality which structures the human personality. This aspect of the developmental, rather than the biological and instinctual, was adopted and reworked by Freud's disciples, so that the emphasis shifts from the id to the realm of the ego.

Freud's diagnosis of mental disintegration or sickness is linked to the analysis of what drives the human being. The existence of the *hidden, unconscious* dimension is central to the diagnosis, which seeks to unearth the seemingly inaccessible causes of humans' mental anguish deeply embedded in the dark recesses of the mind. These are so unpalatable to the conscious mind as to remain repressed, yet still liable to determine the person's active, seemingly irrational, behaviour. In Freud's view, the concept of repression in diagnosing an individual's ills constitutes the foundation of psychoanalysis. Methodologically, psychoanalytical therapy aims to dislodge the particular locus of repressed feelings and experiences as they manifest themselves in outwardly inexplicable behaviour or through dreams and fantasies. We encounter the social tension of the individual's anxieties and pain especially in the area of repression. This is the site of combat between the id and the ego, the individual juxtaposed to the society. Individual and civilisation are inviolably in conflict with each other (Freud, 1930) just as the Hobbesian atomistic human directed by instincts cannot find a home in the confines of the stable, organised society. The logical culmination for humans' capacities to change would seem to be a determined pessimism. Yet *Civilisation and its Discontents* may serve as a springboard towards a combination of socialist humanism and historical Marxism. Freud's own work is limited by the strictures of his analytical tools. Erich Fromm (1900–90), however, welds the Freudian to the social.

Fromm (1941; 1955) manipulates the concept of alienation to probe the tensions of the individual in society, forging a humanist perspective of human beings' capacities. He strives to transform the Freudian pessimism into a moral optimism, extending the Freudian analysis beyond the absorption with sexuality to a concern with the human condition's other attributes found in particular types of society such as alienation, anxiety and loneliness. Fromm's theory of human nature is meant as a bridge between the psychoanalytic theory of human nature, humanism and humanistic therapy, spirituality and the Marxist theory of human nature. But his particular synthesis, predisposed towards the spiritual inner urges, tends to dilute the radicalism of the Marxist theory. Starting from a more radical position, Wilhelm Reich (1897–1957) develops the revolutionary potential of Freud's focus on the power of the sexual drive (as Marcuse was to do at a later stage) and the confining moralistic forces in society. Reich (1942) considers the primary life force to be sexuality and the ability to articulate and feel one's own sexual natural impulses. The basic source of repression is in the authoritarian family structure, which blocks the healthy biological urges through heterosexual orgasm (liberty derived from the essentially sexual human nature). Unlike Freud then, Reich perceives the repressive sexual condition as subject to change, with sexual revolution holding the key to potential revolution (Frosh, 1987). However, although the Reichian picture of human nature is a potentially liberating one, it is actually narrow; it begins and ends with the sexual. As such, it scarcely projects beyond the individual.

Finally, the Freudian theory of human nature constitutes one of the key areas of debate in contemporary feminist literature. Freudians such as Melanie Klein (1882–1960) and Karen Horney (1885–1952) represent an early challenge to Freud on the issue of his androcentricism (centred on the male). They criticise the dogmatic way he assumes a universal acceptance of the significance of male organisms in a child's development and emotional disposition. Mounting the case for an independent psychology of women, these postFreudians argue for the existence of female instincts separate from males' nature. Such critiques nevertheless remain wedded to Freud's biological essentialism and conventional ideas of *natural* heterosexuality. The debates arising out of Mitchell's later critique (1975) produce a more comprehensive feminist challenge to the Freudian biological thesis of human development examined in Chapter 6.

To summarise, the Freudian model of human nature's strong biological orientation accords a central role to unconscious sexual and aggressive urges, but it also highlights the human tension implicit in the conflicts between the forces of love and those of hate, and between the individual and human culture. The obsession with sexuality implies at one level an emphatic reductionist theory of human nature; Freud's assumptions are also transparently those of a deeply patriarchal society. Yet the theory's ambivalence enables combination with other, often radical, perspectives. In the next section we encounter a theory that on the contrary denies the inner facets of the human being, whether conscious or unconscious.

Behaviourism and Psychology

Behaviourism's importance in this century must be seen in the context of psychology's status and its claims to be the scientific specialist study of 'man' *par excellence*. It has cast off the aims of understanding consciousness or concern with the sphere of mind, and unambiguously focuses on *observed* and usually measurable behaviour. Experimental psychology and the behaviourist methodological approach to the study of human beings have frequently developed together. The behaviourist definition of existence, intertwined with environmental determinism and the drive to control, has shaped modern perspectives on what it is to be human. Behaviourism, concentrating on the outward manifestations of human phenomena, carried the nineteenth-century metaphor of empirical science into the twentieth century, though its machine-like model of human nature closely resembles the seventeenth-century Hobbesian model. But it displays a far greater concern with the *external* workings of the environment, in contrast to the Freudian theory, where an inner biological subconscious steers the human being's demeanour. Manipulation of the environment in order to control changes in human nature harks back to Owen's model of human nature in the nineteenth century (Chapter 1). Yet it has also provided an academic rationale for modern behavioural strategies in corporate management.

The early years of the twentieth century nurtured a generation of empirical science and experimentalism. Under William Wundt (1832–1920) experimental psychology resisted the perspective of William James (1842–1910) that psychology is really knowledge of consciousness (James, 1880). In Russia the psychological behaviourist study of human beings was seen as a mode of physiology. The work of Ivan Pavlov (1848–1936) exemplifies behavourism's intrinsic connections with the precepts of nineteenth-century science. Pavlov's experiments with a dog demonstrate how changing the conditions can displace or modify human beings' behaviour, by operating upon the physiological mechanisms of body chemistry and associationism (the theory that the association of ideas is the basis of all mental activity). The dog is taught to salivate to the sound of a bell by associating it with the expectation of food, a method known as classical conditioning.

Behaviourism, with its emphasis upon control and human conditioning, came to hold great appeal for Soviet Union apparatchiks under the Stalinist epoch. Their social engineering policies reflected an intensely materialist concept of human nature, and a highly reductionist interpretation of Marx's concept of social being. For four decades Pavlovian ideas of conditioned human behaviour held sway in the official Soviet academy and the area of psychological research.

The behaviourist persuasion also became dominant in American psychology through the research and ideas of James Watson (1878–1958), an animal psychologist who argued that the subject matter of psychology ought to be human behaviour so as to counteract the unhealthy concern with consciousness, which he considers to be little more than a throwback to belief in witchcraft (Stevenson, 1987, p. 92). Psychology's appeal to American capitalism, ironically, was no less than Pavlov's to the Soviet Union. Watson approaches the human personality as subject to change, given the human being's automatic way of acting in situations (Watson, 1930, in Marks (ed.), pp. 416, 419). The human may be taught new ways to live and think, through the acquisition of *learned* responses:

> For the universe will change if you bring up your children, not in the freedom of the libertine, but in behavioristic freedom – a freedom which we cannot even picture in words, so little do we know of it. (Watson, in Marks (ed.), p. 341)

Through conditioning, any person can be transformed into any kind of personality type, regardless of inheritance. This certainly poses a challenge to the genetic reductionism of Freud and the horrific applications of eugenics propounded in the century.

B.F. Skinner (1904–90) another American psychologist, and one of the most influential experimental psychologists in the tradition, became the best known of the modern behaviourists. Skinner's whole *oeuvre* bears testimony to the very *plasticity* of human nature. In his laboratory experiments with rats, he demonstrates how a variety of animals may be taught to solve a vast array of physical problems through methods of reinforcement of learned behaviour. His techniques of operant conditioning, originally conceived by Thorndyke in1898, produce modifications in behaviour through the reinforcement of learned patterns.

Skinner (1953) considers animal and human nature as synonymous. Furthermore, animals' nature may be located through studying their behaviour. Accordingly, nature and behaviour also become virtually identical. Of course, Skinner has to reject any form of metaphysical dualism (that is, the notion that there is a mental world existing independently of the body) from his intellectual frame of reference. 'Individual choice' plays little part in the explanation of human behaviour, according to Skinner. Humans are not able to decide their own fate, which is determined by events, both past and present, in the external world but also by genetic endowment. Consciousness is determined entirely by the environment, subject to mediation by physiological responses. Because of its very inaccessibility to observation or study, consciousness which separates us from animal or mineral cannot be the constituent of a human being. And indeed it is psychology's 'scientific' method to discover the laws of behaviour, not vainly to chart the realms of consciousness.

The venture comes across as hugely ambitious. Skinner is claiming more for scientific method than even the physical sciences claim. The latter *do* allow for unobservable theoretical elements such as magnetic fields (Stevenson, 1987, p. 108). Skinner, then, conceives behaviour to be changeable and malleable, based on the assumption that there is *no* fixed human nature, and no independent consciousness. The environment in which the person operates may be manipulated, and the person may be taught to *adjust* to the new environment through responding to different stimuli with new patterns of learned behaviour. This may be effected by programmed learning, based on the principles of operant conditioning which means altering behaviour by using *reinforcement* after eliciting a desired response. The method breaks down the individual's response to the external environment into discrete, identifiable parts. For instance, programmed learning in the educational sector operates on the principle of question and answer, reinforced by reward, founded on a Stimulus(S)–Response(R) series of progressions on successful performance to the next stage (Hardy and Heyes, 1987, pp. 50–1). The reinforcing element in this case is the encouragement to proceed in pursuit of the desired goal, strengthening the conditioned response.

Much of Skinner's experimentation was conducted with rats and pigeons. Animal behaviour in his experiments is explicitly subject to control by manipulation of the environment. The corpus of his work is intended to demonstrate that the very process of learning constitutes a relatively permanent change of behaviour as a result of experience. *Science and Human Behaviour* (1953) and *Beyond Freedom and Dignity* (1971) are the two major representations of Skinner's empirical work transposed into a prescriptive view of human purpose. His main proposition is that a technology of behaviour is able to solve the problems of human life and society provided that we surrender our illusions about individual freedom, responsibility and dignity. He applies his theories to language, arguing that human speech is due to the environmental conditioning of the speaker.

Skinner's harnessing of the individual to the environment and environmental change serves as a welcome antidote to the individualistic, uncontrollable Freudian unconscious. Nevertheless, Skinner's theory of human nature may be questioned on a number of counts. First, the '*tabula rasa*' approach to the human being leaves any particular individual at the mercy of whomsoever exerts control over a specific environment. This idea of all behaviour as purely a function of occurrences in the environment remains highly dubious. Presumably, anyone may be taught to be *anything* (Stevenson, 1987, pp. 110–11).

Chomsky (1968) attacks Skinner's application of the concept of operant conditioning to language acquisition (Skinner, 1957) which purports to show that language is subject to explanation through reinforcement processes. In Chomsky's view, behaviourist psychology, with its empirical bent and its focus on external environmental stimuli is insufficiently equipped to deal with the complexity and abstractness involved in understanding how humans learn language (Chomsky, 1968, in Stevenson, 1981, p. 245). Skinner's deterministic science of behaviour, Chomsky reasons, is clearly ideological and claims too much for itself, given *its* lack of evidence (Chomsky, 1968b, pp. 104–32).

Chomsky suggests that there is a systematic 'linguistic competence' underlying human behaviour which does not manifest itself behaviourally in any straightforward or direct manner (discussed further in Chapter 3). And 'this system of linguistic competence is qualitatively different from anything that can be described in terms of ... the concepts of S–R psychology ... or the theory of simple automata' (Chomsky, 1968, in Stevenson, 1981, p. 241).

The behaviourist method regarding human behaviour also comes under criticism from an explicitly structuralist perspective which does not entirely coincide with Chomsky's position. Jean Piaget, an educational psychologist, is highly critical of behaviourism's 'genesis without structures', arguing that the mind is not simply a passive entity for the processing of inputs affecting the senses, but a mechanism which actively transforms the received inputs by performing a set of exploratory operations. To explain a human being's mental development requires taking into account inner mental states, even though they are unobservable. For Piaget, a child moves through a number of stages of mental evolution which involve cognitive symbolism (symbols registering in the brain) and later, social communication. Where Skinner places all emphasis upon environment, denying mental states and the base of language, Piaget (1971, pp. 52–73) calls for removing the duality between environment and hereditary. A dialectical construction of human knowledge makes up the human psyche – a *dynamic* development missing in behaviourism which is only about receiving (learning).

Similarly, Lev Vygotsky (1896–1934), a cognitive and educational psychologist, sees the environmentalism of the behaviourists as a crude expulsion of consciousness in its reduction of all our behaviour to reflexes. His work draws on a synthesis of behaviourism and consciousness in his significant *Thought and Language* (1962, cited in Morris, 1991, pp. 226–30). Guided by Marx, he points to the interplay between the external world and consciousness mediated by human practicality, and shows a concern with changing historical factors not present in Chomsky's own theorising (discussed in Chapter 3).

Evidently, the refutation of consciousness as a constituent in human nature is an absurdity which enables Skinner (and as we shall see in Chapters 3 and 5, the ethologists) to ignore the differences between human beings and animals, which is not to say that Skinner actually advocates the oppressive control of human beings. Indeed, in his utopian novel *Walden Two* (1948) the behavioural concepts are directed at improved social structures, whilst his ideas have been applied in the form of a Mexican commune designed to promote practices such as sharing, pacifism and equality (Nye, 1992, p. 53).

Nevertheless the method and technology imply a state of manipulation where some people exert control over others. In this sense, this is hardly a pure environmental determinism, but in the final analysis this mediated determinism represents a conscious act of power. Furthermore, the concentration upon the external manifestations of behaviour turns human beings into objects – a dehumanisation that allows *anything* to be done to others. As Stevenson (1987, p. 117) asks, '… when (if ever) does anyone have the right to try to condition someone else's behaviour?' Skinner's experimental method, emphasising the empirical collection of data, reflects an eschewal and suspicion of theory which he deems useless compared with fact. Yet his assertion that all behaviour is governed by laws (and hence subject to scientific methodology) is transparently a supernatural (metaphysical) belief.

It may be argued that contemporary psychology has travelled far away from Skinnerian behaviourism (Stevenson, 1987, p. 118), substituted by a cognitive psychology which rectifies the previous imbalance in its assiduous mapping of the human mind's contours. Certainly, more recognition is given to theory; greater attention is paid to mental states and by definition to consciousness as distinct from behaviour (Donald, 1991). But just *how* different is cognitive science in its treatment of the mind? Computer imaging in treating the human mind as a sophisticated computer returns us once more to the metaphor of human as machine. It suggests a technological determinism (the idea that technology *per se* causes humans to act in particular ways) which relentlessly bears upon the human nature debate concerning our potentialities and abilities to shape our own world (Chapter 7). For instance, cognitive science, in making direct analogies between human thought and the computer, is applied on a vast scale by the American Department of State for purposes of state surveillance in the development of military scanning equipment, whilst behaviourist techniques remain popular with practitioners in psychological practice and in industry. Technology's impacts upon social relationships (Chapter 4), mass violence (Chapter 5) and policy decision making (Chapter 7) are analysed later.

We have seen, then, that the behaviourist theory of human nature, notably in Skinner's work, reflects the continued pursuit of empirical scientific methodology for studying human activity, and the modernistic endeavour to control and plan the environment and direct patterns of learning. However, its focus on the observable eliminates all vestiges of an inner nature or a biologically evolved essence; its view of human nature as totally malleable prepares the way for social engineering and human abuse. The section below, in this respect, offers a diametrically opposed theory.

Existentialism

The twentieth century's existentialist picture of human nature, most notably the one painted by French philosopher Jean-Paul Sartre (1905–80), springs from nineteenth-century thought, but was also an impassioned response to developments in a mid twentieth-century world whose social and political landmarks stood in a state of total flux.

In the nineteenth century Kierkegaard and Nietzsche had most cogently expressed the impending anxieties of human beings living in the world. The Nietzschean idea of humans trapped in a vacuum presages the twentieth-century philosophical engagement with the alienated, 'angst'-laden human condition. Nietzsche demonstrates the problematic character of the nature of humans who have ostensibly broken free from the animal world and animal nature and pose the question of their own *meaning* as their destiny (Barrett, 1962, pp. 179–80). This Nietzschean nihilistic thinking belonged to a writer who viewed himself as communicating in an age of moral vacuum (MacIntyre, 1966, pp. 222–3). If anything, the ontological chasm had become even wider in the later context of Sartre's own writings. The theme of conscious and active commitment, a defining aspect of a human nature which demanded full expression, was taken up by the French philosopher in a climate of global warfare, Fascism in Spain and Italy, and Nazi rule in Germany, mass destruction of the Jews and other 'undesirable' groups, Stalinism in the Soviet Union. Such events had been made feasible by the deployment of science and destructive mass technology exceeding the horrors of World War One.

In the years leading up to World War Two, and of course during the war, great disillusionment reigned with regard to political and social systems upon which citizens had relied for centuries. The whole way of life and the human purpose associated with such systems came under attack. A fresh readiness to question the legitimacy of the beliefs, principles and institutions surrounding them emerged, coupled with a greater preparedness to search for psy-

chological and subjective truths than would be the case amid more
secure institutional structures (Mairet, 1948, p. 10). In this climate
the existential view of human nature was attractive for its hostility
towards a determinism which had engendered almost indescrib-
able consequences in Europe. Sartre's Marxist humanism in the
form of profound disillusionment rather than a nineteenth-century
optimism was more attuned to the modern world. Thus he became
the contemporary world's most articulate representative of the
existentialist conception of human nature. From his personal
experience in the French resistance movement against Fascism,
Sartre portrays the human obsessed by a search for meaning amid
despair which nevertheless emphasises the significance of *freedom*.
Sartre's formal philosophising of human nature was strongly
influenced by the phenomenology of Husserl (1859–1938), the
German philosopher who identifies human consciousness as the
kernel of being human, and Heidegger (1889–1976) whose main
work *Being and Time* (1927) is directed at the possibility of humans
able to lead an authentic existence faced with death's certainty
(Stevenson, 1987, p. 9).

Sartre's use of the personal and the specific example is neither
accidental nor idiosyncratic. It reflects the rejection of a *generalised*
portrayal of human beings, replaced by the perspective that existence
precedes essence. All that we *are* is decided for us in the process
of living, extending further than the evident properties necessary
for survival (eating, sleeping) in every human being. Sartre unequivocally proclaims that the quest for human freedom defines human
'nature' since humans possess the capacity to imagine other possibilities. There is no way of denying the responsibility of
self-definition; to be a free being means *acting*.

Being and Nothingness (1943), a detailed exposition of the
alienated, subjective individual symptomatic of the twentieth
century, portrays human beings in the world as unavoidably
alienated; that consciousness which makes them human reduces
their significance, disconnecting them *from* the world. He distinguishes between being-in-itself (*en-soi*) and being-for-itself (*pour-soi*)
as two modes of being related by an unbridgeable separation.
Seeing an object or a person means being defined by the other. We
only exist through separation from some condition. Implicit in this
condition is the separateness of each individual.

These insights may well have fuelled Simone de Beauvoir's *The
Second Sex* (1974) but she transposes them into an unprecedented
critique of male thought. Her feminist categories are specific and
unique in demonstrating how woman becomes 'other', distinct,
separate *and* inferior to the male. Man is seen as self, woman as
'other' in de Beauvoir's existentialism. But the inability of women
to develop their selfhood becomes a *social* construction, so that

women have internalised the idea that man is the essential, woman the inessential (examined further in Chapter 6).

In its deep subjectivism (focus on the inner human subject), Sartre's philosophical mode of analysing the human condition constitutes psychology. Sartre reaches back in the process to psychoanalysis, replacing the Freudian method with an existential psychoanalysis which has in turn been adapted and developed therapeutically by psychotherapists such as Rollo May (1953) and psychologist Abraham Maslow (1968), whose ideas are discussed in Chapter 9.

Sartre refutes the Freudian perspective of a psychologically determined human being imbued with unconscious mental states which produce human behaviour, on the grounds that all aspects of our mental lives are intentional, chosen and our own responsibility (Stevenson, 1987, p. 95). Any attempt to deny this is considered 'bad faith' by Sartre. The set of choices that a human being makes brings the meaning to a person's behaviour or way of life, and defines the nature of that person. For Sartre, life or the human personality is not an unconsciously channelled object. Rather, a person *is* that life. Human beings are nothing more and nothing less than the totality of all their acts comprising such lives. Yet the *consciousness* of this 'fact' is derived from the consciousness of the other, so that I am separate and nothing for myself.

Escape from this alienated condition is through commitment. However, a weakness of the existential philosophy is that this commitment is not self-evident; it is created by the situation in which humans find themselves, frequently one of class oppression. Unless this is recognised and acted upon, the commitment is vacuous. To this extent, Sartre's existentialism must incorporate a social model of human nature. Otherwise the existentialist theory cannot facilitate the types of change demanded by Sartre's personal situation and political commitment.

Consequently, Sartre's later synthesis of existentialism and Marxism, based upon the Hegelian dialectical method, is more politically targeted. This notion of the dialectic implies that the motor of existence is a whole series of opposites and denials. 'Never in the thought of the West has the Self been so pervaded by negation' suggests Barrett (1962, p. 247). On the other hand, it may be contended that the Sartrean human being, acting and striving for human freedom, exceeds the realms of negativity and nothingness towards a revolutionary (as opposed to spiritual) transcendence of the human conciousness.

Once the external world and action becomes part of a dialectical (two-way) equation, one confronts the strict limitations of existentialism's individual-centred theory. Having recognised the human importance of class oppression in society, Sartre meets a considerable dilemma. Existentialism's preoccupation with individual freedom does not admit external 'givens' or conditions of scarcity socially created in the course of history. Sartre's wartime experiences, however, cannot be satisfactorily explained solely in terms of an inner sense of alienation and separateness and theorised through a psychology of the self and subjective consciousness. Thus Sartre wheels in the direction of a Marxist-based theory of *social* being.

His other major theoretical work, *Critique of Dialectical Reason* (1976), openly engages with the outside world and Marxist themes, and attempts to import into the Marxian panoply philosophical insights regarding human beings and the human condition. He notes that inhumanity does not derive from any 'human nature' but is an interiorised scarcity (lack of an inner nature) which is produced by humans destroying themselves as a species throughout history; in this manner we may begin to explain the seeming permanence of war, violence and aggression.

Sartre's brand of Marxism, initially stimulated by the existentialist theory of the human being, contributes an important voice in the modern Marxist debate. Doubts linger as to whether the Sartrean existential picture of human nature *can* be validly imposed upon a Marxist analysis, especially if one views existentialism's model of human nature as grounded in pessimism and a non-spiritual nihilism. Alternatively, we may construe these very features as potential truths about our 'humanity' which a Marxist determinism is incapable of recognising.

Existentialism, then, gives us a crucial picture of the twentieth-century human being, bereft of earlier certainties, encountering an existential vacuum as the familiar social structures are sundered apart, and thus forced to develop through the resources of self. It has offered the antidote to the reductionist biological, instinctual theories of human nature and acted as an antidote to a crude Marxist determinism which developed the picture of the oppressed human being driven inexorably by systemic forces to her/his destiny. Its model of human nature has stood opposed to behaviourism, and whilst saturated with pessimism at one level, at another level the Sartrean emphasis on personal decision making and commitment gave it a sharper, more optimistic twist. The existential concern with the subjective, inner core to human nature has not only provided a critical dimension in psychology's development, but through phenomenology has proved an important influence in social and sociological theory (discussed in Chapter 4). However, its assumption of personal autonomy is questionable and causes problems in attributing unshackled power to the human will; a Sartrean commitment to changing the individual's situation necessitates overarching alterations to the external social fabric which suggests a more holistic model, as discussed below.

Marxism

The Marxist theory of human nature, formulated by Marx and Engels in the nineteenth century, was subject to major conflicts in interpretation during the twentieth century. The predominant materialist perspective emanated from the revolutionary success of Bolshevism in 1917 and the fierce struggles for political power during the Stalinist epoch from the 1920s onwards. Marxist ideas on human nature were initially propagated within an overwhelmingly optimistic set of beliefs in science and the progressive forces of social change.

At root, the Marxist conception of human nature is a materialist one which asserts that the human being is part of nature. Marx conceived of human nature as imminently changeable, and adopted the essential tenets of Darwin's *The Origin of Species*, challenging prevailing beliefs in the immutability of human life. The dialectical materialism of Marx and Engels, clearly antimetaphysical (not recognising the autonomy of ideas), is grounded in biology. First, the human is seen as an organism, but a self-conscious one. But secondly, an essential condition of being human rests in the relationship to social production. Classical Marxism deems human behaviour to be ultimately determined by the mode of production employed by humans in sustaining their existence. Hence, human nature emerges along with changing productive *systems*. The Marxian approach of historical materialism assumes that any understanding of what we are as beings must contain an explicit *historical* dimension. The Marxian schema thus places great stress on the augmentation of people's *capacities*, both physical and mental, in the development of productive resources. Marxists contend that the manipulation of nature is a way of transforming humans' own nature. Therefore the individual human's nature must be grasped as a *social* nature.

A third component of the classical Marxist theory of human nature is the element of needs, which Marx and Engels considered as changeable in a practical sense, but basically universal and deep-rooted. In certain societies and at particular historical moments they become submerged and repressed. Writers then take recourse in abstract notions of humanity which appear to stand *independently* of economic systems, but the ability fully to express human needs has been badly damaged and diminished by the capitalist economic system which treats humans simply as labour.

Within the Marxist debate the human side to human nature vies with the naturalistic and scientifically reductionist. The political balance of forces was instrumental in influencing what became accepted as the official Marxist version. Hence, those works concerned with alienation, *German Ideology* (1947) and *Economic and Philosophical Manuscripts* (1963), were swept aside during the Stalinist years in favour of scientific laws relating to the motor of historical change and revolution's inevitability. Perhaps this was because of their obliqueness, but it is more likely to have been due to their greater susceptibility to manipulation. The deterministic 'laws' of change were fitted into the Russian Bolshevik Party orthodoxy after the 1917 seizure of power.

Faced with burgeoning poverty and economic hardship, the Soviet Union increasingly affirmed the building up of the industrial economic system's productive capacities according to the laws of dialectical materialism, so as to reflect the rise of the industrial proletariat. The planned system was to determine the new 'man'. Objective science was placed on a pedestal, whilst the state forged the behaviour of human beings. Stalin's writings expound the tenets of Marxist-Leninist thinking to illustrate that 'everything changes'. Lysenko's approved biological science and his work on plant breeding was used to exemplify how human beings, and particularly 'Soviet Man', could transfer nature at will (Kolakowski, 1981, pp. 102–3).

For many the 'hard' materialist stance which exalted industrial power and might was the only feasible bulwark to Nazism and fascism, given that the more individualistic and romantically inclined nineteenth-century notions of liberalism and social democracy had been effectively and brutally quashed (Biddiss, 1977, p. 217). What seemed to matter was the totality of human production and the transformation of the environment. Such large-scale economic and social engineering released no space for the person's inner nature which was viewed as a luxury.

Dialectical materialism's proclaimed laws, outlined by Bukharin (1888–1938), Lenin (1870–1924) and Stalin (1879–1953), placed all the theoretical weight on the *scientific* nature of Marxism, and the 'fact' that humans do not possess free will; all human action is causally determined. Any ethical content in human nature is similarly ignored. Lenin's interpretation of Marxism thrust to the fore the knowledge of 'reality' and action conforming to that reality, instead of concern with the critical consciousness of one's action and conduct (Lenin, 1908).

The reductionism which characterises the Marxist-Leninist model of human nature was reflected in the formal Soviet Union approval of a Pavlovian behaviourist psychology reliant on physiological explanation. The Russian was praised for his belief in human beings' incredible plasticity and potentiality (a belief not unlike that of American behaviourist psychology, which has always been criticised by the Soviet Union!). At the other end of the scale, the Soviet leadership deliberately suppressed Vygotsky's ideas of consciousness and people involved in *creating* their environment (Bottomore et al., 1983, p. 403). The Freudian psychoanalytic theory of human behaviour and its associated therapies were also officially censored as a response to Freud's denial that economic structural change begets basic changes in human nature.

This is an untenable perspective of the human carrying serious consequences. As interpreted by the Soviet apparatchiks, the rigid notion of dialectical materialism and reductionist science led to totalitarian policies, human oppression and the sacrifice of untold numbers in Stalin's work camps. However, those Marxists ranged against such Soviet distortions sought to present a humanist or a critical version of human beings.

The Marxist humanist account is based on an acceptance that one cannot deny a basic form of human nature, and that Marx's writings do in effect support this view. Otherwise, they ask, where is the benchmark for assessing what is negative in human behaviour? How does one know? They argue for the existence of a morality which transcends relativism. Again, they mount their critique on the supposition that human history, whatever its twists and turns, includes one common ingredient which is the human being.

Marx does not come to reject the idea of human nature after the writing of his *Economic and Philosophical Manuscripts* (1844). Geras (1983) demonstrates its key explanatory role; he contends that historical materialism itself, Marx's wholly distinctive approach to society, sits squarely upon the idea of a human nature (Geras, p. 107).

Members of the Frankfurt School were especially prominent as critics of Marx's economism, though different approaches to specific classical Marxist prognoses on the future of society and the possible improvement of human potentiality existed within the School. Certain of its members felt that Freudian insights carried revolutionary potential if grafted on to a Marxian framework.

For any analysis concerned with Marxist or psychoanalytic thought, Fromm is an important figure. Initially a Freudian, he believes that human beings possess impressive creative potential for overcoming their alienation from fellow human beings and nature. A deep capacity exists for co-operation and friendship. Hence, Fromm's model is antithetical to Freud's biological instinctually motivated individual impelled towards acts of aggression fundamentally antisocial by nature. Fromm notes (1961) that there *are* anthropological constants, and that humans are not infinitely adaptable to changed conditions. But he also considers that one ought to differentiate between what is constant in human nature, and what is historically pliable. Human needs are not equated with individual satisfaction but with common creative needs that have *de facto* clashed with historical tendencies, for example capitalism's discordant fragmentalising forces of competition. The Freudian analysis of history resulting from psychological and ahistorical pressures is displaced by Marx's concept of history and the Hegelian-Marxist framework of alienation.

Alienation is the central theme which runs through from the prime exposition in the *Economic and Philosophical Manuscripts* (1844) to the later *Capital* (1868–94) but its human meaning is more pointedly explored in the former. Alienation in Fromm's eyes does represent the accumulation of oppression and unhappiness, but not all of it arising from capitalist society. The communist bloc regimes shared little in common with what Fromm perceives as Marx's *humanistic* vision encompassing solidarity, expansion of human beings' creative powers, freedom from constraint and freedom from irrational authority. Fromm's own list of expanded human needs includes relatedness, transcendence, rootedness, sense of identity and the need for a frame of orientation and devotion. But Fromm is more deeply entrenched in moral thought and spirituality. He situates Marx in a tradition of German humanism and Zen Buddhism, and sees the Marxian analysis as applying universally and not only to the working class. Human beings are capable of perceiving their own nature and thus, through the act of love, of shaking themselves free from false needs.

The problem with this avowedly humanistic and spiritual world view is that it evacuates the whole universe of external pressures bearing upon the isolated individual, and thus distances Fromm from the *revolutionary* implications of Marx's sharper focus of an economic alienation integral to the system of capitalist production. Fromm removes human struggle from the social arena into the spheres of the 'soul of man'. Kolakowski, the Polish philosopher, suggests that such a selective treatment of Marx renders Fromm's Marxism:

> little more than a series of trite aspirations … His picture of Marx is thus almost as one-sided and simplistic as the one he criticizes, which presents Marxism as a blueprint for Stalinism. (Kolakowski, 1981, p. 387)

Other representations from the Frankfurt School advance a more critical theory in the face of Marxist dogma, on the surface seemingly more pessimistic than Fromm's rather fuzzy optimism. Herbert Marcuse (1898–1979) became the most celebrated of the School in the 1960s. His concern with human nature excavates the Hegelian tension 'between potentiality and actuality, between what men and things could be and what they are in fact' (Marcuse, 1968, p. 69). Humans may realise their possibilities, but have so far been constantly alienated in society from achieving such possibilities; society regiments the individual into a *One Dimensional Man* (1964). Capitalism prevents the articulation of human needs. Alienation is manifested in repression of the individual, but Marcuse argues that the new technology and wealth in the west can release the surplus suppression by enabling more time to be devoted to the eroticisation of the whole person.

Geoghegan (1987, p. 108) proposes that Marcuse's picture of the human being is revolutionary by dint of its utopianism. Marcuse brings a refreshing perspective to Marx's notion of self-realisation through work by positing new opportunities for life *outside* the workplace. Clearly, the Marxist idea of human nature is ambivalent and has itself been subjected to much internal debate in the twentieth century. Such debates are evidently not about an abstracted philosophy but chart future directions for human society.

To sum up the discussion, orthodox practical Marxism has in many respects proved as deterministic and reductionist as the behaviouristic model's human plasticity. Marx's own theorising on human nature certainly implies a historical materialist formulation but is more fluid than any model of dialectical laws. His thought is also more dynamic than the static development in behaviourist thinking, in the gestation from his earlier philosophy to the later more specific political economy. The emphasis upon a critical awareness of human consciousness means that self-activity is attributed an important role. Internal Marxist debates juxtaposing the humanistic as against the reductionist theory of human nature are still of immediate concern, notwithstanding the formal transfer of power in former communist societies.

Summary and Conclusions

In concluding the chapter, we have seen how the Freudian model's picture of determined instinctual drives builds upon the biological metaphor but then suggests that much of our nature is submerged and hidden from us in the realms of the preconscious, always ranged against culture and civilisation. This presents a considerable challenge to moralistic assumptions of cultural consensus. The Freudian theory certainly runs the risk of biological reductionism, but its incorporation into social theory suggests its critical potential. Behaviourism's scientific claims, preoccupied with externally observable, verifiable behaviour as the hub of an infinitely malleable human nature, cannot be divorced from the social implications. The behaviourist theory of human nature gives short shrift to human consciousness and thus the human subject's inner life. By gaining command over the environment, it is argued, people may control the human individual – hence its appeal to political systems both east and west, and hence its dangers. The tenor of existentialism, however, posing a distinctly antiscientific prospect for human nature, challenges those deterministic and manipulatory theories of human nature (most notably positivistic psychology) which depend upon the scientific metaphor. Sartre's portrait of human nature *begins* with the inner being whose essence has to be authentically created through commitment. But the difficulty remains that an exclusively existentialist focus which also fully recognises that humans are in society is a logical absurdity. Finally, the Marxist model, the social model of human nature *par excellence*, is far from monolithic, politically dominated by the Stalinist materialist interpretation. Yet it is countered by an alternative humanist vision incorporating existential and spiritual insights into the Marxist corpus. Clearly, any feasible optimism about human change is reliant upon interpretations of human nature that recognise the capacities of human beings to relate to each other, to shape, and be shaped by their environment. In the following chapter we turn to the specific role played by biological theories of human nature in juxtaposition to those theories and models concerned with the role of culture.

Further Reading

General Surveys

Michael Biddiss, *The Age of the Masses* (Penguin, 1977). Modern European thought in the context of historical events.

Robert Nye, *Three Psychologies* 3rd edn. (Brooks/Cole, 1986). Freud, Skinner and Rogers; specific sections on human nature.

Leslie Stevenson, *Seven Theories of Human Nature* 2nd edn. (Oxford University Press, 1987). Covers the main thinkers of this chapter.

Freudianism

J.A.C. Brown, *Freud and the Post-Freudians* (Penguin, 1961). Freud's theories, Horney, Fromm, Stack Sullivan and others.

Sigmund Freud, *Five Lectures on Psycho-analysis* (Hogarth, 1957).

Robert W. Marks (ed.), *Great Ideas in Psychology* (Bantam, 1966).

Existentialism

William Barrett, *Irrational Man: A Study in Existential Philosophy* (Doubleday, 1962). A historical exposition.

Jean-Paul Sartre, *Existentialism and Humanism* (Methuen, 1948; 1973). An accessible statement on human nature.

Leslie Stevenson (ed.), *The Study of Human Nature* (Oxford University Press, 1981). Excerpts from Sartre's *Being and Nothingness.*

Behaviourism

John Dewey, *Human Nature and Conduct, 1922* (Southern Illinois University Press, 1983).

Barry Schwartz and Hugh Lacey, *Behaviorism, Science and Human Nature* (Norton, 1982). A sympathetic account of Pavlov, Thorndyke, Skinner and others.

B.F. Skinner, *Beyond Freedom and Dignity* (Penguin, 1971). Essays on his technology of behaviour approach.

Marxism

T.B. Bottomore and Maximilian Rubel (eds.), *Karl Marx: Selected Writings in Sociology and Social Philosophy* (Penguin, 1963). The most useful starting point for beginners.

T.B. Bottomore (ed.), *Karl Marx: Early Writings* (McGraw-Hill, 1963). Necessary reading for Marx's major statements on human nature.

T.B. Bottomore, *The Frankfurt School* (Tavistock, 1983). The critical theory side to the debate.

Herbert Marcuse, *Eros and Civilisation* (Beacon Press, 1964).

Biology or Culture?

Introduction

We have just examined the complexities of twentieth-century philosophies and theories of human nature; the sociopolitical connotations of their approach to the human subject have been significant enough to shape the course of major ideological struggles. But the human nature debate, frequently posed as nature/nurture, presents itself perhaps more familiarly in the terms of biology versus culture, setting out the evidence from biological science as against the cultural creations of group life explored by anthropologists. Undoubtedly, the scientific paradigm has ruled the twentieth century, shaping our ideas of what it is to be human. And to a large extent this paradigm has produced a myriad of specialisms, including offshoots of nineteenth-century Darwinism and evolutionism. Scientific dominance was apparent in the majority of the key ideas of the early twentieth century relating to human nature. Behaviourist psychology has been driven by the scientific approach to human behaviour, exemplified by Watson and Skinner. Freudianism conceptualised human actions through instinctual biological forces. Marxist theory took as its starting point the evolution of human beings in relation to the evolution of social systems. Only existentialism denied human nature as 'given'.

But as the century has progressed our ambivalence towards scientific knowledge and method has intensified along with science and technology's growing power. Certainly scientific discovery has been put to such horrific *uses* as to question our whole *raison d'être*. On the other hand, the biological sciences such as molecular biology have enabled unparalleled knowledge of the nature of human life, and indeed have facilitated cures for disease, for example the study of hereditary disease based on findings from genetic evolution. As we shall discuss in Chapter 5, the issue of just *what* is inherited has proved politically controversial – particularly the issue of inherited human intelligence.

A prime issue relating to the modern scientific view of human activity is the perennial danger of determinism and reductionism, whereby physical or natural science characterises the human purely in physical terms – humans driven by animal instincts or humans nothing more than atoms, a frame of mind characterised in extreme form by molecular biologist Jacques Monod: '... everything can be reduced to simple, obvious, mechanical interactions. The animal is a machine, and there is no difference at all between men and animals' (Monod, cited in Lewis, 1974, p. 9). This perspective has been attacked by humanists, theologians and social theorists. But it has also been questioned by scientists and philosophers of science particularly on the grounds of determinism and the absence of human consciousness. Such challenges, however, have themselves fallen prey to reductionist thinking.

This chapter explores these debates and their associated tensions. It probes the idea that human nature is 'given' or determined, and discusses the polarity of human beings as advanced primates and humans as *essentially* different from animals. The chapter moves on to explore further the biological sciences deriving insights into human nature from the study of animals – ethology and sociobiology, examining the consequences of the sociobiologists' findings re: genetic evolution for theories of human nature and for the progress of the social sciences. Addressing the nature/nurture debate, we then turn to those ideas illustrating the role that culture plays in the development of human nature. Writings from social anthropology are used to illuminate on the one hand the 'search for human universals' in human cultures, and on the other hand the diversity of social cultural forms.

Animal or Human?

The question of whether or not human beings are animals is tied to the question of whether nature is different from culture, and *vice versa*. It means evaluating ideas that humans are essentially different from animals, that humans are simply later versions of apes, and are inextricably related to the primates and hence not essentially different, and that studying human nature is synonymous with the study of nature (animal life), that is, investigating human nature as a natural science, treating human beings as basically the same.

The proposition that 'man' is essentially different from animal is integral to spiritual models of human nature suggesting a freedom from the naturally given, a self-consciousness, and an ability to attain knowledge of ethical truths (Stevenson, 1987, p. 47). Humans can exercise moral choice. 'No animal can sin, man can fall far below the animal level, to almost unimaginable wickedness, cruelty and degradation; or he can rise to the fuller realisation of human potentialities. The choice is his', states Lewis (1974, p. 189). The human is *unique* in such experience, in the 'highs and lows', distinctive features of the human condition which extend 'far beyond anything to be found even in the highest primates' (Peacocke, 1986, p. xix).

A philosophical approach would argue that humans' ability to conceptualise makes them unlike animals, and this ability in turn is tied to language – seen as an exclusively human capacity which the primates do not possess. Cultural and social constructionists have also tended to characterise the 'social' or 'culture' as possessing an autonomous existence defining the human.

Such a position of 'uniquely different' is a difficult one to maintain in the face of counter-evidence and the opposed argument that humans are *not* essentially different from the primates. Darwin's work, described in *The Origin of Species* (1859), demonstrated continuous development from animals to humans, so that the features of the human species may be traced back billions of years. Humans have evolved through the process of natural selection, whereby those types of animal most adaptive to the environment, that is, the more intelligent and the quicker, survive, live longer, breed, and pass on their superior characteristics to the next generation (Hirst and Woolley, 1982, pp. 5–22).

Given that humans are undoubtedly the product of evolution, one would expect to unearth a continuous and close connection between nature and human beings. As Reynolds (1973, p. 144) notes:

> ... man the thinker is only a part of man; however meaningful our actions they contain a strand of behaviour. We are flesh and blood and nervous system organized in very much the same way as the apes with whom we share a common evolutionary origin.

Indeed, we are similar *physically* in a number of respects to the apes. In the Darwinian scheme, human beings are seen to be part of the higher mammals (those able to learn from experience) – the primates, whose origins go back 70 million years. Both apes and humans have common origins in their evolution. The cultural use of tools and tool making has affected the process of natural selection and led to the physical structure of modern human beings by dint of emphasising features crucial to survival (Hirst and Woolley, 1982, pp. 5–21).

Contemporary field studies of the 1960s (de Vore, 1965, p. 26, cited in Hirst and Woolley, 1982, p. 63) demonstrate that one can locate a 'fundamental primate way of life' common to humans, apes and monkeys, essentially an organised *group* life. Such primate social organisations – baboon, chimpanzee and orangutan models – differed from each other and from those of humans. Along with tool use, they clearly played a significant role in controlling the environment and in survival. As the human species emerged, cultural development became more intensified, and so the human became greatly distinguishable from the primate. One of the impressive divergencies has been the size of the human brain, considerably larger as a proportion of the body than that of the most intelligent ape.

Evidently, the study of human nature cannot omit the natural origins of the human species, and hence the biological sciences are pertinent in any debate purporting to define what human beings are, in recognition of a set of needs common to humans and other animals – that is, an acceptance that humans are not basically different, but that the differences are more a matter of degree. How far, then, has the 'new biology' offered us the requisite insights regarding human nature and the interconnections between nature and the human species? Answering this question leads us to concentrate on ethology and sociobiology.

Ethology

Ethology has proven to be a widely popular school of biological thought, perhaps due to its propensity for wide publicity given the ethologists' intense focus on human aggression. In more recent years it has become more or less subsumed under sociobiology. The human ethologists' portrayal of human nature is wholly based on ethology's natural science investigations which assume that all factors identified in animals must also be present for humans, since we are effectively nothing more than animals.

Konrad Lorenz and Robert Ardrey, two of ethology's main exponents, took as their prime focus innate aggression and competitiveness. Since the assumptions they make are so central to the human nature debate, the specific ramifications of their rather crude biologism, especially concerning the prognoses of violence and warfare, are examined more closely in Chapter 5. At this juncture we are interested in the general outline of their theories.

Zoologist Lorenz views behaviour as evolving from that of other animals, as part of a bodily and physiological continuum, and subject to the same natural causes. He advances what he deems the four big drives – feeding, reproduction, flight and aggression. The latter, however, is presented as the pivotal drive. Even love is 'explained' or defined in relation to aggression, which is the starting point. Without hostility there can be no love, since 'love is constructed out of the forces of hostility' (Reynolds, 1976, p. 7). Lorenz's studies of fish and birds identify battles and threatening behaviour between members of the same species. Aggression between the rival males of a species is shown as leading to the strongest both leaving their offspring and available to defend family and the herd. By claiming and defending territory through devices such as bird songs, animals are able to ensure their access to food and space. On Aggression (1966; 1974) fixes the emphasis on the *evolutionary* facets of aggression, for instance social ranking and sexual selection, mediated through the ritualisation of aggression. Aggression is redirected away from our mates towards our neighbours and outsiders. This deflected antagonism, contends Lorenz, is genetically grounded (Lorenz, 1973, p. 49).

For Lorenz, human beings possess an innate drive to behave aggressively towards their own species, an instinctual mechanism which explains all sorts of historical conflicts in human history involving ostensibly rational human beings. Militant poses and actions are seen as comprising basic human nature essential for survival purposes, features evolved from the prehuman response in defence of the 'community'.

By stressing innate instincts, Lorenz suggests a rigidity of nature which counters Skinner's environmental behaviourism. At the same time, the concept of an innate drive towards aggression does have an affinity with the Freudian id and its invocation of aggressive instincts and death wish, deemed to disempower reason. 'Man is the creature of reason', Lorenz concedes. But he (she) is also subject to innate behaviour. 'He is not exclusively a creature of reason; his behaviour is by no means so thoroughly determined by reason as is assumed by the majority of philosophical anthropologists' (Lorenz, 1971, cited in Stevenson, 1981, p. 228). To this extent the explanations of the ethologists are, as noted by Reynolds (1976, p. 3), Freudian in their emphatic conception of the human individual as a biological, as distinct from a wholly cultural, entity.

At one level, ethology correctly recognises the import of the animal–human connections. But there are definite problems. Simon (cited in Lewis, 1974, p. 95) enunciates four major objections to the ethological approach: that it fails to do justice to distinctively human characteristics (the aesthetic, religious and philosophical sides of nature); it ignores the significance of language and communication; it oversimplifies human beings' social behaviour, especially aggression; and that humans' social behaviour is *not* at all instinctual (borne out by human beings' very adaptability and lack of fixed behavioural patterns).

A more specific methodological critique may be made. Stevenson (1987, p. 129) points to the unscientific binding together of Lorenz's four big drives. Improbably, everything about behaviour is held to be tethered to aggression, and thus cannot be tested. Given such circular reasoning, it is unsurprising that nothing in the way of changeability is attributed to human beings, or that humans' socially constructed practices are seen as the irrevocable natural condition. Hinde (1982, p. 20) also points to the dangers for ethologists in drawing false parallels between humans and animals, in the light of human capacities for cognitive functioning, the cultural diversity among humans and the many animal species.

Ethology, then, makes no distinction between animals and humans, and conflates the instinctive tendencies of each. However, reading off animal behaviour such as patterns of aggression to infer the fixity of human nature is methodologically and ethically crude, leading to a static picture of human nature wrenched from human reflectiveness. Sociobiology claims to have overcome such crudity.

Sociobiology

In this section we analyse the defining components of sociobiology and its relationships to ethology, examine the pertinence of genetic evolution within the human nature debate and assess its perspective on the purported biology–culture disjuncture. Where sociobiology has moved beyond ethology is in refuting the viability of reading off animal behaviour for observations about *human* nature, in challenging the centrality of instincts, and in bringing culture and adaptation into the study of human life. Sociobiology is a new version of ethology, and indeed a modification of Darwinian evolutionism. Its novel feature is a concentration upon the 'gene', seen as the predominant mechanism for reproduction and the growth of animal and human life; a gene as opposed to a species or an individual. A sociobiological definition of the human is considered by its proponents to be radically different from the ethologist version. Sociobiologists attack the notion of group selection and replace it by gene selection. It is the gene that drives for survival, not the group. Gene behaviour provides the foundation for the understanding of social patterns. Dawkins (1989) perceives gene behaviour as the thrusting mechanism directing social and individual behaviour.

As individuals, we are survival machines for genes which are nearly immortal. The model of the evolutionary gene constructed by Dawkins and other neoDarwinians revolves around the non-human species. The importance of the focus upon the gene is that evolutionary change occurs because certain genes increase while others decrease in number. Differential breeding success is measured and analysed by mainstream biological science; individuals carry certain genes which increase in number while individuals carrying other genes slowly diminish. Thus 'the physiological and behavioural adaptedness of any particular organism to its natural and social environment is defined through its ability to contribute more than the average number of its genes to future generations' (Dickens, 1992, p. 97).

Earlier we commented that the ethologists' reading off from their punctilious detailing of animal behaviour to generalise about the human world is a suspect exercise. Nevertheless, despite the fact that the new evolutionary biologists in the 1960s were studying the genes of non-humans, E.O. Wilson's *Sociobiology: The New Synthesis* (1975) claimed to be 'the systematic study of the biological basis of all social behaviour', and to integrate biology into sociology and the social sciences. This effectively professes to explain the human *per se*, and of course this condition is allegedly explained scientifically as a naturally competitive urge ranged against the materiality of scarce resources, a contest of strategies which produce stability through the survival of the fittest.

The 'tempered' aggression is dealt with differently from the ethological approach, in that both aggression and co-operation are accounted for by *evolved* cultural co-operative behaviour, Wilson's explanation incorporating 'evolutionary stable strategies' and forms of 'altruism' nevertheless harnessed to genetic composition. Such strategies represent both learned and inherited forms of social and individual behaviour. One does not divorce the individually inherited from the socially learned, since the selfish genes of an individual lead to socially compatible preservation. In a later work, Lumsden and Wilson (1981) propose that mind and culture have to be integrated with the sociobiological account, culture representing more than a passive element, strong enough to influence the course of genes and vary the natural selection process ('gene-culture co-evolution'). Culture is able to produce the climate for genetic evolution. However, genes are still capable of holding culture 'on a leash', so that genetic evolution remains the overriding factor in understanding culture.

The organic approach to human beings stands directly in the line of Darwinism and social Darwinism, but also predates the latter in its Hobbesian atomism and the mechanical model of the human being (Chapter 1). Rose et al. (1984, p. 242) trace the survivalist tradition from Hobbes through Malthus and Spencer in the nineteenth century to Wilson's speculations regarding human qualities. Wilson's sociobiological synthesis insists on projecting an image of *human* nature even though the scientific basis of his own *Sociobiology* and Dawkins' work was conducted with animals and insects.

Human Nature (Wilson, 1978) presents a picture of a single human nature shared by humanity over many generations, 'within which relatively minor hereditary influences recycle through ever-changing patterns, between the sexes and across families and entire populations' – a biological unity (Wilson, 1978, p. 50). On the basis of sociobiological theory Wilson details four of the 'elemental categories of behaviour': aggression, sex, altruism, and religion (Wilson, 1978, p. 97).

Aggression in human nature is represented by the practice of war, 'a straightforward example of a hypertrophied biological predisposition' (p. 116) through hundreds of thousands of years of evolved learning rules followed by our programmed brains, that is, programmed for aggression (p. 119). With respect to *sex*, 'males are characteristically aggressive, especially toward one another and most intensely during the breeding season' (p. 125), whilst 'women as a group are less assertive and physically aggressive', the magnitude of the distinction depending on the culture (p. 128).

Altruism in human nature is interpreted by Wilson as a self-preserving feature – whether related to kin or 'allies of the moment' (p. 155). Here Wilson conceives human kinship as a biological, universal feature. It can be 'hard-core' – based on kin selection – and 'soft-core' – more like a general social contract. Higher ethical values in human beings evolve culturally, but at the end of the day '[t]he genes hold culture on a leash' and hence, '... [h]uman behaviour ... is the circuitous technique by which genetic material has been and will be kept intact. Morality has no other demonstrable ultimate function' (p. 167).

Finally, Wilson delineates the 'deep structure of religious belief' subject to natural selection as three successive levels: the ecclesiastical, the ecological and the genetic (p. 176). The highest forms of religious practice confer biological advantage, and also 'congeal identity' (p. 188).

Critiques of sociobiology range from the methodological to the political, and it has been argued that differences depend on whether or not one feels affinity or empathy with the biological discipline. The waters have also been muddied by noted sociobiologists transgressing the territory of scientific description and explanation of animal behaviour to theorise on human nature. Such speculations are open to question on a number of grounds (Stevens, 1990, p. 159).

First, although the model is able to predict, it is usually used to explain what is already there. Second, there is little *direct* evidence that genes influence human social behaviour, although they obviously shape the operation of the nervous, sensory and hormonal system, bearing upon how we feel. Third, sociobiology fails to recognise the extent to which capacity for language makes humans unlike other species. One might add that the existence of consciousness in humans and the intrinsic meaningfulness of human action constitute a convincing refutation of sociobiological reductionism.

Reynolds (1980, cited in Hirst and Woolley, p. 73) observes that in 30,000 years the human species' genetic composition has scarcely changed, whereas human life has moved from a hunting and gathering to a technological society. 'At the most,' states Stevens (1990, p. 160) 'sociobiology can offer only a *partial* explanation of human social behaviour. The complexities of social and economic life cannot simply be reduced to biological principles ...' There remains an ineluctable determinism whereby mental symbols are reduced to the physical (Lumsden and Wilson, 1981) and indeed such a physicalist reduction reveals the sociobiological definition as narrow and deplete of any real anthropological description. To quote Trigg (1985): 'Their reductionism leaves little room for any notions of culture or of mind which can themselves act on the brain as well as be constrained by the physical characteristics of the brain' (Trigg, p. 174).

Whilst such judgements are guarded, and clearly sympathetic, other prognoses have rejected the applicability and relevance of sociobiology in understanding a 'human nature' in modern cultures and complex societies. Anthropologists and sociologists have placed emphasis upon the culturally based meanings of social life, and within such a 'paradigm' *some* schools of thought have argued even against the proposition that evolutionary principles hold any explanatory power *at all*.

In summarising sociobiology's contribution to the biology:culture debate, the emphasis shifts from raw animal group instinct to gene survival which incorporates the cultural yet nevertheless restrains it. Sociobiology finally reaches back to biology and genetic impulses; although it may explain *some* human action, it ultimately banishes consciousness, language and human culture to the sidelines. In the following section we survey the study of culture and cultures in locating human beings, postponing until later (Chapter 5) an examination of explicitly political criticisms of biologically based explanation.

Culture and Society: the Search for Universals

In looking at the culture side of the biology:culture debate, one encounters two sorts of approach in anthropology. The first trawls human cultures and history for signs or evidence of a *common* human nature, expressed culturally – an approach which may admit biological scientific corroboration and insight. The other searches for the wealth of human diversity, unearthing the historical and geographical multiplicity of human behaviour and practices.

The 'search for universals' is a pursuit of some common human nature which marks us out as human. Functionalist anthropologists have been most engaged in the search for the natural, and contend that there *is* a human nature. Culture is not seen as contradictory to our inner biological needs but complementary to them. Midgley (1978, p. 285) remarks that the blank opposition of nature to culture may make sense *pace* an individual, but not in analysing groups or the human species. 'Culture is not an alternative or replacement for instinct, but its outgrowth and supplement,' Midgley (1978, p. 286) affirms.

The universal attributes making up our 'human nature' or humanness are usually 'structural', and anthropology has claimed that a number of universals exist, namely language, speech, family systems, symbolic communication and myth (Brown, 1991). Taylor (1985a, p. 215) considers language an overriding area of concern in the twentieth century, reflecting the modern world's intense interest in meaning. '[The] question of language is somehow strategic for the question of human nature ... man is above all the language animal' (p. 215), not least because of language's puzzling and enigmatic qualities (p. 216). Noam Chomsky's linguistics work, largely from a stance of counteracting Watson and Skinner's behaviourism (Chapter 2), characterises the human mind as innately capable of building language. Chomsky attacks Skinner's application of the concept of operant conditioning to language acquisition, which aims to show that language is subject to explanation through reinforcement processes (Skinner, 1957). In Chomsky's view, behaviourist psychology's empirical bent and orientation towards external stimuli are inadequate for handling the complexity and abstractness involved in understanding how humans learn language (Chomsky, 1968a, in Stevenson, 1981, p. 245). Skinner's deterministic science of behaviour, Chomsky reasons, affirms too much for itself, given *its* lack of evidence, and is clearly ideological (Chomsky, 1968b, pp. 104–32).

Chomsky infers that a systematic 'linguistic competence' underlies human behaviour which is not manifested in outward behaviour in any simple or direct manner. 'This system of linguistic competence is qualitatively different from anything that can be described in terms of ... the concepts of S–R psychology ... or the theory of simple automata' (Chomsky, 1968a, in Stevenson, 1981, p. 241). It is the existence of certain *innate* features, a highly 'explicit and detailed schematicism' that guides the human child in acquiring language. This instinctive knowledge which enables the derivation of 'complex and intricate knowledge on the basis of very partial data' is a fundamental constituent of human nature. Language's role is pivotal to communication, expression of thought and personal interaction. We all speak some language, and each language has a set of rules. When we learn a foreign language we soon realise there are definite rules, yet it is not clear how we acquire the rules for speaking our own language so efficiently at such an early age. Chomsky assumes that this must be the case in other spheres of human intelligence, cognition and behaviour: 'This collection, this mass of schematisms, innate organising principles, which guides our social and intellectual and individual behaviour, that's what I mean to refer to by the concept of human nature'(Chomsky and Foucault, in Elders, 1974, pp. 137–38). For Chomsky, then, human beings are not pieces of blank paper to be filled in by external environmental stimuli. A human nature does exist, accepting the biological structuring capacities of the mind. That is why individuals are able to use language creatively; the attribute of creativity constitutes the precise distinction between human language and nature (Benoist, 1973, p. 37). A biophysical structure underpins the mind, enabling us 'to deduce from the multiplicity of individual experiences a unified language' (Rabinow, 1984, p. 3). Considering this biological imprint, Chomsky's perspective is a challenge to the sharp distinction between human and apes.

Chomsky's basic rationalist thesis, following Descartes's dualistic concept of the independence of body and mind, is that humans are *innately* endowed with a deep structure of grammar. Unlike apes, we can follow a complexity of rules. For example:

> ... it seems that dialects that are superficially quite remote, even barely intelligible on first contact, share a vast central core of common rules and processes and differ very slightly in underlying structures, which seem to remain invariant through long historical eras (Chomsky, 1968a, in Stevenson, 1981, p. 247).

Children possess an 'innate grammar' in their developing minds. Their recognition of mistakes suggests a knowledge of the rules of some universal, organic grammar inscribed on the structures of the brain which underlie the basic edifice of all languages (Reynolds, 1976, pp. 191–2).

Children look for regularities in the speech they hear around them, making guesses about any rules underlying the sound patterns. They develop and refine hypotheses about these sounds, until they arrive at a complex set of rules which make sense of the regularities, and facilitate the formation of meaningful sentences with words in the correct order. Hence, for Chomsky there exists an internal innate device for making hypotheses regarding sound patterns or speech. But in addition children possess extra information – information additional to that required to learn a particular language, because babies are able to learn all languages equally well, for example a Chinese baby nurtured in Britain learns English just as quickly and efficiently as a British baby (Aitchison, 1976). Thus, reasons Chomsky, there are also 'language universals' enabling children to learn language so well because they 'know' what a language looks like in outline, and eventually can turn sounds and words around to make sense through sentences. Yet the final outcome is achieved only by children's ability to *evaluate* all the different possibilities. For instance, a child is able to move from a concoction of words such as 'have eat up large brown cows the grass' to 'large brown cows have eaten up the grass'. Chomsky's scheme becomes a Language Acquisition Device (LAD) which enables any child to acquire any language with relative ease (Aitchison, pp. 90–104).

But whilst the insights of Chomsky and his universalistic perspective on human nature are hugely influential, they have by no means produced a consensus of support. Leach (1982, pp. 110–11) has expressed scepticism of the alliance between theologians and 'the hard-nosed scientist' advancing the 'innate'. More specifically, Piaget's structuralism (1971) demonstrates the unidimensional quality of Chomsky; just as behaviourism is bereft of structures, Chomsky's linguistic analysis ignores the social and environmental structures through which the human subject is able to construct meaning. The child becomes active in the world; hence thought cannot be reduced to language.

Midgley (1978, p. 251) offers a philosophical critique of Chomsky's clear distinction between animal and human, noting the inconsistency between Chomsky's correct insistence that humans' linguistic faculties are innate (and thus, presumably, in need of a physical basis) and his argument that only humans, and not apes, possess this innate capacity for language. The validity of such a position is by no means unequivocal, in that apes have been shown to have learned *some* language, although no ape has been taught speech of a competence approaching that of a human being.

Benoist (1973, p. 43) objects that Chomsky's attempt to deny cultural diversity erects *ethnocentric* (culturally bound) limits to human nature which are defined in western terms. Chomsky's system of grammatical rules which he assumes is common to *all* languages, is based on investigation of European languages. Chomsky's method also eliminates the dimension of *historical* changes made to language codes and cultural systems (Benoist, 1973, p. 45). His structures of the mind are, for Carrithers (1992, p. 71), basically 'asocial and individualistic'; they take no account of human beings' necessary social interrelationships. Consequently educational researchers such as Bruner have explored more interactive and social perspectives. Bruner (1983) suggests that a child's intrinsic capacity for learning language (LAD) cannot fully operate without assistance from an adult and the social interactions occurring in any linguistic community. Again, acquiring language depends on social skills which are learnable and changeable.

Recognition of the family system as a universal has served to highlight the social nature of human beings, and demonstrates the human need for co-operation. The stress upon functions in functionalist anthropology (and sociology), as in Malinowski's work, has illustrated the bonds between human needs and culture. For Malinowski, a major anthropologist of the early twentieth century, certain needs are produced by culture; the family holds crucial significance in the satisfaction of fundamental human needs (Malinowski, cited in Trigg, 1985, p. 48). The family embodies custom, order and authority. Although it may take on different forms in different cultures, *universally* it performs similar functions in relating to human reproduction, food and order. It is the *common* function that is seen here as the basic expression of human requirements.

Social acts of symbolic communication make humans more than simply an animal; they join with the structures of language to convey meaning. French structuralist Levi-Strauss has been a consequential figure in modern anthropology and the study of human attributes, but he gives faint credence to biological evidence in analysing human society. Instead he devotes vast attention to categorisation, symbolism and rules. Humans are basically categorising and rule-making creatures, unlike other creatures (Levi-Strauss, 1966).

Levi-Strauss, like Chomsky, explores the interface between nature and culture through the study of language and structure, debunking in Rousseauesque fashion traditional metaphysical concepts of human nature (Benoist, 1973, p. 23). Levi-Strauss posits that some kind of latent opposition between nature and culture inhabits the customs, attitudes and behaviours of humans in societies. Human beings from the Levi-Strauss perspective are predisposed to formulate a 'we' which stands apart from 'others'; we perceive the latter as uncultured and savage. So as to unearth the nature of humans, one must turn back in comprehending how the human is related to nature, and this may be accomplished anthropologically through focusing upon myths and symbols. Structural anthropologists are thus engaged in a deciphering and formalising of an underlying logic (located beyond the actors' own conscious awareness) in human beings' seemingly random and haphazard cultural practices. This use of a social *unconscious* by Levi-Strauss clearly negates humanist conceptions of human nature as consciousness and subjectivity. Structuralism's methodology constructs formal relationships between the elements in a social system, for example the structures of kinship, myths and totemisms (Benoist, 1973) and is not really concerned with the individual elements.

Responding to the question, then, of what constitutes a human, or where does the boundary lie between culture and nature, Levi-Strauss contends that it is language that differentiates humans from others, and that humans can become aware of themselves as social creatures only by using metaphors (totem systems) which juxtapose and compare themselves with others. Categories of speech transform the human brain's structural characteristics with universal human *cultural* characteristics, which thus must be considered innate. As a result, humanly evolved patterns exist which have been internalised by the psyche, a process which finds its parallels in the specialised parts of the brain which generate speech formation. It is *symbolic* thought that differentiates human beings.

These represent hidden recesses of human nature which for Levi-Strauss have reconciled the contradictions between human nature and culture. Levi-Strauss's denial that human nature is situated in the spheres of consciousness (as with Chomsky's 'deep structures') resembles the Freudian concept of the unconscious, its symbols refracted through the 'animal' id clashing with the superego. Determinism is common to the two theorists, the Freudian unconscious behaviour depending upon instincts, whereas Levi-Strauss's unconscious structure is 'determined by the logic of nature written in the circuitry of the brain' (Badcock, 1975, p. 109). Where Freud emphasises the body's irrational instincts, Levi-Strauss prioritises the mind, a collective 'cogito' reflecting and created by nature, but a nature which is mainly an abstract principle.

But whilst his picture of human nature indicates affinities with Freudianism and seemingly with scientific Marxism, Levi-Strauss distances himself from Sartre's existentialist version of human nature, and in particular the idea that human nature is historically and perpetually made and remade. To this extent, Levi-Strauss's view of human nature is strongly anti-individualistic in the sociological functionalist tradition of Durkheim (Chapter 4). Sartre is overly subjectivist, and in Levi-Strauss's eyes cedes too much importance to historical explanation. He accuses Sartre of being ethnocentric by divorcing his society from others. Human nature is not to be found at the central point of the universe in human subjectivity.

Benoist (1973, pp. 27–8) construes this assault on Sartre as Levi-Strauss's attempt to displace humanism. Certainly Levi-Strauss, along with poststructuralist Foucault (Chapter 4), has come under fire for decimating the human subject by the adoption of an anti-humanist stance. However, it may be argued that Levi-Strauss is not so much dismissive of the *notion* of a human subject as critical of the empiricist idea that human consciousness counts for more than collective cultural universals. His focus on the intellectual, cognitive structures inherent within the mind, mediating the transformation from animal nature to human culture, has also been faulted for its marginalising of political, economic and social organisational factors. Goldmann (1969) claims that history and all human praxis disappear from Levi-Strauss's structural forms. Glucksmann (1974, pp. 88–93) detects an implicit psychological reductionism which understands primitive cultures in terms of the brain's physiological structures, and fails fully to explore the interactions between conscious behaviour and unconscious structure.

The political implication of this model of human nature is that a Marxist anthropologist by reputation, Levi-Strauss advocates a position militating *against* human change. 'Society cannot be *acted upon* purposefully since the social actors can never have a correct account of its workings' (Glucksmann, 1974, p. 92).

A cardinal misgiving with the structuralist anthropological strain relates to the problem of the nature:culture rift in Levi-Strauss and the related assumption that such a split is universally mirrored by the gender distinction of female = nature : male = culture. Earlier in his writings Levi-Strauss rejects the nature:culture fracture, an implied biological reductionism emphasising the role of the brain. But later he argues that the nature:culture split is an artificial construct of *culture*. Thus Levi-Strauss theorises nature alternately as the perceived phenomenological world (excluding culture) and as *human* nature to which cultural codes are reduced (MacCormack, 1980, pp. 3–4).

MacCormack claims that Levi-Strauss's efforts to situate the nature:culture contrast 'in a timeless, value-free model concerned with workings of the human *mind*' is itself a myth and helps to cultivate shaky ideas about females and 'human nature'. Conceptions of nature and culture cannot be value free. Our ideas remain distinctly European and historically situated; MacCormack, echoing Ardener (1975), notes that the pairing of nature with wildness and with femaleness seems logical only from within an industrial and Judaeo-Christian tradition. Even in the historical mould of European thinking, for instance the eighteenth-century Rousseauan intellectual framework, nature has not always been attached to wildness (MacCormack, 1980, p. 9). The coupling of nature and female is not a 'given'. In Gini culture it is *male* essence that is associated with the spirits and birds of the wild (Gillison, 1980, pp. 143–73). The idea that women's destiny is to be biological must be subject to close scrutiny based not on 'universalising' European categories. MacCormack suggests that anthropological work on attitudes to nature in various cultures, for example in Papua New Guinea, and historical studies of western European thought highlight the danger of Eurocentricism (MacCormack and Strathern, 1980). Whilst all the groups used a series of binary opposites in their symbolic constructions of reality, none could be reduced to either the simple nature:culture or female:male analogies (MacCormack, 1980, p. 21).

Definite human features, then, such as language, myths, metaphors and abstract symbolism, have been universally produced through human cultures, a set of innate unconscious structures leading to differences in social behaviour. The implication is that culture or nurture cannot leave biology or nature behind, and that the natural is not necessarily that of the aggressive animal but of the specifically human. Transparently, this anthropological discourse reinforces the point that culture is never independent of some deeper underlying human nature. However, the matter does not rest there. Another perspective within the anthropological discipline resists the position that a human nature exists apart from culture.

The Quest for Human Diversity

The particularity of human behaviour has inspired social anthropologists to investigate the shaping of human beings by their culture. Clifford Geertz, a leading modern cultural anthropologist, states that:

> without men [sic] no culture, certainly; but equally, and more significantly, without culture, no men. We are in sum, incomplete or unfinished animals who complete or finish ourselves through culture – and not through culture in general but through highly particular forms of it. (Geertz, 1965, pp. 112–13)

Appreciation of the diversity demands an awareness of the plurality of cultures and the changing systems, the different values and norms of behaviour, even the distinctive approaches to the sort of human person one is, the different kinship relationships, the constructions of sexuality and sexual relationships, including incest. What we regard as against human nature turns out to be merely against our own culture or society's values, practices and beliefs. Anthropological evidence amassed from premodern societies (Giddens, 1989) does alert us to the pitfalls in accepting the idea of a fixed human nature. Individual cultures exhibit idiosyncratic ways of being human, and different values are placed upon diverse practices. Even when, from a singular ethnocentric vantage point, we imagine that certain approaches to the human *must* be universal, reverence for the child as life, say, we may then encounter opposite attitudes which encourage infanticide (for example, female children were frequently strangled at birth, viewed as a burden to the family in traditional Chinese culture). Additional illustrations embrace outlooks towards food, a basic need. Some religious cultures aver the eating of pork whilst others prohibit it.

Conflicting world views are held by Melanesian and English societies on the question of persons and relations. For instance, the former do not consider babies to be new persons. Melanesian inhabitants of the Papua New Guinea island of Gawa possess a matrilineal system of kinship. On the other hand, they utilise techniques for imagining foetuses which lie external to the material body (Munn, cited in Strathern, 1992, p. 56). Trobrianders view babies as old people, ancestors returning as spirit-children in contrast to the English notion of children born 'new' people (Weiner, 1976, pp. 120–3). The total antithesis of a non-genetic perspective of children, 'the uniqueness of the child lies in the fact that it appears as its parents in another form' (Strathern, 1992, p. 60).

Ruth Benedict's *Patterns of Culture* (1935) is a model of the non-biological and non-universal anthropological conception of human nature which binds the latter to integral, specific cultures. Examination of the Pueblos of New Mexico, the Dobuans of eastern New Guinea and the Kwakiutl Indians of the north-west coast of America reveal variable understandings towards such facets of life as possessions, sexual behaviour, and warfare, products of a cultural selection process drawn from all the possible varieties of human traits. Some cultures have exaggerated or played down similar traits, with no real consensus *across* the cultures as to the selection's validity. Benedict employs the metaphor of an arc to illustrate the manifold range of human interests and possibilities, from dealing with life to dealing with death. One society 'builds an enormous superstructure upon adolescence, one upon death, one upon after-life' (1935, p. 17).

The precise parameters defining adolescence and adulthood remain in dispute. Biological puberty does not condition the puberty rites. Rather, it is what adulthood means in the specified culture. Benedict draws attention to the meaning of adulthood as warfare among central North American tribes. In Australia it meant participating in a specifically male cult entailing the exclusion of females. Nor is the notion of war a universally accepted prescription embedded in every human culture. Benedict notes the disparity between cultures that can accept periods of peace in between war and those who find it impossible to admit the possibility of peace with other groups whose members would then have to be transposed from the category of 'other' to that of human being. Further, a people may consider a state of war equally implausible. The thought of Eskimo villages engaged in organised, deliberate battles with each other is a concept alien to Eskimos, although the act of killing is recognised and understood (Benedict, 1935, pp. 21–2). Where north-west coast Indians honoured violent experience, Pueblo Indians' aggression was strongly frowned upon. Benedict argues that the act of studying 'other', more simple, 'primitive' cultures equips us to recognise elementary features about ourselves hidden from us within our own culture – those 'fundamental and distinctive cultural configurations that pattern existence and condition the thoughts and emotions of the individuals who participate in those cultures' (Benedict, p. 39).

Sexuality's cultural and historical diversity has formed a central enquiry of much social anthropology. Margaret Mead's approach to understanding human life parallels that of Benedict in that she uses her fieldwork studies as 'natural laboratories' for the under-

standing of human nature. *Coming of Age in Samoa* (1928) investigates emotional stress and adolescence and the naturalness of sexual
relations, counterposing the young Samoans' relaxedness and
casualness to more neurotic attitudes in western culture. The study
of primitive cultures and sexuality was used to throw light upon
the western psyche and its own cultural assumptions, for example
those of American society.

More recent studies on the relationship between sexuality and
gender have articulated sexuality as a cultural construction. Case
studies in the west, in Jamaica, Fiji, Kenya, India and Mombassa
unpick the mosaic of sex, gender and sexuality producing a set of
diverse identities (Caplan, 1987, p. 22). For instance they show
the flesh–spirit dichotomy to be absent in African thought, contrasting with the Christian belief in the ascendence of spirit over
flesh, and Gandhi's celebration of sexual abstinence. Again, the
control of human fertility is intimately bound up with constrain-
ing humans' sexual behaviour in Eurasian societies of the
Mediterranean, Fiji and India. The studies find women's sexuality
less subject to such constraints in cases where childbirth is expressly
welcomed. Such anthropological revelations serve as an antidote
to the biological portrayal of 'woman nature' and sexual identity
in general (an aspect which receives further attention in Chapter 6).

Yet Benedict's and Mead's handling of cultural diversity does
not avoid determinism. It suffers from cultural determinism in a
number of ways. Initially, the personality is inviolably dissolved into
culture. Benedict and Mead present humans as plastic, to be
moulded into their respective societies, and grant no consideration
to the cultural universals. Hence, human biological evolution and
indeed the notion of *any* sort of human nature is discounted. The
significance of conflict between society and individual is played down
in similar fashion to sociologist Durkheim's holistic perspective
(Chapter 4). Psychological factors bearing upon the act of being
human, and Freud's insights into the psychic tensions between the
unconscious and civilisation hold no relevance for cultural relativism.
The human individual simply becomes a receptacle transmitting
cultural attitudes and values down the generations. What is more,
class antagonisms are unlocated in the process of mapping and
patterning dissimilar cultures. In the absence of historical analysis
this seems a logical outcome.

We cannot assume away the interconnectedness of cultures and
global history, especially with our knowledge of imperialistic
conquest and ideology. From this angle, Benedict's portrayal is an
ahistorical one, where human behaviour is totally determined by
the culture in question. Human beings are on the contrary
changeable and temporal, yet also causal. Carrithers (1992) suggests
that human life possesses metamorphic, interactive and temporal

qualities, and that such qualities serve to differentiate humans from animals. They have the capacity to produce, invent and reinvent new relationships in producing their existence, and to yield fresh insights into what we are and what we might become. In this sense, as we shall discuss further in the next chapter, human life is mutually and therefore socially constructed. Unlike plastic beings conforming to tradition, humans are active, inventive and intrinsically social animals with a history (Carrithers, 1992, pp. 12–33).

Summary and Conclusions

On the question of animal or human, it is undeniable that humans have biologically evolved. The close relationship with the physical structures of apes is immediately apparent, although the human's brain size has become distinct. Human nature has to be seen as humans linked to nature, although the strength of the linkages is a matter for dispute. Ethology's position that biological, genetic, innate instincts evolving from animal instincts ('human nature') reflect an *essentially* animal nature, is too reductionist and basically represents a rather simplistic 'reading off' process, leaving no space for change, for cultural particularity or the consciousness of human thought.

Sociobiology's replacement by the concept of genetic group selection is similarly reductionist, given the expulsion of language, cognition and consciousness. Nor does it conceive of truly unselfish, ethical behaviour. Although seeming to embrace human culture, 'genes' remain deterministic. The anthropological search for universals and 'innate' humanness, however, exchanges the determinism of the biological body or environmental determinism for the determinism of the mind – a structurally determined human nature. Mind is seen as the bridge from animal nature to human culture, yet without reference to historically changing social and political structures. The search for cultural difference reveals the many pathways to being human, and eludes the notion of an indefinable, mentalistic, ungrounded unconscious nature or a way of seeing the world. Nevertheless, the problem for those cultural anthropologists seeking cultural distinctiveness is the assumption of a cultural consensus and the associated total integration of the individual human being into the culture. A human *nature* is substituted by a cultural determinism, and the endlessly plastic human psyche melts and reforms within the cultural collective. By denying biology, such a world view treats humans as containers bereft of content.

As well as failing to engage with the rich, social interaction between individual and social which renders humans more than animals, both culturalism and cultural multiplicity reject or denigrate historical change. The following chapter considers the ways in which modern sociological theory handles such tensions in the creating and fragmenting of the human subject in society. This will place us in an advantageous position to examine the ideological and political ramifications of biological and cultural conceptions of human nature for issues relating to 'race' and gender.

Further Reading

General Surveys

Paul Hirst and Penny Woolley, *Social Relations and Human Attributes* (Tavistock, 1982). Part I devoted to the human:animal debate.

Steven Horigan, *Nature and Culture in Western Discourses* (Routledge, 1988). Debates on nature and culture, human and animal, and how the boundaries are intellectually constructed.

James J. Sheehan and Morton Sosna (eds.), *The Boundaries of Humanity: Humans, Animals, Machines* (University of California Press, 1991). The biology–culture debate, as well as whether mind = machine.

Ethology and Sociobiology

Ted Benton, *Natural Relations: Ecology, Animal Rights and Social Justice* (Verso, 1993).

Richard Dawkins, *The Selfish Gene* 2nd edn. (Oxford University Press, 1989). A highly popular and readable exposition.

Konrad Lorenz, *On Aggression* (Harcourt Brace World, 1966). The behaviour of fish, rats, frogs equals human instincts.

Roger Trigg, *The Shaping of Man: Philosophical Aspects of Sociobiology* (Blackwell, 1982). Raises philosophical issues such as altruism and determinism.

Edward Wilson, *On Human Nature* (Cambridge University Press, 1978). Sociobiology's most explicit statements on human nature.

Culture and Anthropology

Michael Carrithers, *Why Humans Have Culture* (Oxford University Press, 1992). A lively discussion on social relativism.

Merlin Donald, *Origins of the Modern Mind: Three Stages in the Evolution of Culture and Cognition* (Harvard University Press, 1991). Psychologist's analysis of mind:culture and consciousness debate.

Clifford Geertz, *The Interpretation of Cultures* (Basic Books, 1973; Fontana, 1993). Collection of writings on ideologies, mind and cultures.

Edmund Leach, *Levi-Strauss* (London: Fontana, 1970). A succinct exposition of Levi-Strauss's structural anthropology.

Carolyn McCormack and Maralyn Strathern (eds.), *Nature, Culture and Gender* (Chicago: University of Chicago, 1980). Anthropological studies of gender's significance.

Mary Midgley, *Beast and Man: The Roots of Human Nature* (Harvester, 1978).

4

Sociology, Social Theory and Human Nature

Introduction

Debates about our human essence were viewed in the previous chapter through the lens of biology on the one hand and cultural anthropology on the other. But the discipline of sociology, too, has played a considerable part in the debate. Sociology's distinctive approach to the idea of human nature by definition places the emphasis upon humans as social beings, and upon cultural and social structures. One of sociological theory's main methodological objectives of explaining human social behaviour scientifically through the organicist metaphor reflects its historical origins as a discipline during the late nineteenth century, when social evolution was construed as the parallel to the Darwinist natural evolution. However, perspectives clearly diverge over the extent to which the social structure holds sway over the individual, and it is such differences that have shaped the formation of schools of thought within sociology.

Whilst each tradition has seen human *life* and behaviour as socially constructed as opposed to spiritually conceived, discrete models of human nature have underpinned each. We encounter the human as 'social being', but also human nature as environmentally determined, individually oriented and subjectivist. Hence, sociological theorising in the twentieth century cannot be understood apart from its relationship to the century's major theories of human nature – behaviourist, Marxist, Freudian and existentialist. It is unhelpful to study human beings in society from the angle of a single academic discipline. Sociology has served as the archetypal social constructionist discipline, yet it is not unequivocally socially reductionist. Its growing interest in the 'self' is a philosophical issue at one level, but at another level the juxtaposition between 'human nature' and the pursuit of the issue of 'identity' by social and cultural theorists demonstrates the centrality of social context. The chapter discusses Durkheim's functionalist and holistic approach to human nature and Weber's more individual focus on human understanding and agency. It then examines the issue of the human subject, self and the significance of 'other' in the social behaviourism of G.H. Mead, and the later existentialist-oriented social interactionist school of thought. We investigate the recasting of the human nature debate in postmodernism, the ideas of Michel Foucault and finally the interweaving of history, social theory and the human subject. Although Marx is clearly recognised as one of sociology's three classical founding figures (with Durkheim and Weber), his basic approach to human nature is not discussed again here, so as to avoid repetition of pertinent material from Chapter 2.

Durkheim and Functionalism

Emile Durkheim (1858–1915) makes his prime contribution to the human nature debate through his ideas on the social collective, dual human nature and anomie. His holistic perspective, concerned with groups rather than individuals, places the social in the overriding position; there are autonomous 'social facts' which scarcely leave space for the individual, who stands merely as a pliable entity subject to moulding and shaping into a social group collectivity. Durkheim's sociology speaks of the social as distinct from the individual in the explanation of human behaviour; it is indeed argued that no room is made for any *psychological* explanation of the individual human being. By the same token, the psychology of the individual cannot offer any explanations for social phenomena. Psychology is about individual consciousness; Durkheim's individual human has *no* human *nature*.

Durkheim interpreted his sociological task as demonstrating the very malleability of humans in the diversity of their belief systems and social structures. Hawkins (1977, pp. 229–52) argues that the fractures within the individual human, *because* they are autonomous, occur within the psyche, and thus do not constitute a mind:body dualism. However, Durkheim worked towards a position of the 'dualism of human nature' later in his *Elementary Forms of Religious Life* (1912) and *Dualism of Human Nature and its Social Conditions* (1914). Durkheim (1912) identifies a characteristic peculiarity of human nature: its constitutional duality.

> On the one hand is our individuality and, more particularly, our body in which it is based; on the other is everything in us that expresses something other than ourselves ... [This] duality corresponds to the double existence that we lead concurrently: the one purely individual and rooted in our organisms, the other social and nothing but an extension of society. (Durkheim, 1912, in Wolff, 1964, p. 337)

Hence, the human individual's life is a double existence comprising individual organic forces and social collectivistic determinants. The *conflict* between them is represented by the clash of the sensations with intellectuality and morality (Durkheim, in Wolff, 1964, pp. 337–8). Such conflicts and tensions embedded in the duality are full of pain; the social fulfils the task of quelling some of the individual's most powerful inclinations.

> [Since] the role of the social being in our single selves will grow ever more important as history moves ahead, it is wholly improbable that there will ever be an era in which man is required to resist himself to a lesser degree, an era in which he can live life that is easier and less full of tension. To the contrary, all evidence compels us to expect our effort in the struggle between the two beings within us to increase with the growth of civilization. (Durkheim, 1912, in Wolff, 1964, p. 339)

The pain of the individual inside and outside of the social collective (sentiments which find their echo in Freud's *Civilisation and Discontents* – Mestrovic, 1991, pp. 184–200) is aptly captured by the Durkheimian concept of 'anomie'. Anomie (Durkheim, 1893) refers to the unregulated, pathologically inclined economy in which individuals are thrown into opposition against each other. But it also refers to individual human beings' state of mind, to their pathological mental state, humans without stabilisers vainly attempting to adjust to an increasingly uncontrolled social environment, unhampered by religion or state regulation. Pushed to the edge, the agitated and disoriented individual turns finally to suicide or murder (Durkheim, 1897).

Durkheim conceives of society as an organ which, in the process of evolution, develops specialised, more complex functions to maintain the system. But his theory is dependent on the use of the organic model of the human individual as metaphor for a *social organism* which possesses functional or dysfunctional qualities. The prognosis of increased organic specialisation in society furthermore extends to the organic constitution of the sexes, whose biological and psychological features become progressively differentiated. Sydie (1987, p. 34) argues that Durkheim's conclusions (1893; 1897) with respect to the nature of the sexes are conditioned by his 'dichotomized view of the development of the sexes', itself founded upon the assumption of an evolutionary divergence of the sexes biologically, psychologically and socially. But Sydie (p. 38) suggests that any benefits from the greater specialisation in organic society facilitating individuality and self-realisation accrue to males but not to females.

A functional specialisation between male and female is a recommendation by Durkheim stemming from the duality of human nature. The aesthetic functions are accorded to females, and the instrumental functions allotted to males, paralleling the duality of the sensory and organic *nature* and the regulatory rational *culture*.

The more 'primitive' qualities of the female suit them less for the intellectually oriented corporate occupations. 'The duality of human nature is common to men and women, but the dichotomies are unequally developed and represented in the sexes' (Sydie, 1987). Regardless of the fact that Durkheim, the first professional academic sociologist, refutes patriarchy as the basic social and political form of organisation, he nevertheless makes the conventional assumptions of natural hierarchy regarding male nature:female nature held by his society (Chapter 6 explores further the issues of social constructionism and female 'nature').

From Durkheim's perspective, then, society precedes individual; any individual human nature is subsumed by the social collective. The tension between this collective and the human condition of the modern anomic individual is the modernistic archetypal theme. But Durkheim's organic metaphor becomes a reductionist model whereby individual human nature is subsumed by the holistic universe of social 'facts'. The organic metaphor not only reinforces the 'whole', and hence militates against systemic change, but reinforces traditional patriarchal assumptions about female and male 'nature'.

In the following section we scrutinise Weber's methodological individualism which also expresses from the individual's subjectivist standpoint the tension between impending fatalism, the rationality of the social, and the striving for an individual autonomy.

Weber, Social Actor and Human Agency

Max Weber (1864–1920), a German sociologist, developed a highly influential school of sociology, at the base of which sits a model of human nature immersed in the idea of *meaning* and meaningful activity. Following Nietzsche, Weber situates meaningful individual action at the centre of his theory, an approach distinguishable from classical Marxism and functionalism. Weber accords a prominent position to the human subject in society, guiding the ideas of the later symbolic interactionist school of sociology mediated through the work of G.H. Mead and Goffman. Here we will consider Weber's basic concepts of 'meaningful action', 'bureaucracy' and 'charisma' in the context of his perspectives on human nature.

For Weber, meaningful action is what it is to be human. The major forms of human conduct – the 'goal rational', 'the value rational', the 'affective' or emotional, and the 'traditionalist' – convey the meaning in human beings' actions. Making *sense* of our lives is a basic ingredient in humans' nature. The goal rational calculates the probabilities and possibilities in adopting any particular mode of behaviour – the kind of instrumental self-motivated calculation in which nineteenth-century utilitarians like Bentham engaged.

Nevertheless, humans strive for ideals beyond self-interest. All rational human action presupposes a teleology (the pursuit of some goal to which human actors attribute value). The ethical dimension here renders a strong antidote to Hobbes's blindly self-directed human being. Weber does acknowledge a spiritual element within the human being in this 'rational orientation to an absolute value of some ethical, aesthetic, religious, or other form of behaviour, *entirely for its own sake* [author's italics] and independently of any prospects of external success' (Weber, 1947, p. 115). He also recognises the actor's emotions as non-rational action (Weber, 1947, p. 116). Nevertheless, poised at the edges of meaningful and non-meaningful conduct, it may closely approximate the other two categories of the calculative and the value-driven. Weber gives examples of the affective as 'the satisfaction of a direct impulse to revenge, to sensual gratification, to devote oneself to a person or ideal, to contemplative bliss, or ... the working off of emotional tensions' (Weber, 1947, p. 116). Traditionalist action is situated at the boundaries of the meaningful and non-meaningful, action carried out habitually although not necessarily consciously intended, but which may count as an implicit, subconscious intentionality (Weber, 1947, p. 115). Weber's 'ideal-type' model of human nature infers that an individual will comprise any one of a variety of combinations of such human attributes. The final human result is indeterminate, and clearly depends upon the exercise of choice. Weber hereby adopts an existentialist model of human nature, each person making her or his own nature through choice of values and the creation of meaningfulness. However, such open decision making is circumscribed by a society's authority structures.

But the prognosis of such circumstances, the estimation of their strength, the extent of their power to determine, remains subject to debate, and indeed offers a useful springboard to the questions of modernity and fatalism. Weber's outline of the nature of bureaucracy and bureaucratic authority highlights the dangers of the rational, the striving for the scientifically objective in the lineage of the Enlightenment.

Bureaucratic organisation, an essential ingredient for any industrial society, reflects a superior and essential form of human rationality for Weber; the very distancing from the personal elements in humans is a virtue. The formalisation of human interrelationships is seen as necessary not just in the economic sphere but through the institutionalisation of other areas of society through formal rules and procedures and tiered authority structures. Yet he also concedes that the 'developed' western world is becoming increasingly *dominated* by technical-rational action and its accompanying imper-sonality, and is thus in danger of squeezing out the other forms of human action which make up human nature. Human society erects for itself an iron cage – industrialisation experienced as the *fate* of the modern world, but a fate by which humans may dominate their own system, rather than the other way around. Mommsen (1974, pp. 95–115) suggests that Weber was a liberal in despair, able to accept the historical significance of persons with special qualities, but *not* able to accept their role as *antagonistic* to the mass of the population (p. 106).

Weber's interest in the special human being was expressed through his concept of charisma and the charismatic personality – the natural leader capable of sustaining the essential creative activity of human nature as a corrective to the fatalistic tendencies of bureaucratic and rational routine. This was Weber's answer to how humans in society could break out of their iron cage – the focus on individual free initiative as a constituent of human nature, although Weber's attitude to the related concepts of bureaucracy and charisma was alternately one of repulsion and attraction (Hughes, 1958, pp. 288–9). However, the whole notion of the charis-matic element in human nature is somewhat vague, even mystical (Blackburn, 1969), rooted in a chemistry of personality which attributes a religious inspiration and a certain magnetism to leaders (Marcuse, 1968) or innovative qualities imputed to a limited range of 'God'-appointed individuals (thus by inference suggesting the absence of potential in most humans).

This charisma is an attribute, though, which is incapable of self-perpetuity, and inevitably becomes routinised: the *fate* produced by industrialisation and domination by laws above and indepen-dent of the individual. But why these processes should be fate is not immediately obvious. Marcuse (1968) asks who it is that decrees the fate, given that society is not 'nature'. Forms of control, needs, satisfactions are not 'fatal' but only become so when socially sanctioned. That is, they result from material, economic and psy-chological coercion (Marcuse, p. 214). These are issues that bear heavily upon modern society. As such, they re-emerge in the Chapter 5 discussion of the Holocaust, whilst the policy implica-tions of Weber's 'iron cage' are explored in Chapter 7.

To summarise, Weber's focus on meaningfulness and human understanding in his model of human nature reflects more than a passing concern with the inner reality of an individual's social action. The point is that he attributes to individual action intrinsic *value*, more than a simple reading off from social collective moral imperatives. Weber's model is a challenge to functionalism and a crude Marxist structuralism, yet his theorising of humans' rational powers in creating their own forms of imprisonment poses a key dilemma of the century: the extent to which technical rationality produces fatalism in thought and action. The belief in powers of charisma which naturally reside in selected individuals, however, has to be questioned as an unsubstantiated, vague and politically conservative antidote to bureaucratic determinism. Below we turn to related schools of thought that have built upon Weber's concern with the individual actor.

Modern Sociology and the Social Self

Examination of modern sociology's treatment of the self requires an exposition of G.H. Mead's social behaviourism and the notion of a mediating social self; a charting of the relationships between the existentialist theory of human nature and Mead's tripartite schema of 'I', 'me' and 'other'; Goffman's symbolic interactionism; and the underpinnings of phenomenological sociology.

Mead (1863–1931) in *Mind, Self and Society* is concerned with the issue of human beings creating a self and identity in their interactions with each other. His social psychology or social behaviourism emphasising *reflexive* behaviour is historically significant in that Mead 'broke from the mechanical and passive notions of self and consciousness which had dominated early twentieth-century American psychology and sociology', in undertaking a continuous investigation into how self is generated externally (through its practical social experience) and internally through its experience as consciousness (Swingewood, 1991, p. 264). Mead draws together the natural biological aspects, the environmental influences and the cognitive elements of the human subject; and opposes the dualistic thinking of conventional philosophy which accepts a clear disjuncture of mind and nature. Rather than seeing human nature as body and mind, different but in some fashion connected together, Mead treats mind as a *natural* phenomenon, part of nature, and focuses on its emergence out of humans' behaviour (Cuff et al., 1990).

How do we square our knowledge so far of deterministic behaviourism with such a view of mind? Mead's social behaviourism was unlike Skinner's behaviourist model of the human (Chapter 2), which denies the utility of studying mental states. In the tradition of Weber and phenomenological philosophy, Mead describes human conduct as saturated in human meaning. The self comprise three parts – the 'I', the 'me', and the generalised 'other'. The 'I' is that part which looks at myself, the subject acting and thinking, biologically and socially. The 'me' constitutes myself as other humans see me, indicating an awareness of self which exists for others as an object, but closely related to the 'I' through social experience.

The generalised 'other' is the development of a social conscience (similar to the Freudian concept of the superego).

How children *see* the world deeply interests Mead. Possession of a sense of self is dependent on the development of children's ability to see their own actions through the perspective of a 'generalised other' (that is, seeing through other persons' eyes). Thus, our sense of human identity is socially constructed by our powers to conceive of ourselves as distinct from another, in an 'objective' socially situated position. Since human beings are social beings, feedback is highly germane for affecting what people *do* and think. Knowing what I am like is tied to the existence of others (which takes the form of hell in Sartre's drama *No Exit*). Our lives are lived out in performance, playing dramatic roles; in fact, Mead's philosophical metaphors have been likened to those of the playwright Pirandello (Baumann, 1969). A universal, independent human nature is unplaced within this schema. Even our inner *characteristics* and unique composites as individual human beings may be touched by our beliefs about them, such as when a personal feeling of one's own gaucheness is reinforced in the company of others (Glover, 1988, p. 177). Mead's concept of sociality, in deference to the parameters of the external objective, counters the Hobbesian atomistic individualistic model of the human subject; self and self-consciousness are organised around the *social* individual, whilst our knowledge of humans is of paramount importance to the way we behave.

Craib (1976) shows how Sartre's existentialism offers 'the means for grasping the complex transformation of interpersonal relationships undertaken by Mead and the 1960s symbolic interactionist challenge to a predominantly conventional, functionalist sociology' (Craib, 1976, pp. 35–6). The respective portrayals by Mead and Sartre of self and self-determination are crucial to the task of understanding the nature of the self (Aboulafia, 1986). Separately, each presents a partial account accompanied by strengths and weaknesses. Mead identifies the development of human reflexivity and the self as a social object 'first and foremost', whilst the French philosopher's account focuses on the non-cognitive arena of the human self, defined by existential choice. These two sides of the same coin, the social psychological and the existentialist (Aboulafia, 1986, p. xiv) may be synthesised to produce the concept of the mediating self, skewed towards Mead's 'sociality' to demonstrate how the human self is mediated and defined 'through its relationship with others', but comes to determine the course of its own life. This is justified by the existentialist position that the self-consciousness is undetermined and free because it is aware of all kinds of possibilities.

Mead's project to comprehend a dialectic between individual consciousness and socially constructed forms of behaviour have also led social theorists to suggest overt linkages between Mead and Marx, in that both eschew the idealism of the human subject and a rigid social determinism, share an emphasis on the human subject's sociality, a dialectical understanding of human beings and their social context; and a stress on human thought as a *dynamic* socially mediated process essential for human life (Goff, 1980, cited in Morris, 1991, p. 310).

There are problems with Mead's model. Whilst Mead focuses on a self which exists and develops only within a network of 'others', he is nevertheless wedded to a behaviourist view which does not appear to take account of language's role in defining self and relationships. Conversations with others surely aid us in the task of achieving our self-definition (Taylor, 1989, p. 36; n., p. 525).

The issue arising of feedback from the 'generalised other' which tells us what we *are* is not unproblematic. Feedback itself can be manipulated so as to affect a whole set of beliefs about ourself. In this context, analysis of postrevolutionary China reveals the process whereby prisoners were taught to see themselves as criminals of the people, fabrication becoming reality; guilt feelings overpower the prisoner 'because all of the time you have to look at yourself from the people's standpoint' (Lifton, 1967, p. 86). In such cases, the 'inner' is overcome by the power of sociality. No independent core of a human nature is available to resist because, argues Glover (1988), the 'thought manipulation' ministers to the human being's need for recognition by others. Therefore, we are prepared to acquiesce in the external control over our thoughts and beliefs *because* our nature is social rather than biological, atomistic or individualistic.

Concepts of the 'other' and their political implications have been prominent in the analysis of social and human conflict and co-operation. A major problem, however, is that the generalised Other simply *is*, which does not deal with the issues of differentiated *power* to create other (aspects considered more fully in Chapters 5 and 6). Later symbolic interactionists and phenomenologists also grounded their sociology of knowledge and socal constructionism in Mead, for developing a social psychology, and in Marx for theorising the historical dialectic between social reality and individual existence (Berger and Luckman, 1967, p. 186). A fixed biological human nature is dismissed in favour of admitting a human nature only in the sense of

> anthropological constants ... that delimit and permit man's socio-cultural formations ... While it is possible to say that man has a nature, it is more significant to say that man constructs

> his own nature, or more simply, that man produces himself.
> (Berger and Luckman, p. 49)

In forging the dialectical connections, Berger and Luckman detect an inadequate sense of social structure in Mead and his followers, and a total ignorance of Mead among neoMarxist social theorists. Mead above all, for Berger (1969, p. ix), is able to offer a dialectical understanding of individual consciousness and society.

The idea of the self-conscious social self in sociology became prominent in the late 1950s and 1960s. Goffman's *Presentation of Self in Everyday Life* (1958) focuses upon the communicative, interactive elements in being human. Following Mead, he expands the dramaturgical metaphor of life as a stage. Goffman's human beings are engaged in the pursuit of a self and the creation of identity, inviting the allegation that his is a cynical perspective on human nature; Goffman's humans are presented as manipulating performers. What we see of each other's social 'front' is always false. The important question for Goffman is how we act in situations, performing our allotted role, like Orwell's waiters in *Down and Out in Paris and London* with their incessant changes of persona and bearing as they glide from chaotic kitchen to the stage-managed dining room.

All life is acting; for symbolic interactionists there is no substance to the self *per se* (Cuff et al., 1990). Acting defines the nature of interactionism. The nature of humans, it seems, may be understood from what they do, and how they pragmatically *choose* what they do in the social context. The emphasis falls on meaning, rather than upon structures, which are taken as given but which circumscribe the possibilities for human expression and freedom. Goffman's application in *Asylums* (1961) of the interactionist position on how the individual human being is defined is discussed in Chapter 8 in the context of models in health.

One of the most damning criticisms of the Goffmanesque theoretical frame is that it lacks an analysis of structural power. The defect arises out of Mead's social behavourist approach to the self which at root assumes a common core of values in a common culture representing the generalised 'other'. This is close to the conservative position in that it neglects culture's repressive character, omitting the conformist nature of modern industrial society (Swingewood, 1991, p. 267).

Before concluding this section we should note that the existentialist human nature model has also manifested itself in ethnomethodology and its phenomenological roots. Space does not permit a detailed exposition of phenomenological sociology. Basically, the work of Schutz (1899–1959) highlights the subjective experience of acting in the everyday world as essential to the human condition. Only through reflection and looking backwards may we understand the meaning of a human life; humans impose socially constructed meaning. The sensations of life *as lived* cannot be reflected fully but constitute a 'pre-phenomenal' world of action basic to human social life. 'Human nature' is created through activity setting and the solving of problems to overcome. To survive, human individuals specify their situation through their own conscious knowledge, and construct their *particular* world in an undetermined manner. Only in retrospect does the actor's conduct seem determined (Campbell, 1981, pp. 200–5).

In summarising this discussion of interactionism, the school's focus on self, placing existentialist models of human nature to the fore, has constituted a fundamental stream of modern sociological thinking. G.H. Mead's cognitive self incorporates the world of external others. However, it insufficiently accounts for the impact of linguistic communication between human beings, and remains uncritical of the external world; it avoids explanation of how the self may be specifically distorted, 'othered' and oppressed (Chapter 5) by the assertion of unequal social and political power. At the same time, it may be argued that the synthesis of Mead's insights with a Marxian consciousness of social structure and ideology facilitates a greater holistic appreciation of the self–society dialectic. Goffman's symbolic interactionism helps us to comprehend more easily how the self can consciously handle socially oppressive institutional processes, but it too readily assumes the power of the individual self to achieve full self-consciousness and control. In the end it offers a rather cynical, self-calculating picture of human nature. Finally, phenomenological sociology's human nature model, perhaps of all the subjectivist models in social theory, is unduly unaffected by the objective external domain. The following section leads us into another kind of territory altogether.

Social Theory and the Death of the Subject

The whole idea of the self-conscious social actor meets its antithesis in Foucault, whose main body of work (with exceptions towards the end of his life) evacuated the human subject, contesting the very concept of a unitary self. We will look at the specific statements and discourse of Foucault's perspective on human nature which take for granted the submerging of subject: the role of contingency; the historical development of social institutions; the role of social scientific knowledge in marginalising the human; and the modifications to his thinking. Foucault does not recognise a human nature *per se* as no constant subject has existed through history. If this may mimic Sartre's stance that there can be no given human nature, humans are seen by existentialism as making their own human-ness; Foucault's human subject plays no such self-conscious and central role.

Foucault's world view also contraposes the notion of *innate* humanness as presented in Chomsky's structural analysis of the mind. Debating with Chomsky on human nature (Elders, 1974, pp. 133–98), Foucault articulates a mistrust of the notion of human nature, one which has been displaced by other constructs of scientific knowledge and discourse. The concept simply reflects a certain point of pre-scientific knowledge:

> It was not by studying human nature that linguists discovered the laws of constant mutation, or Freud the principles of the analysis of dreams ... In the history of knowledge, the notion of human nature seems ... to have played the role of an epistemological indicator to designate certain types of discourse in relation to or in opposition to theology or biology or history. I would find it difficult to see in this a scientific concept. (Chomsky and Foucault, 1974, pp. 139–40)

Creativity *is* only possible through social rules, concedes Foucault, but the principle of such regularities should not be placed 'in the interior of the mind or of human nature' (Chomsky and Foucault, 1974, p. 160). Such regularities should be sought, *outside* of the human mind, in social forces and relations of production. For example, social institutions such as mental asylums and prisons predominantly serve a policing function through which humans come to identify their relationships. These public forms and institutions become the expression of human beings' essential activity; through the social construction of our action and discussion we shape our conception of human nature (Foucault, 1970). 'Foucault has it in for man' is Piaget's clipped response (1971, p. 129).

In Foucault's narrative of social institutions in history, the individual subject without certainty is caught up in a web of contingent events. The human cannot escape, because there is no essential nature or being to guide or direct (Philp, 1985, p. 78). If anything, the human subject lives in a state of discontinuity rather than continuity.

Social pragmatic and subjectivist writings (discussed earlier) emphasise a self-consciousness sometimes to the point of manipulation of self. However, Foucault conceives the structure of the *unconscious* as crucial, evoking an affinity with Freud's structural psychoanalysis although differing in its approach to the mind. Foucault sees the Freudian unconscious as prefiguring the end of the human being; it dissolves the human objective status of consciousness. By denouncing the human viewpoint of knowledge, Foucault's thought also converges with that of Levi-Strauss's anthropological structuralism; yet Foucault is far more attuned to tracing the *historical* journeys of the human mind through means of social discourse. Such historical analysis is an indispensable underpinning for social psychological and social interactionist accounts of the fractured self, such as Goffman's dramaturgy (Parker, 1989, p. 67). Foucault claims that selves and their construction are themselves subject to power-laden discourses through social roles. Where G.H. Mead takes the 'other' as a given, Foucault's 'other' is historically constructed; for instance, the modern 'I' is made aware of 'other' as state-led surveillance. Human beings are caught between their objective position in the social environment, and their knowledge of such.

Knowledge is derived through the human sciences, especially ethnography, psychology and linguistics, which afford the means to investigate *how* human nature as concept has functioned. Scientific evaluation has been carried out to provide positive knowledge about the human being. Developments in scientific investigative methods into human mind and behaviour also foster categorisations of 'other', for instance the racialised 'other' of the nineteenth century (Chapter 5). Foucault' s *Order of Things* (1970) studies the significance of phrenology, IQ testing and crime testing as if they were human-less structures objectifying the world, and in the process making an object of the human being.

Because Foucault considers discourse on the human subject as demarcated by the historically conditioned level of knowledge (we can't talk about what we don't know), he is able to argue that the human (his term 'man') is a recent invention in post-sixteenth-century western cultural history, and indeed is now due to 'disappear' (Foucault, 1970, in de George, 1972, pp. 284–5). How far are we prepared, however, to accept this account of the evacuated human subject?

Taylor (1985, p. 177) concludes that at the end of the day,

> the final basis of Foucault's refusal of 'truth' and 'liberation' seems to be a Nietzschean one ... there is no order of human life, or way we are, or human nature, that one can appeal to in order to judge or evaluate between ways of life. They are only different orders imposed by men on primal chaos following their will to power.

However, Dews (1989) proposes that a total removal of the human subject from history was not Foucault's unmodified position. The late Foucault did come to 'reinsert' the human subject following his own reading of the Critical Theory Marxists (Chapter 2). His last works reflect an unexpected turn towards 'a positive evaluation of the individual cultivation of the self' (Dews, 1989, p. 46). The antihumanist stance weakens with his advocacy of historical events 'that have led us to constitute ourselves and to recognise ourselves as subjects of what we are doing, thinking, saying' (Foucault, 1986). In his final interviews Foucault conceives of his own role as helping to make others freer through an understanding of social and historical processes. It is evidently impossible to submerge the human.

Many criticisms of Foucault's work stem from the alleged lack of commitment to the human subject, and the invisibility of human persons in history's social strategies theorised by Foucault. Who co-ordinates the human agents? Social power, it is hypothesised, causally commands human individuals' psyche, a case of social determinism offering no leeway for the individual's resistance to institutional oppression that Foucault suggests occurs inevitably (Sarup, 1993, pp. 80–5; Taylor, 1985b, p. 174). Foucault's allegiance to resistance does imply a commitment to some conception of the human good which, in turn, is usually based on a view of human nature and human subjectivity (Philp, 1985, p. 79). Nevertheless, he cannot admit to this position, which for Philp (p. 79) 'so clearly sits uncomfortably with his repudiation of the human subject and his denial of a constant human nature'.

Foucault's writings, then, are crucial in demonstrating that how we see human nature and identify the self is contingent upon historical knowledge. Indeed, the idea of a self-conscious human subject is evacuated, annulled by the role of unconscious structures, social regularities and the exertion of social power through the construction of knowledge. Yet the relativistic theory reflects a highly reductionist model of human nature, in that 'human' ceases to hold significance and resistance is a contradiction in terms. Foucault himself is thus forced to recant by reincorporating the human self and conscious human commitment back into history. As we shall see below, the conscious self is far from dead.

The Fragmented Self and Authenticity

Despite the Foucauldian denials of the human subject, the late twentieth century has witnessed a concerted search for *some* self, to forge an individual identity, to connect with an authentically unique self in the face of a relentless technicism and impersonal rationality. This search is patently bounded by socially and culturally constructed versions of selfhood. But the preoccupation with individual identity and an *authentic* self indicates a reaffirmation of Sartre's existentialist position on being human in an inhuman world.

Where, however, lies the authentic? In the modern context, the centring upon the self has meant a distancing from others. The current epoch has spawned a 'culture of narcissism' (Lasch, 1979) heralding self-fulfilment as life's major value, a self-protective reaction to the threatening elements of an uncertain modern world, a culture of uncertainty (Hoggett, 1992, pp. 40–52) inducing the slide into subjectivism (Taylor, 1992, pp. 55–69).

With no human nature of significance or certitude, the social self takes over. Formation of a specific identity within a social context turns itself into an obsession – humans manufacturing their own identity. The value of difference (Weeks, 1991) is declared amidst the incessant flux of individual and social needs ranging from the ethnic to the sexual. We may view this fabrication of self-identities in its highly individualistic form as securely locked into economic and commercial markets, the meeting point of Thatcherite individualism and the commodity-driven consumer culture (Chapter 7), a world view which submerges any alternative community-oriented ethic of human life beneath its own tumult.

The restructuring of contemporary sociological theory reflects these concerns. Giddens (1991) explains the self-directed ethically vacuous obsession as a 'survivalism' confronted by the threat of the meaningless. 'Potentially disturbing existential questions are defused by the controlled nature of day-to-day activities within internally referential systems ... Mastery, in other words, substitutes itself for morality ...' (Giddens, p. 202).

Philosophers and social theorists argue such ethical vacuity and self-directedness constitute the hallmarks of postmodernism, but Rosenau (1992) suggests that we may distinguish between sceptical and affirmative postmodern approaches to the human subject. The former's assemblage of the postmodern individual seeks to replace the human subject by an individualised *personage* (with human *nature* having no relevance).

Features of the postmodernistic humans as identified in the literature are neatly encapsulted in Lipovetsky's 'ideal type' which includes a number of defining characteristics: concern with one's own life; lack of a singular identity reflected in the fragmentary self; the tendency to opt for the temporary and the spontaneous instead of the permanent and the planned; the acceptance of all values as equally valid; and an antipathy to collective and communal ethics (Lipovetsky, 1983, cited in Rosenau, 1992).

On the other hand one may interpret the quest for some internalised reference point as an antidote to the ephemera of the contemporary world, more purposeful than the above profile suggests. Indeed Taylor (1992) construes a *moral* force behind notions like self-fulfilment: 'the moral force of the ideal of authenticity' which is 'somehow being implicitly discredited, along with its contemporary forms' (Taylor, pp. 16–17). But where in the postmodern climate of a moral subjectivism is space made for any ethical judgements concerning human behaviour?

Taylor (1992) infers that reason is able to play no part for those who adopt the contemporary culture of authenticity, a blow to the rationalist philosophers who believe there is *a* human nature, and that a full understanding of this will conclusively demonstrate certain ways of life and values to be right and wrong. But the latter have been locked into the notion of a 'standard' derived from human nature, and have simply disregarded the ideal of authenticity as a 'mistaken departure from such standards rooted in human nature'. To this extent, and also due to the 'objectivist social scientific procedures – the normal fashion of social science explanation' the *importance* of authenticity as a moral ideal has been obscured (Taylor, 1992, p. 17).

Identities and the search for self do *not* have to be narcissistic or crudely individualistic. Giddens (1991) too is sceptical that a postmodernistic turn (or late modernity) has augured the disappearance of the human subject. Despite the expulsion of the self or subject by postmodernism, the self reinstates itself in the appearance of life politics: '... repressed existential issues, related not just to nature but to the moral parameters of existence as such, press themselves back on to the agenda' (Giddens, 1991, pp. 209–31). Life politics presupposes a degree of emancipation and develops an ethics as to how we should live (1991, p. 215). The trajectory of Giddens's recent ontological concerns with personal identity, the self and intimacy, a departure from the almost complete attention previously accorded to structures and the political state (Giddens, 1990; 1991; 1992) reflects this revised agenda.

The quest for identity as a potentially progressive force in life politics is also explored by Weeks (1991). The issue of worldly created identities is an intensely political one *per se* by virtue of its dynamic social nature and the recurrent clash of individual and collectivities: the polarity of the atomistic and the social models of human nature. Identity, far from being an innate or natural quality, 'is striven for, contested, negotiated, and achieved, often in struggles of the subordinated against the dominant ... put together in circumstances bequeathed by history, in collective experiences as much as by individual destiny' (Weeks, 1991, p. 94).

Affirmative postmodernist positions call for a return of the subject as a person, a renewed recognition of the human subject in society. The returning subject is conceived by Megill (1985, cited in Rosenau, 1992, p. 37) not as a conscious, purposeful and feeling individual but as a 'post-modern subject with a new non-identity ... focused ... on daily life at the margins' (Rosenau, pp. 57–61). Community is reaffirmed by progressive postmodernists including disillusioned Marxists who have distanced themselves from Marxist structuralism's overpowering anti-humanism of the 1970s, and its denial of subject. Touraine (1988) seeks the revival of the subject based on 'resistance' faced with a world where autonomous self-definition apart from society is a momentous task. The plea is for an activist human agent in search of life, personal freedom and creativity. Postmodernism's policy ramifications are discussed later (Chapter 7).

In summarising the above argument, although structuralism has denied the significance of the human subject, social theory is replete with the return of the subject and the individual's search in society for the authentic self. This may be seen in one respect as purely narcissistic; viewed differently, it reflects the increasing uncertainty of the modern world. Whilst consumerism pulls the individual towards vacuous modes of signification, the search may still be deemed a genuine quest for the expression of some inner human nature. Sceptical postmodernism's efforts to refute the notion of a human self beyond the current moment may be offset by affirmative postmodernists' reaffirmation of the human agent's right to resist. Yet in the final analysis this position too seems to bow to a fragmented view of humans severed from their social being.

Summary and Conclusions

To summarise, the classic sociologists Durkheim and Weber handle human nature as the human *in* society, human nature as social being. Durkheim, acutely conscious of the tension between the human and the social structure, conceptualises a society's institutional functions, particularly moral structures, as determining the parameters of human expression. Any nature lies in the *socially* constructed. In this respect his heavily anthropological treatment of the human sets the tone for an overfunctionalised sociology during the first half of this century. Durkheim's organic metaphors are both reductionist and sexist. Weber's methodological individualism counterbalances the functional and the Marxist stress upon the structural by the social actor's subjective experience and understanding of *inter*acting in society. The existential features of our humanity necessitate the conscious affirmation of goals and values. Human beings' unique powers of purposeful rationality may well lead them to erect objective bureaucratic structures, but whether these stand fatalistically above human control must be questioned, as must Weber's notion of the 'natural' quality to charismatic leadership.

Mead's social behaviourism formulates the social impact upon ideas of self, but the undifferentiated nature of Mead's generalised 'other' suggests a rather universalised model of the human being which expunges the significance of power and thereby misses the details of the repressing and the repressed; it eludes the specific ways in which certain categorised groups are socially 'othered', their identities *imposed* upon them by racist (Chapter 5) and sexist (Chapter 6) representations (both powerfully influenced by the biological model). Foucault's replacement of the subjectivist by the structural and historical facilitates a deeper appreciation of the more unconscious determinants structuring human action. Foucault's framing of human action as subject to the state of knowledge and institutional power provides a sharp corrective to Goffman's totally self-conscious, calculating, reflective actor. Yet Foucault's deval-uation of the currency of human nature as an inexorable concept clearly results in the unwarranted expulsion of the human subject from history even in his own estimation. Notwithstanding his intentions, it renders the human self indelibly pragmatic and contingent, bereft of judgement. No appeal to any form of a human nature is possible other than a Nietzschean call for some superhuman residing far above the multitude.

Confronted with such uncertainty and contingency, the re-emergence of the human subject wears an individualistic cast, rationalised on the one hand as a preoccupation with self emptied of ethical content, subject to a cultural and materialistic narcissism, and on the other reflecting an inner urge to connect with the authentic self. An imperative survives to plumb the depths of some rational substantive human nature which postmodernist culture constantly denies, refusing to prioritise human values. Space, however, is available for new values. The progressive postmodernists affirm human subjects as able to define their nature in terms of reasserted identities through striving for personal freedoms. But we must ask ourselves if a personal freedom is sufficient. What of the social self and communitarian values?

Having examined so far various biological, cultural, and social theories and their handling of human nature models, the following chapter will investigate particular political and ideological uses of human nature theories which have constituted the foundations of racism.

Further Reading

General Surveys

Tom Campbell, *Seven Theories of Human Society* (Oxford University Press, 1981). Relates social theories of society to theories of human nature; covers Aristotle, Hobbes, Adam Smith, Marx, Durkheim, Weber, Schutz.

Milton Gordon, *The Scope of Sociology* (Oxford University Press, 1988). Chapter on sociology and human nature.

Paul Hirst and Penny Woolley, *Social Relations and Human Attributes* (Tavistock, 1982). A defence of social constructionism.

Axel Honneth and Hans Joas, *Social Action and Human Nature* (Cambridge University Press, 1988). Densely written, relates sociology to philosophical anthropology.

Rosalind Sydie, *Natural Woman: Cultured Man: A Feminist Perspective on Sociological Theory* (Open University Press, 1987). A feminist critique of male sociology which engages with the human nature debate; focuses on Durkheim and Weber.

Charles Taylor, *Philosophy and the Human Sciences* (Cambridge University Press, 1985). Essays on philosophy, social science and human nature.

Social Theory and the Self

Mitchell Aboulafia, *The Mediating Self: Mead, Sartre, and Self-Determination* (Yale University Press, 1986). Attempts to synthesise existentialism and social behaviourism.

Anthony Giddens, *Modernity and Self-Identity: Self and Society in the Late Modern Age* (Polity Press, 1991). A shift in this major sociologist's focus towards the individual.

Erving Goffman, *The Presentation of Self in Everyday Life* (Penguin, 1958). A classic of symbolic interactionism.

Charles Taylor, *The Ethics of Authenticity* (Harvard University Press, 1991). A crisper version of his vast, but hugely readable, *Sources of the Self.*

Structuralism and Post-Modernism

Paul Rabinow (ed.), *The Foucault Reader: An Introduction to Foucault's Thought* (Penguin, 1991). A good starting point for engaging with Foucault.

Madun Sarup, *An Introductory Guide to Post-Structuralism and Post-Modernism* 2nd edn. (Harvester Press, 1993). Highly succinct.

5

Biology, Racism and Aggression

Introduction

Up until this point the discussion has counterposed theories and models of human nature as they have developed historically, assessing the specific contributions to our self-knowledge made by the disciplines of biology, philosophy, anthropology, psychology and sociology. The political ramifications are implied by the positions adopted as to whether we are individual as opposed to social by nature, and the extent to which we accept the conceptual splits of human:animal, mind:body, self:society or science and culture. At this juncture, however, it is incumbent on us to probe further into the issue of human nature and political manipulability, to study the full and terrible consequences of 'othering' by analysing antisemitism and racism in relation to biological theory. Certainly, racism brings into razor-sharp focus the biological reductionist picture of human beings. Biology and racism have often gone hand in hand since the nineteenth century with the implicit acceptance of the biological metaphor, the founding of eugenics, and the justification of white imperialism by social Darwinists. The biological metaphor re-emerged in the twentieth century in the context of advances in genetics, the mobilisation of mass and state aggression, global warfare, general economic depression, and genocide. This chapter will show that in spite of the horrific dehumanising destructive consequences of biological theory as applied to the essence and nature of human beings, the ideas did not *disappear*: they simply remained dormant, only temporarily losing respectability. Biological and genetic models have been more readily adopted in psychological explanation, for example aspects of educational psychology and traditional criminology. Their reappearance appealed more to sociological explanation through the incorporation of cultural factors into the explanation of behaviour and the denial of biological determinism.

The biological model is especially controversial: first, because of the disastrous human consequences in categorising human beings into higher and lower; second, because of its pessimistic conclusions regarding human potentiality; and third, because of the political and policy implications. The chapter initially surveys the earlier portrayals of biological ideas as applied to human behaviour, before examining the notions of genetics and race, and the Nazis' model of human beings which served as *raison d'être* for their programme of genocide for blacks, Jews and gypsies and the mentally sick. In the case of the Jews, the racism was based not only upon a biological conception of human difference. Historically, antisemitism has also been underpinned by theological 'arguments' and an interminable hatred directed by non-Jews against Jews. The chapter goes on to analyse theories of human aggression, including sociobiology and related models of human nature in the particular context of racial hatred and genocide, before exploring ideas of the new right and the new racism which have intellectually justified theories of human nature and human instinct. Notions of the 'natural' defensive group are pinpointed in an analysis of the contemporary resurgence of racist ideas across Europe.

Genetics and Nazism

This section looks at the Nazis' application of genetic theories and 'human nature' as biological hierarchy to the political and social treatment of the Jews and the role of the body in characterisations of the 'natural' and 'unnatural'. Genetics and eugenics flourished in the nineteenth century. Early biological explanations of criminality and aggression emphasised features within the individual as the main cause of such conditions as mental disorders arising from the body (Aggleton, 1987). Human nature was seen as little more than bodily attributes or natural function. Lombroso (1911) placed emphasis on bodily features which were later (Kretschmer, 1951) causally linked to particular aggressive behaviour; Lombroso and Ferrero (1895) provided a crude link between facial look and criminality from their analysis of the facial characteristics of 20 criminals. Having noted their physical irregularities such as large jaws, they accordingly labelled them *born* criminals and identified them as 'throwbacks' from an earlier evolutionary stage in their physical resemblance to apes (Rubington and Weinberg, 1989, pp. 23–4).

Carl Gustav Carus related race to bodily organs, white to the brain, black to the genitals, in the early nineteenth century, whilst Gobinau's racial hygiene theories argued that white, yellow and black races were of unequal value. Yet Darwin's *The Origin of Species* had a much greater impact in a manner scarcely intended, becoming 'the involuntary progenitor of racist ideology' (Burleigh and Wipperman, 1991, p. 28) as filtered through the writings on selective breeding by Haeckel and Schallmeye, zoologist and physician respectively.

In racial antisemitism, however, we face not just another discrete characterisation of the nature of certain human groups; it is symbolic of the *non*-human. The 'theory' of antisemitism itself was introduced by the Englishman Houston Stewart Chamberlain in his *Foundations of the Nineteenth Century* (1899, 1936, cited in Staub, 1989, p. 106) which integrated racial-hygienic and social Darwinist ideas with anti-semitism. His attack on Jews was based on the belief that they threatened Germanic peoples' intellectual abilities and were infused by the Devil. Hence, Jews were personified as *demonic* in nature, and thus their nature was deemed capable of virtually anything. Cohn-Sherbok (1992) describes how the demonic image of the Jew stretches back to the fourteenth century when Jews, viewed as 'vermin of the earth', were relegated to a 'sub-species of humanity'. All western Jew hatred has spotlighted the *difference* of Jews (in existentialist terms, their 'otherness'). Physiological portrayals have 'ratified' the alleged distinctiveness.

For many centuries all parts of the 'Jewish' body, for instance the nose (especially), foot, brain and voice have been mythologised as personal and social facets of degradation and decay and associated with the Jew's nature (Gilman, 1991, p. 5). Hence, by the time of the Nazi upsurge these ideas were tranformed with ease into an extensive racial political programme advocated in Hitler's *Mein Kampf* which synthesised racist and antisemitic ideologies (Burleigh and Wipperman, 1991, p. 42). During the period of Germany's Third Reich eugenics became a fully fledged official state ideology. Hitler's disease metaphors helped to rationalise the wholesale extermination of the Jews. *Mein Kampf* affirmed racial category as the focal principle of human existence. Viewed as an essentially biological entity, but a subspecies, the Jews were perceived by Hitler as the ultimate 'Anti-Race' aiming at the complete demolition of Ayran culture (Biddiss, 1977, p. 231).

'Race' became 'race' science in Nazi Germany. Hans Gunther, an academic, viewed 'race' as the key to understanding all the human sciences, and his writings still circulate among postwar Nazis (Seidel, 1986). Medical experiments conducted by doctors in the *Lager* (concentration camps) were directly related to such ideas of disease. The research on 'racial stock' constituted a part of the Nazi racial health policy, 'scientific procedure' theoretically grounded 'to determine man's exact place in nature through observation, measurements, and comparisons between groups of men and animals' (Mosse, 1978, p. 2, cited in Bauman, 1989, p. 69).

Arguments for genocide policies were offered in the language of 'biological pollution' and racial hygiene:

> Because the body is part of nature, the fight to kill 'the Jewish bacillus' is presented as 'natural'. It follows that antisemitism itself may also be seen as 'natural'; and, indeed, the urge towards 'racial purity' in *Mein Kampf* is assumed part of 'the iron logic of Nature'. (Seidel, 1986, p. 21)

Social and political phenomena are often presented on the political right in biological terms, as if biology were destiny (Seidel, 1988a; Rose et al., 1984). Curtis (1986, p. 6) suggests that the primacy of racism may be found in Marr's precise coining of the term 'anti-semitism' in 1879, implying that racial characteristics rather than religious beliefs were being opposed; it was the myth of Jewish biological inferiority that justified the systematisation of anti-semitism in a secular age:

> The argument of biological differences propounded by anti-Christians marks the emergence of the genocidal strain in modern antisemitism. The world, it was concluded, must be saved from Judaization. (Curtis, 1986, p. 7)

Konrad Lorenz, discussing domesticated animals and maintenance of purity of the stock, felt able to write *in 1940* (with Nazi racism and genocide fully operating):

> The selection for toughness, heroism, social utility ... must be accomplished by some human institution if mankind, in default of selective factors, is not to be ruined by domestication-induced degeneracy. The racial idea as the basis of our state has already accomplished much in this respect. (Lorenz, 1940)

Borrowing a number of ideas from Eugen Fischer's *Racial Characteristics of Man as a Phenomenon of Domestication* which juxtaposed the so-called perfect specimen Nordic against the ostensibly mis-shapen deviate Jew, Lorenz also published an article in 1942 for the *Zeitscrift fur Tierpsychologie* under the title of 'The Innate Forms of Possible Experience', promoting the principles of ethology to recommend a self-conscious, scientifically based race policy. A sobering postscript is that despite the vociferous international protests, Lorenz was awarded the Nobel Peace Prize for his scientific endeavours.

Whilst 'race' has been a highly significant element in biologically oriented theories, gender has also been a related component and used to similar effect through differentiation and oppression. In this respect both have been central to fascist and new right ideology. As we shall see in the following chapter, female nature has been portrayed as unlike that of the male. Females, like people of Afro-Caribbean and Asian origin, oppressed on the basis of biological difference and assumed human inferiority, were assimilated into the Nazi 'theory' of genetics and sound stock. Those women categorised as racially inferior and untouchable were subjected to brutal treatment, tortured and murdered in Nazi Germany. 'Natural' may indeed be identified as the shared characteristic of racist, anti-semitic and sexist discourse by which minority groups are treated as a 'natural group' (Guillaumin, 1972).

The knowledge of the dangers of Nazi philosophies and their logical culmination would have led, one imagines, to the complete discrediting of any conceptualisation linking social life and behaviour to genetic factors. This was not to be the case, shown first by the events and debates over general intelligence, and secondly by the claims of genetic determinists in the 1990s. After World War Two, in the wake of revelations of the Jewish Holocaust and the Nazi biological genetics master plan, scientific racism was given no public or academic credibility. However, explanations of genetic inheritance especially relating to educational attainment received wide coverage within two decades. Clearly, although the more optimistic socioeconomic climate had ensured that spurious racist scientific ideas failed to emerge, in effect they had lain dormant until their propitious re-emergence. Rose et al. (1973) suggest that the 'ideological truce' which paralleled Britain's end of empire and the emergence of the new African states was shattered by the events of the 1960s including the racist overtones of the Vietnam War, intensified racial conflict in the USA, and the major influx of migrant workers into western Europe. Such events heralded 'the re-emergence of scientific racism in its contemporary form' (Rose et al., 1973, p. 241).

In America in 1969 educational psychologist Arthur Jensen claimed that blacks' poorer educational performance could be explained by their innately inferior intelligence. Herrnstein (1971) maintained that class difference determinants were genetically produced, whilst a physicist William Shockley contended that national intelligence levels were in decline due to higher population growth rates among blacks and the white working class than among middle-class whites. In Britain, behaviourist psychologist Hans Eysenck's case studies implicitly supported Jensen. But Rose and his colleagues (1973) showed that the ideas of the biological IQ theorists and the resultant social policies scarcely deviated in essence from earlier social Darwinism and eugenicists Galton and Pearson's biological 'laws' of inferior races. They also mirrored the implied links made by eugenicists between genetics and intelligence, and intelligence test measurement techniques. However, the noted educationist Sir Cyril Burt's findings and research methodology were largely discredited in the 1970s as a result of the discovery by Leon Kamin (1974) that Burt had fabricated data to fit the theory of inherited IQ.

The IQ concept, then, perpetuates the biological notion of human nature whilst accepting the idea that the environment has *some* impact in shaping individual behaviour. Notwithstanding the body of literature illustrating the racist implications and untenable *non*-scientific nature of the 'inherited intelligence' school of thought (Richardson and Spears (eds.), 1972; Kamin, 1974; Rose et al.,

1973; Rose et al., 1984) IQ testing has remained a stock in trade of education psychologists which arguably reinforces inequality through the concept of an educational meritocracy and basically supporting the idea of an inherited general intelligence.

Developments in modern genetics raise anew prospects of the scientific manipulation of our human nature. The £2 billion Human Genome Project makes feasible an understanding of the genetic code responsible for many of our human features and biological traits, and concomitant cures for many inherited diseases. Gene therapy, however, still raises ethical issues on the human nature question, and looms particularly large against the historical backcloth of eugenics and the Nazi state. Apprehension reigns that the technique may be used for the enhancement of general human characteristics. Scientific competence to preselect a child's sex raises the spectre of genetic engineering's recurrence (Sattaur, 1988). Are we now confronted with the Frankenstein prospect of engineering our human nature, manipulating how we may reproduce ourselves, what we may reproduce, and what we may achieve in life?

Wide publicity (the 'gay gene') was recently given to US research findings that homosexuality in males is affected by genes and appears to run in families through the mother, seeming to suggest that sexual orientation is natural and not socially constructed (although the researchers did not claim that the genes could *determine* sexual orientation) (*Guardian*, 1993). In spite of the ambiguities and counter claims over the full scientific, moral and social significance of these findings, crediting biological explanation for social difference or 'deviance' has led to anxieties that eugenics and Nazi genetic engineering will be accorded a revitalised credibility.

A basic cause for anxiety is the extent of genetic biology's ambitions. Stent (1978, p. 227) describes the field as one which deals with the whole western cultural traditions in suggesting the necessity for the destruction of western culture by enhancing human qualities and changing human nature. To quote Kaye (1986, p. 94):

> No longer committed to the value-salvage operations of their social Darwinist and biological-humanist predecessor, they have directed their scientific and interpretive efforts elsewhere: toward the curing of modern Western souls and their sick societies and toward the establishment of a non-Western, non-Christian culture.

Despite the ambivalence of new genetics' findings, antireductionist scientists such as Robert Young and Steve Jones (BBC2, 22 August 1993) have expressed concern for the Genome Project's social implications. The whole of life and human nature are not reducible to molecules. Inestimable potential human consequences arise from the genetic reductionist perspective. 'If there is a gene for human sexuality,' questions a physiology professor, 'then why not one for creativity? If cystic fibrosis, then why not conscious intention?' (Noble, 1993).

To summarise and conclude this section, eugenics and social Darwinism were central to Nazi ideology and practice whilst the *bodily* characterisation of the Jews functioned to turn them into inferior non-humans who, by lacking a *human* nature, may be more readily exterminated. Further, antisemitism was authenticated by the 'scientific' stamp of racial categories, marking a transposition from the historical Christian antisemitism to modern antisemitism's ultimate logic in the form of the gas chamber. 'Race' and genetic qualities were central to the Nazi platform, part of the crucial juxtaposition between intrinsically 'superior' and 'inferior' groups. Genetics as a science was used to differentiate and oppress. Yet the rejection of genetic science was a temporary phenomenon. As we have seen, the educational psychologists' embrace of the IQ notion and the measurement of a general intelligence still imply an acceptance of social Darwinist and eugenic suppositions; their findings have served to justify inequalities between groups as natural. More contemporary breakthroughs in genetic therapy must be treated critically and with caution. Modern geneticists' ambitions to manipulate new forms of human nature too easily cast shadows of the past. Scientific selection soon becomes exclusion of the 'outgroup', the unwanted group. Finally, given that so far we have concentrated on narrating the particular characterisations of one group by another, how do we account for such aggression and destructiveness targeted at the 'other'? Is it explicable in terms of a given biological human nature?

Aggression, Human Nature and Racism

We now turn to a range of theories of aggression which strive to deal with violence and destructiveness against 'out groups', covering instinctivist or naturalistic theories, including ethology and human sociobiology, and the Freudian psychoanalytic theory of human destructiveness; behaviourism's approach to the debate; personality characteristics; the existential engagement with the emotions; and the analysis of victimisation as a cultural phenomenon.

Instinctivist theories basically comprise those of the ethologists, and Freud's theory of destruction and the death wish seen as a biological drive (Chapter 2). As we noted in Chapter 3, Lorenz's complete conceptualisation of human nature is premised upon instinctual aggressiveness activated by external stimuli. It is instinct gone wild in humans, and thus no longer of a preservative nature but a *danger* to survival. More contemporary ethologists have added to Lorenz's insights with their own studies of animals and human tribes, showing how human beings' biological heritage and killer instincts lie at the roots of war. Innate aggression instead of social or economic factors, they reason, explains modern warfare. Basically, human beings are tribal animals ranged in permanent conflict with other groups, a state of affairs created by the release of aggressive energy. Morris (1971) justifies war between nations as well as group aggression of the kind between rival football gangs in such terms, whilst Morris and Marsh (1988) pronounce that 'man is a tribal animal. We must fully appreciate this fact if we are to understand one of the most important facets of human nature' (p. 30). They argue that the need to differentiate ourselves from those groups with considerably different characteristics complements a basic need to define oneself by identity with a group possessing identifiable habits, values, attitudes and styles (1988, p. 11). Such a position is soon translated into the language of natural (and national) antagonisms. Thus we are led to believe that 'in groups' and 'out groups' are only reproducing natural life. Furthermore, runs the ethological argument, animal nature lies at the root of capitalist nature and the persistent drive to acquire private property. This behaviourist tendency mirrors that of animals fighting for their own piece of property or territory, conceptually transcending the earlier notion of biological instinct (Ardrey, 1966). But Ardrey's thesis that property and territoriality derive from animal life, a revival of the seventeenth-century 'property instinct' in human nature (Montagu, 1968, p. 9) gains little support from observation of most mammal behaviour, including the *non*-territoriality of great apes.

Sociobiology, as we saw in Chapter 3, treats aggression (in common with ethologists) as instinctual, but also as *culturally* evolved through the selfish gene's evolutionary stable strategy. Culture transmits aggression which, regardless of its incidence, is considered natural. Aggression's absence is seen as transient or an aberration. Genocidal warfare is universal although we can expect some isolated cultures to escape the process temporarily by reverting to pacifism (Wilson, 1980, p. 299). The biological and the cultural do not function as distinctive processes. Culture reflects the adaptation of genetic evolutionary behaviour, serving biology. Nationalism, wars and violent aggression are the exaggerated outgrowth ('hypertrophy') of an underlying biological tendency towards tribalism or kin altruism (Chapter 3). But this hypertrophy is now assumed in the modern period to have taken on a monstrously destructive form. Yet it is not clear how one equates modern nationalistic world wars with simple tribal loyalties which have to be quelled internally by national governments for nationalism to operate. Socially constructed political strategies are qualitatively different from 'hypertrophied tribalism' (Kaye, 1986, p. 122).

As with many reductionist approaches to human nature, the socio-biologists have avoided justifying their own selection of *the* universal traits in human nature, such as aggression, which is culled from an immense diversity of individual and cultural characteristics (Rose et al., 1984, p. 246). In the final analysis, despite its claim to scientific status, sociobiology is ideological in its rationalisation and justification of existing selfishness and individualistic capital-istic competition. Its biological determinism suggests that 'this is how we are', hence justifying the status quo and appeals to con-servatism.

The Freudian model is the second type of instinctual theory of aggression (Chapter 2) charting the conflict between the death and life instincts. Freud saw humans in the final analysis destroying either themselves or others by a biological drive rooted in the make-up of the human organism. One may detect various similarities between Lorenz and Freud in one respect. Each cultivates an image of human beings incessantly reproducing an uncontrollable aggression which leads to destruction. Nevertheless, Freud based his obser-vations on human beings and not on animal behaviour. By reading off the behaviour of animals to explain that of humans, ethologists missed the differences *between* human individuals and groups. To quote Fromm,

> ... it is an untenable scientific procedure to claim, without even trying to muster evidence for it, that this is a universal human reaction, or that it is 'human nature' to commit atrocities during war, and to base this claim on an alleged instinct based on the questionable analogy with fishes and birds. (1977, p. 53)

Freud on the other hand *was* interested in the predisposition of *certain* human beings for aggressive behaviour, in pursuing their motives and making sense of their emotional conflict. He wished to help individuals change their behaviour through recognition of the nature of their impulses.

The work of writers such as Bettelheim and Fromm who built upon his ideas and integrated them into the analysis of social conditions suggests the heuristic power of Freud's theory of aggression. Bettelheim, a child psychologist and concentration camp survivor, adopts the Freudian model of the death drive suf-focating the life force (1986). This power of human beings' destructive tendencies represents an internalisation of the totali-tarian superego by individuals evading too many externally produced conflicts. George Steiner also argues that the death drive was not specific to Hitler but affected the Jews themselves (1971). To quote Bettelheim (1986, p. 211): 'The Nazis murdered the Jews of Europe. That nobody but the Jews cared, that the world, the United States, did not care, was why Jewish life drives lost the battle against death tendencies.'

Bettelheim's account, however, does not rely exclusively on the death wish. He also couples the Freudian explanation with, first, technologism and technological mass society, and second with the latter's obsession with the pseudo-scientific delusion of improving the human's genetic inheritance. Indeed, we must query any wholesale acceptance of the Freudian conception of instinct with its associated biological reductionism. René Girard's deeper examination of cultural process and his concept of mimesis (Girard, 1972) represents a challenge to the model of biological life and death instincts as expounded in Freud's *Beyond the Pleasure Principle* (1920). In Girard's schema a *mimetic desire* is culturally embedded, through rivalry seeking out an inevitable victim. The desire is embedded in the brain and transmitted *culturally* rather than biologically; such destructiveness has expanded within culture as the brain capacity of hominids has increased (Williams, 1991, pp. 6–7). Koestler (1973) mounts a similar sort of argument with his thesis of the brain's missing parts, explaining the events of unparalleled aggression and cruelty as: 'the failure of the neo-cortex to control the ancient, emotion-ridden part of the brain. Our sensory equipment has become poverty-laden.' In such circumstances, the power of the 'word' and language can be hugely destructive in its capacity for convincing people to see others as not belonging to the same species.

Skinner's behaviourism, we recall (Chapter 2), concedes nothing innate within the human, since every personal contour is shaped by environmental stimuli. Behaviourists study and explain aggression through observation of outwardly manifested behaviour. Often this is vindicated as human beings' response to frustrating events, overpowering them with aggressive or destructive behaviour. A seminal psychology experiment probing into the psyche of Nazi murderers illustrates authority-manipulated aggression and human destructiveness. Stanley Milgram's classic study on social obedience (Milgram, 1974) shows how *anyone* is capable of barbarism. 'Nice' is soon convertible into cruel and brutish; 'concerned' young men are 'no better and no worse than human beings of any other era who lend themselves to the purposes of authority and become instruments in its destructive processes' (Milgram, 1974, p. 180). The experiments with 'ordinary' volunteers prepared to inflict pain on command of a 'leader' found inhumanity to be a matter of social power relationships.

The apparent conclusions are horrific but highly plausible, and seem to mirror a reality including the Nazi experience. Hannah

Arendt, from her documentation of the Adolf Eichmann trial (Arendt, 1963), certainly not an artificial laboratory experiment, concludes that the Nazi leaders were 'terrifyingly normal'. We can all be steered into destructive behaviour; humans are malleable, lacking inner moral constraints. Yet doubts exist about the Milgram experiments themselves, not least the implicit disobedience (untestable in a behaviour-focused experiment) of a number of participants, the feelings of guilt and moral concern (conscience) in most of the participants. Hence, the experiment may, at the behavioural level, provide further proof of the *ease* with which humans, plastic in their nature, can be dehumanised, but it may also demonstrate the existence of inner pressures rendering cruelty insufferable (Fromm, 1977, p. 86).

Behaviourism, in common with the sociobiological, naturalistic theory of aggression, eschews inner mental and organic motivational states. Thus, it is prone to miss the uniquely human displays of hatred and destructiveness towards others, communicated through qualities of the human personality, where again one confronts the matter of authority and the proneness to obey. Personality theories of aggression project on to the attributes of an individual personality the human species' capacities to act. Fromm's (1977) Freudian-existentialist synthesis reacted against the supposition of universal, animal instincts in human beings, noting that in the course of their *existence* humans exhibit a range of passions marking them out from animals. These passions, present in diverse personalities with different character structures, help us make sense out of our lives. Alternatively, they may contribute to the formation of the aggressive, authoritarian, sadistic personality. Theodor Adorno's *Authoritarian Personality* (1950) yielded results to demonstrate the plausibility of the *born* Nazi recognisable by certain identifiable personality characteristics (but this is only tenable in the absence of socially constructed character formation).

Fromm's analysis points to a variety of factors leading to aggression and destructiveness, premised upon a set of *existential* human needs and the various *character-rooted* passions which, in striving to escape the existential void, may end in destruction of the 'other'. The necessity for a framework of orientation and devotion to, for example, some idol or the acquisition of power *impells* the incumbent to achieve the goal, regardless of the means. The need for roots can lead to a person's heightened sense of isolation, and a craving to destroy all others. 'By destroying the world I am saved from being crushed by it,' states Fromm (1977, p. 313). The existential quest for unity in oneself and with the external world may be met by a passion for destruction where the anxious, fragmented human individual 'loses' oneself in striving to overcome the existential dualistic split (Fromm, 1977, p. 315). Our impulse in life to feel effective may transform itself into the search for power over others and their eventual demise. Other passions which may end in untrammelled aggression include the excitation and stimulation of the human brain, and the avoidance of boredom. Finally, certain character structures, for instance sadism, may point towards fearful destruction *if* facilitated by a supportive social structure.

The connection between character and existential compulsion has been explored by Sartre. His existential psychological explanation of the pathological obsession with Jews employs the concept of projection. *Anti-Semite and Jew* (1948) defines antisemites as those who are afraid and thus project their own anxieties, drives and aggressions on to the scapegoated Jews. In demanding rigorous order for others, they wish to place themselves above the law, simultaneously fleeing from the consciousness of their liberty and their isolation (Sartre, 1948, p. 31).

This analysis is echoed by Flory (1986) who discusses the projection of guilt, but approaches prejudice as an essential innate force in all human beings. Prejudice itself becomes a manifestation of what Flory describes as:

> the most fundamental and instinctive of all human drives – 'self-ishness' – which persists because of the *pride* that makes us ready to go to almost any length to avoid admitting to ourselves that we were in the wrong. (Flory, 1986, p. 240)

Antisemitism and racism, then, are the results of a selfish attempt to inflate one's sense of self-worth by downgrading others (Flory, 1986, p. 240).

Bettelheim and Janowitz's study of antisemitism and racial intolerance (1975) also finds projection to be an essential ingredient in prejudice. Aggression against an outgroup is seen as individuals' projection of their own questionable behaviour on to the 'other' – behaviour which has contributed to personal failure (Smith, 1988, p. 193). Charny et al. (1982) characterise the easily led and deeply suggestible genociders as using the anonymous group for an escape route from apprehension at their own non-aliveness and ontological death, projecting these anxieties on to 'non-human' scapegoats.

But this projection, the act of scapegoating, would appear to be grounded in more than the particular individual's personality features. In Chapter 3 we saw that culture must play a part in the formation of our human characteristics and responses. Girard argues that victimisation is culturally created to meet needs and resolve conflict through mimetic desire (the process of imitating and desiring). Once the conflict reaches a certain level, then one must displace or eliminate the rival possessing the desired characteristics. The injunction to maintain a cultural cohesiveness generates the necessity for victim. Mimetic activity resolves itself in the differentiation, exclusion and victimisation of *one* so that the *all* (the group or community) may co-exist. Hence, 'human beings are universally, if not at all times and necessarily, caught up in the mimetic desire that is potentially destructive' (Williams, 1991, pp. 9–10).

Fromm has pointed to the limitations not only of the behaviourist focus, but also of an exclusive concentration upon personality. The very strength of 'normality' in major genociders intimates the limitations of psychological analysis. In his psychoanalytic evaluation of Hitler's autobiographical profile Fromm shows that even Hitler's drive to destroy the 'other' was not unlike that of many 'normal' heads of state. He was not *evidently* 'evil' and not the only destroyer. Hitler's case was special in the 'disproportionality between the destruction he ordered and the realistic reasons for it' (Fromm, 1977, p. 532). It is the scale of this disproportionality that signals to us the urgency for historical understanding and social evaluation. The disproportionality cannot be reduced to universal personality attributes or to other properties of an alleged human nature like existential angst. Hitler was *able* to wreak such awesome annihilation of humankind because of the circumstances. 'What was unique was the socio-political situation in which he could rise; there are probably hundreds of Hitlers among us who would come forth if the historical hour arrived' (Fromm, 1977, p. 574).

Instinctual, behaviourist and existential psychological theories are unable to tap the sheer magnitude of cruelty and total destruction of the 'other' through racial and antisemitic hatred. Biological or psychological nature only partially explain horrific violence on the mass scale. Genocide of ethnic 'outgroups' cannot be elucidated in psychological terms. For example, the social and cultural preconditions had to exist for the Jewish Holocaust to happen (Staub, 1989). One must engage with the sociopolitical connections of mass violence. Heller (1979) has argued that aggressive forms of behaviour are *only* rendered possible in the context of external sociopsychical patterns which express a historically developed 'second nature' (Heller, 1979, p. 96, cited in Honneth and Joas, 1988, p. 100).

We must be prepared to grasp the multifaceted quality of human nature which is, contends Charny (1982), a paradox whereby human beings can be both good and bad, creator and destroyer. The fact we find almost impossible to come to terms with is that genocides result from people just like ourselves, functioning with initially quite healthy natural processes which grow wild; unintentionally and pathologically they turn into murderous violence (Charny et al., 1982, p. 25). Despite this horrific internally generated impetus, however, modern rationality and society from Charny's perspective is able to overcome it. Charny's conclusions, though, fall short of the analysis. The Holocaust, so inviolably *bound up* with the nature of modernity, cannot simply be associated with the endurance of barbarism. Bauman's sociological study (1989) rejects the thesis that the Holocaust was born out of premodern uncivilised behaviour: 'the hidden, lurking pre-social beast'. Its real context was the modern, '*civilised*' society.

Bauman proposes that the idea of the modern state replacing the Hobbesian model of 'man' in a state of nature is myth. Rather than interpreting the Jewish Holocaust as the failure of civilisation (that is, of reason and purpose), historical evidence on the events discloses human nature's weaknesses such as an abhorrence of violence in the face of calculating, rational, cold, technical efficiency, amply reinforced by the scientific intellect:

> The Hobbesian world of the Holocaust did not surface from its too shallow grave, resurrected by the tumult of irrational emotions. It arrived (in a formidable shape Hobbes would certainly disown) in a factory-shaped vehicle, wielding weapons only the most advanced science could supply, and following an itinerary designed by scientifically managed organization. (Bauman, 1989, p. 13)

Jordan (1991), a scientist, warns of the human dangers of the paradigmatic mind:body split and the extraction of emotion from rational thought:

> The question ... arises: once we have molded our scientists to think in a mode without feeling, why should they shift values when they come to questions of human life? ... I do not think we recognise how easy it is for reason to get off track. And when it does go wrong, when it does get beyond wisdom, may heaven help us. (Jordan, 1991, pp. 200–1)

His description of how scientific experiments with gypsies, Jews, Poles and Russians at Dachau were clinically conducted and recorded in the pursuit of knowledge concerning the length of time human beings could survive in cold water (Jordan, 1992, p. 201) is echoed by the words of a camp survivor, Primo Levi, in *Drowned and the Saved* to the effect that 'alongside Cartesian logic there existed the logic of the SS' (Levi, 1988, p. 144).

To summarise, efforts to comprehend human aggression and the inhumanity of genocide lie at the heart of the human nature debate. Instinctivist theories have argued from an untenable biological reductionist perspective in accounting for human destruction. The ethologists' reading off from observation of animal behaviour ignores the social and political motives and actions of human society, whilst socobiological studies of modern forms of warfare employ a crude unsubstantiated convergence with tribalism. The Freudian brand of instinctivism does begin with human behaviour, but the more penetrating analyses of the 'death wish' attempt to connect with social context. Behaviourist approaches to the main-springs of Nazi aggression and cruelty deliver a sobering picture of environmental conditioning in the shape of the mechanical, unquestioning human, but miss the universe of self-conscious human motives, emotions and reasoning behind acts of violence. Human personality, existential needs and the condition of emotional anxiety confronted by the perceived 'other' seem pertinent factors in the creation of aggression. Yet too strong a focus upon person-ality leads us away from understanding mass hatred and ethnocentric violence and the politically motivated social construction of an 'enemy'. Without an appreciation of the role of the state and political cultures we cannot even begin to understand such events of human destructiveness as the Jewish Holocaust. Understanding human nature cannot be abstracted from the specifics of social and political power.

The Resurgence of Racism, Sociobiology and the New Right

In this section we probe further into the social and political context of the racist ideas since the 1970s, and the extent to which socio-biological ideas have been instrumental in fuelling the rise of a new right racism; we look at the importance of culture and nation, and then at the politically inspired elision between nation, nature and human nature. The ideas of sociobiology have relied less upon the biology of individual personality and more upon group and cultural processes, although they are nonetheless political in their claims and implications. It may be debatable how far one may directly read off any overt right-wing extremism from sociobiology's scientism. Ruse (1985) argues that sociobiologists are unjustly accused of being racist, since there is no sign of them directly espousing racist views. Their ideas have been *used* detrimentally by racists. On the surface, Ruse's position seems reasonable – but how reasonable?

The Sociobiology Study Group (1978, p. 282) and Leach (1978) claim that Edward Wilson's model of human nature, knitting the cultural to the genetic, is ethnocentric in its construct – human behaviour viewed highly selectively 'through Euro-American cultural lens'. Wilson's selectivity calls for an abstraction from much historical and ethnographic detail on social behaviour and social organisation. Nevertheless the ostensible abuse of these theories has placed biology back on the political agenda with the termina-tion of economic boom in both the United States and Britain since the 1960s. In spite of the commonly acknowledged horrors of the Holocaust we confront the resurgence of racist organisations in Britain, Europe and the USA. The traditional British Conservative Party has propounded a form of biological racism over the past two decades which incorporates the more subtle versions of biological determinism based on 'cultural' instincts and differences. Such a political position is justified by sociobiological perspectives. We noted earlier Wilson's view of inherited cultural mechanisms as a simple tribalism which vindicates the defensive and aggressive postures of national and ethnic groups against others (Wilson, 1978). But the use of tribalism as explaining aggression is an implicitly ideological position. The Morris and Marsh discussion of how tribal behaviour is acted out by Nazi and racist skinhead groups in Europe and in America by the Ku Klux Klan is devoid of reference to the particular political and economic contours. Naturalist explanation of violence avoids coming to terms with the particular social context. The genetic *natural* imperative in sociobiology becomes racist, in that racism is viewed as genetically functional, virtually a rationalisation of the inevitability of racism (Goldberg, 1993, pp. 145–6). Barker, too (1981), draws attention to this naturalism in the sociobiologists' handling of xenophobia which is interpreted as an evolutionary and innate response to our fellow beings who happen to be genetically unrelated or possess a different skin colour.

Nazi group or racist gang behaviour cannot be understood by isolation of the specific context. In Britain's case, for example, such behaviour is not unrelated to the specific set of *policies* and ideology espoused by the formal government in power, itself feeding upon the 'new racism', a version of the natural or 'common sense' understanding which melds culture to racism, but which also embraces the concept of 'nation'.

Barker (1981, p. 20) outlines a range of specific components which form a theory of 'pseudo-biological culturalism', a theory of human nature inextricably binding race to nation. The new racism embraces the idea of a way of life or a culture, promoting the belief that it is human nature to form bounded communities or a nation aware of its differences from other nations, and implying the existence of a sociobiological *instinct* to preserve identity and defend territory.

The distinction between this type of racial theory and the one so wholeheartedly embraced by the Nazis is the strategic replacement of the notion of 'others' as inferior with 'others' as coming from *different* cultures (and hence better to be kept apart). Such a position is reflected in the language of contemporary right-wing English philosopher Roger Scruton, a leading figure of the new right academic *Salisbury Review* group, which is framed in terms of 'natural prejudice', 'their own kind' and 'group herd instincts'. For Scruton 'illiberal sentiments' are simply those that seem 'to arise inevitably from social consciousness: they involve natural prejudice, and the desire for the company of one's own kind' (Scruton, 1986, p. 14).

Towards the end of the 1960s the Conservative Party's Enoch Powell employed a version of natural determinism and inevitable hatreds, in justifying immigration controls and repatriation, a classic invitation to 'other' an explicitly defined group:

> I do not believe that it is in human nature that a country, and a country such as ours, should passively watch the transformation of whole areas which lie at the heart of it into alien territory. (Smithies and Fiddick, 1969)

During the 1970s the new right within the Conservative Party itself professed a cultural theory of 'natural' difference which actually strengthened the voice of self-proclaimed racist political organisations. The new right incorporated into its thinking 'scientific' insights regarding cultural behaviour; the climate was considered ripe for the perpetuation of racist attitudes, and thus the Conservative Party's new right perspectives became increasingly powerful. A new 'commonsense' racist theory was taken up, refined and disseminated by the press. Margaret Thatcher's 1978 television speech on the subject of the pain undergone by British people because of the extensive immigration into the United Kingdom resonated with the overtones of Powell's earlier speech:

> ... I think it means that people are really rather afraid that this country might be swamped by people of a different culture ... We are a British nation with British characteristics. Every nation can take some minorities, and in many ways they add to the richness and variety of this country. But the moment a minority threatens to become a big one, people get frightened. (*Guardian*, 31 January 1978, cited in Solomos, 1989, p. 129)

The fact that the new right within the Conservative Party was propounding a cultural theory of 'natural' difference actually provided a strength to the voice of the overtly racist political organisation. It was useful for the campaigns of opposition to be able to utilise a reworked theory of Conservatism which was less obviously based on the explicit racist and imperialist social Darwinist theories of evolution and human nature, and founded more on the idea of culture and difference.

Other authoritarian groupings even further to the right than the *Salisbury Review* group emerged in the 1970s, including academics such as David Irving, claiming that Hitler was unaware of the Holocaust. Contributors to the British *Mankind Quarterly* and the German *Neue Anthropologie* explicitly acknowledged the influence of German 'race-science' in their writings (Billig, 1979). Fascist organisations in their literature disseminate various versions of the Holocaust denials, including a refusal to accept the number of Jews that were slaughtered in the concentration camps (Seidel, 1986).

More recent versions argue that the deaths in the camps were not due to gas but to disease, evoking once again the diabolic imagery of the diseased Jew.

Antisemitic and racist ideas of 'human nature' and 'natural attributes' may have remained latent for a period, but they have openly reappeared in the recession of the 1990s with disturbing force. Three elements have been present since the collapse of communism in 1989 and the reunification of Germany: the extension of racist violence across eastern Europe; the most open and vicious anti-semitism since the termination of World War Two, and third, the upsurge of right-wing extremism. Overt antisemitism has once more surfaced in France, with murders and the despoilation of Jewish cemeteries; French Algerians are defined as foreigners. Italy is witnessing the return of fascist demonstrations, whilst Africans there are regularly attacked. Political transformations in eastern Europe have dragged the latent forces of antisemitism and virulent nation-alism to the surface. Hungarian politicians publicly express antisemitic views, whilst the national hatred of gypsies has inten-sified. Fascist organisations have returned in Rumania, where gypsy minorities are labelled impure and virulent antisemitism threatens the safety of the country's remaining Jewish community (Ford, 1992). Britain's contemporary experience of racial harassment and violence includes attacks on Jewish cemeteries, murders of Asian people, and the election of a Fascist Party candidate in a local election, all arguably fuelled by British government policy's setting of the social agenda with a series of immigration laws which define and thus justify exclusion of the 'other' (non-nationals). Finally, Nazi racist and antisemitic attacks have reappeared in the reunified Germany; racially inspired murders and riots with government complicity have violated the country's Turkish community.

These events reverberate to the sounds of the human nature debate over the natural and the national. The state defines what is natural; the portrayal of human features insidiously merges into national-ity. Germany's 1992 riots took as their cue the concept of blood and racial homogeneity which *remains* written into the German Constitution's Article 16, basing German citizenship on blood and defining the German nation in ethnic terms (Sivandan, 1992). The German state certainly retains its biological focus. However, more generally, new right and 'new' racism perspectives and racist actions in Europe are welded together by a racially based theory of nationality encompassing conceptions of nation as supreme authority and attributions of some unifying sentiment. Such sentiment stems from a shared history, common customs, ways of life and sense of belonging (or kinship). This shared history inter-connects with 'nation' and not with the idea of racial superiority. Difference is stressed, but judged as natural. Nations are not formed from the ephemera of politics or economics, runs the argument, but from a *human nature* which directs our biological instincts to defend 'our' life and traditions against others because of the dissimilarities of the 'other'. The precept of the naturally experienced 'nation' becomes the overarching moral value to justify *any* action.

In the above discussion, sociobiology's philosophical foundations have been shown to be politically suspect in their implicit justification of racist and aggressively nationalist behaviour as 'natural' or tribalistic, welding biological notions of race to the idea of national preservation and cultural difference. The replacement of eugenics by 'culture' has reorientated racism with a new racism which equates human nature with unbridled hostility towards the 'other'. The revival of open racism and antisemitism in a period of heightened economic insecurity and rapid political change suggests that affluence only mutes the voices of hatred. Clearly significant is the role played by national states in the justification and rationalisation of the 'natural' other, feeding upon human anxieties.

Summary and Conclusions

To conclude, biological models of human nature, originating in the nineteenth century, have played a great part in the construction of racism and antisemitic ideology and the conduct of ethnocentric warfare. The scientific paradigm may in the end justify the profoundest of horrors. Behaviouristic psychology, too, champions the idea of natural cognitive inferiority among identified social groupings; the genetic metaphors adopted by the Nazi state as policy are recurrent in the 1990s in the form of genetic therapy which may lend 'scientific' weight to social exclusionism. Instinctivist theories, including the Freudian model, may suggest innate aggression and destruction, but the behaviourist thesis of ultimate social obedience, in the perpetration of cruelty, to the authorised 'other' is also reductionist in its denial of the conscious, reflective and rebellious side to human nature. Both the existentialist and culturalist discussions of prejudice, scapegoating and victimisation render us penetrating insights into human nature, although they tend to avoid specific social motivations and policies and socially constructed identities. This is the case, too, with sociobiology which explains cultural behaviour as genetic destiny. Cultural relativism may too easily fall prey to the new right's emphasis on group difference and justification to marginalise the 'other'. The events of the 1990s demonstrate the political character to racist constructions of human nature. In the following chapter we look at the competing constructions of 'female nature' and their place in the human nature debate.

Further Reading

Sociobiology and Politics Debate

Martin Barker, *The New Racism* (Junction Books, 1981). An explicit attack on the sociobiologists' implicit racism and the new right.

Jonathan Benthall (ed.), *The Limits of Human Nature* (Allen Lane Press, 1974). A stimulating set of papers by Raymond Williams, Koestler, Robert Young et al.

Arthur L. Caplan (ed.), *The Sociobiology Debate* (Harper and Row, 1978). Arguments from both sides; special section on human nature.

Howard L. Kaye, *The Social Meaning of Modern Biology* (Yale University Press, 1986). A strong critique of biological and sociobiological ideas.

Michael Ruse, *Sociobiology: Sense or Nonsense?* (Reidel, 1985). Argues sociobiology is not really racist, but may be subject to distortion.

Genetics, Nazism and Antisemitism

Zygmunt Bauman, *Modernity and the Holocaust* (Polity Press, 1989). Argues technical, scientific efficiency facilitated the Jewish Holocaust.

Michael Burleigh and Werner Wipperman, *The Racial State: Germany 1933–1945* (Cambridge University Press, 1991). A clear demonstration of eugenics as applied social policy.

Sander Gilman, *The Jew's Body* (Routledge, 1991). A mesmerising account of bodily imagery and antisemitism.

Gill Seidel, *The Holocaust Denial: Antisemitism, Racism and the New Right* (Beyond The Pale Collective, 1986).

Genes and the Politics of IQ

Steven Rose, Richard Lewontin and Louis Kamin, *Not in Our Genes: Biology, Ideology and Human Nature* (Penguin, 1984). A classic contemporary sociopolitical critique of positivism and genetics.

Leon Kamin, *The Science and Politics of IQ* (Penguin, 1974).

6

Woman and Human Nature

Introduction

Theories of human nature, as we have demonstrated so far, often entail implicit modes of classification which culminate in the 'othering' of specified 'outgroups'. This is most trenchantly illuminated in the case of 'race' as discussed in the last chapter. On a broader canvas, such theories and models have also served to 'other' the female within a patriarchal context. Exploitation and oppression of women's oppression as features in society have continued throughout history. As with racism, they have been underpinned by theories of human nature, particularly the biological model. Hence, many feminists have felt it imperative to engage with the human nature debate. Given that the adopted positions have a direct bearing upon one-half of the global population, the formulations are not only epistemological, concerning issues of knowledge about men and women, and issues of morality, but are explicitly political. Concern with the 'natural' and the appropriate action and behaviour for females circumscribes the boundaries of significant decision making, especially between the public and the private. It defines the parameters of power, and is thus intrinsically normative. It steers the direction of public policy, and determines *who* makes these policies.

Generally, theories of human nature by male writers have marginalised, oppressed and assisted in the exploitation of women. Responses in feminist theory have been compelled to engage with ideas of human nature, a discourse monopolised until recent times by males. That the most vital, ebullient area of social theory emanates from the feminist perspective reflects a historical epoch where for the first time women as a group have been in a position to develop alternative formulations of being human. For example, women have achieved recognition and positions within the publishing industry (facilitating greater dissemination of non-male ideas), and remain an integral part of labour markets outside of the domestic sphere. Most pertinently, women's movements developed in this century to pressure for the right to vote, and then the right to everything else. The nineteenth century's rapid economic and social changes placed the issue of women and liberation on the liberal agenda. Socialist revolutionary movements debated the issue, not usually to the satisfaction of female activists. But the real flowering of counter-male chauvinistic ideas in western civilisation began in the 1960s in a potentially revolutionary epoch which challenged hidebound institutions, educational models and most importantly, the aggressive continuum of war in Vietnam by the world's wealthiest imperialist power, the United States (Kennedy and Mendus, 1987, p. 17). Yet the *revolutionary* potential for women stemmed from the system's unparalleled economic affluence and the concomitant technical innovations which ensured new material conditions to outweigh seemingly 'natural' barriers.

Traditionally, male social and political thinkers from Plato and Aristotle ignored, marginalised or dehumanised females, confining them to the domestic sphere whilst justifying this position 'by reference to women's particularistic, emotional, non-universal nature' (Kennedy and Mendus, 1987, p. 10). Women are portrayed as totally emotional and sentimental. Nietzsche perceives women as natural servants. Rousseau asserts women to be 'fitted by nature to please and be subjected'. Kant presents woman's social conditions as truly reflecting her inherent nature. Hegel sees male and female distinctions relating to family and property relations as universal and natural rather than specifically grounded (Hodge, 1987, p. 148). In all these cases, usually scrupulously logical and analytical philosophers have refused to recognise the distinction between the historically specific and the unchangeable (Kennedy and Mendus, 1987, pp. 12–13).

In the introductory chapter we examined the diversity of models of human nature expounded by the great thinkers. On closer scrutiny it becomes transparent that the 'human nature' they describe and unearth refers simply to *male* human nature. Hence, any rights and needs they identify as essential to being human are not meant for females (Okin, 1980, pp. 6–7). Their writings have engaged with certain central themes. First is the definition of female in relation to the family by virtue of her procreative biological functions; second is the assignation of fixed roles and lack of concern with her potential. The human nature debate in feminist theory, bereft of discrete autonomous philosophical or social theoretical traditions of its own, has built upon earlier philosophies, albeit 'natural' and patriarchal although turning them on their head to women's advantage. The result is an impressive plurality rather than a monolith. This chapter analyses the diverse feminist personifications of human nature and 'woman nature': the essentialist model of biology, sexuality and the body; the conception of woman as psyche; the existential conception of the female as potential; and finally, female nature as a socially constructed category.

Women's Nature, Body and Sexuality

As we saw in the previous chapter, the biological view of human nature characterises the human essence as bodily, instinctual or genetic composition. Tied to this biological essentialism, however, is a focus upon the explicit biological sex differences, which include the ability to bear children or not, the differences in hormones, brain size, chromosomes and the presence of secondary characteristics such as body hair, strength, size and bodily weight. Such male–female biological differences have been rationalised as natural distinctions by male supremacists of the sociobiology school. Notwithstanding the sociobiologists, certain feminist theorists have themselves accepted the essentialist version of woman nature, although internal debate has turned on whether the biological is interpreted as a problem or as a solution for defeating oppression and discrimination. Male nature may be viewed as intrinsically and hormonally violent; female nature may be characterised by the sphere of emotions, at their zenith expressed in the act of reproduction. But it is also argued that unless distinctions *are* made between a woman's sex and her gender, then *all* female activities are subject to a transfixed determinism. Finally, if women's nature is to be understood in terms of specific bodily sexual attributes enabling human reproduction, then what of the very *identity* of those who either choose not to reproduce are who are unable to do so?

Sociobiologists, as we have seen (Chapter 3), argue that the relationships and behaviour between males and females are determined by the impulse of the selfish gene which creates an inviolable division in the investment of energies. Hence, the female 'nature' inclines towards 'mothering' and the family tasks. On the other hand, the father's male 'nature' propels him to invest his energies outside the domestic territory. Tensions are produced by the attempts by each party to force the other to expend more energies in the familial, parenting role (Dawkins, 1976, p. 151). Thus, sex relations become *naturally* a battleground, represented by a whole host of biologically induced strategies amounting to mutual exploitation, and anxiety over the uncertainty of fathering.

But the sociobiological narrative mistakenly assumes that the sexual double standard is universal and transcends history and culture. In focusing upon animals as a means of explaining human relationships, sociobiologists are in effect reading back from the double standards of their own particular society. Men's concern with the investment of parenting in offspring not belonging to them is associated with the bequeathing of property and the insistence on female chastity, casting doubt upon the alleged causal connection between the parental investment drive in *all* societies including those without heritable property. Aries (1965, cited in

Abbott and Wallace, 1990, p. 64) argues that in history the possession of children has been viewed variably; the purpose of children in societies where child labour is common is seen as different from their purpose in societies where they lack an economic function, irrespective of the strength of parental affection. Sociobiologists' perspective on childcare services, which presumes that the labour power required is simply part of a free market, similarly eschews cultural and social differences. But this does not apply in non-market or non-capitalistic forms of society (Sayers, 1982, pp. 51–64).

In Chapter 5 we paid additional attention to the characterisation of human nature as aggressive and violent. Goldberg (1977) argues that there is a natural extension from male:female hormonal differences to patriarchal social organisation and behaviour, citing empirical studies demonstrating expressed preferences for guns (boys) on the one hand and soft toys (girls) on the other. However, apart from the problems surrounding the method (Sayers, 1982, p. 74), Goldberg's thesis, whilst claiming the existence of a logical connection between biologically based sex differences and the universality of patriarchy, also invokes the *psychological* capacity to dominate, a circular form of reasoning (Sayers, 1982, p. 76).

The sociobologists' distinction (on genetic and evolutionary grounds) of male aggressiveness and female passivity has indeed been incorporated and remodelled by feminists who have investigated rape and wife abuse. Radical feminists such as Brownmiller (1975) direct attention to the part played by male violence in the development and perpetuation of patriarchy. According to Brownmiller's biologically founded account, which treats biology as problematic, woman's anatomy is structurally unable to prevent the stronger male from raping the woman. The conscious realisation of male genitalia as weapons of fear has led to the continued subordination of women in wider human and social relations. Firestone (1972) also holds the sexual division of labour to be based upon natural biology, with pregnancy and childcare confining women to the biological family.

However, this explanation must be differentiated from sociobiology by dint of its greater evaluative thrust. As Levitas (1983, p. 122) notes, in spite of sociobiologists' claims, 'there is a strong implication that explanation is legitimation'. Rich (1976), for example, invokes male dominance as *purposive*, in contrast to sociobiology's behaviourism and complete disinterest in human motives, consciousness and purpose.

An added distinction relates to technology. Unlike the sociobiologists who tenaciously hold on to the human nature they have identified, the radical feminist position views reproductive technology as the new means, a revamped nature to deny the formerly natural oppressiveness of pregnancy and motherhood (whilst retaining a commitment to biology as the root of oppression).

But why should woman's biology be seen as a negative *per se*? The radical ecofeminist school indeed treats woman's biological nature as positive. The natural physiological split between male and female becomes a cause for *celebration* by women (Reuther, 1975; Daly, 1978; Starhawk, 1979; Griffin, 1980), a eulogy to female biology's special spiritual power and its intimate connection to the earth's non-human nature. From this viewpoint, women and non-human nature are virtually inseparable. Furthermore, such a position ostensibly endows women with intrinsic powers of knowing and conceiving the world. Ironically, this antihumanist and anti-rationalist picture of woman nature resembles the patriarchal dualism of western philosophy which places the male in culture and relegates the female to nature. Yet whereas many feminists disclaim such a dichotomy, the ecofeminists concede it, but proclaim that culture and rationality have destroyed and damaged nature instead of transcending it. Male values and 'nature' are rejected by the nurturing of intuitive female qualities endemic within a patriarchal society.

Continuous damage to the physical environment strengthens the appeal of this antimale view of the nature/human harmony. The social constructionist conception of environment couched in purely utilitarian objective terms is a false separation between human and non-human nature. But with contraception, the fact of childbearing is no longer essential to women's nature. Males, too, must biologically interact with the natural environment in the act of breathing and of course in the act of reproduction. Rejection of the masculine model of the human does not *necessarily* mean its replacement by a feminist model, a spurious choice. 'The fact that the concept of the human is up for remaking,' proclaims Plumwood, 'doesn't mean that it has to be made in the mould of either the masculine or the feminine' (Plumwood, 1988, p. 22). It merely creates a new hierarchical dualism, replete with dangers in the portrayal of a superior nature which embodies racist hierarchies as measured against the closeness to nature (Griscom, 1987, p. 97; Ortner, 1974, pp. 67–87, cited by Griscom, 1987).

Another variant of the biological 'difference' model is the argument that sex differences in the brain exist, and at least partially determine sexual inequalities by mediating differences in intelligence (that is, females are presented as naturally less intelligent). Although this idea, born out of the imperialist epoch, was shelved in the face of activities which *proved* women to be factually equal to males (Sayers, 1982, p. 95), the hypothesis of difference has shifted to the idea of sex differentials in brain organisation rather than social factors, determining, for example, spatial abilities. These abilities are in turn related to the ability to achieve top performance in certain professions, thereby 'inevitably' militating against women. Tests carried out, however, have revealed only small differences and rather ambiguous results.

Many feminists argue that the best manner of refuting the alleged causal implications of the sex difference in counteracting biological determinism is to forge a distinction between sex and gender. Sex is deemed to be biological, but gender incorporates psychological and cultural properties. Gender refers to the strength of feminity or masculinity residing within a human being. In Oakley's words (Oakley, 1972, p. 158): 'Sex is a biological term; "gender" a psychological and cultural one.' The differential is justified on a number of counts. First, to label mothering as natural loses sight of its social variability and changeability. Second, in order to demonstrate how ideas and practices are male-dominated and how women are marginalised and devalued, one must discriminate between females and their *associated* characteristics. Thirdly, such a disparity is crucial to the refutation of biological reductionism. The distinction performs vital political functions in opening out the system's receptivity to change. Finally, it highlights the subjective significance of biological sex and the role of perceptions of sex in the socialisation process. However, the distinction is not necessarily one of a given and unchangeable biology as opposed to a readily changeable gender.

Failure to make this distinction leads the biological determinists into uncritically accepting the conventions of 'sexuality' as the natural expression of sex relationships, meaning the 'natural' sexual identity. Rich (1976, cited in Eisenstein, 1984, p. 55) fails to understand heterosexuality as a socially grounded and culturally variable political institution. Sex has been indelibly linked to procreation, the latter advanced by Freud as well as the sociobiologists as the wholly natural purpose of sexual behaviour. This may be seen as part of the male supremacy argument, given that males cannot be sexually marginalised if their functions are attached to heterosexual monogamy. Conventional wisdom presents heterosexuality as intrinsic to human nature, a biological *fact* of human nature. Commonsense 'evidence' springs from sociobiology's androcentric view of human sexuality, which explains pair bonding (male control and female sexuality) through the evolutionary loss of the oestrus cycle, an indiscriminate sexual excitation conveying female receptivity to all males, which draws male and female together to enhance the infant's survival chances. Caulfield (1985, p. 345), however, notes that although biologically some signs of the lost oestrus cycle persist, these are overshadowed by the cultural context of sexuality and by research into alternative reconstructions of the evolutionary loss of oestrus which suggest different outcomes for the resultant hypothetical 'human nature'. The upshot of the research is that there is nothing more natural about procreative heterosexuality than non-procreative sexual relationships. Anthropological evidence shows that non-reproductive sex is an indisputable feature of the human species. Hence, lesbianism should not be interpreted as 'against nature'. Nor should male homosexuality. Recent neurobiological research among gay males and lesbians by Simon Le Vay and Gunter Dorner are linking homosexual inclination to brain differences such as shortage of testosterone in the brain. Kohn, however, calls for the exercise of caution, observing that: '... the danger of hormonal explanations for homosexuality is that they are hard to cast in terms that exclude connotations of abnormality. Moreover, many of their adherents might be far less concerned to do so than Le Vay' (Kohn, 1992, p. 32).

Sexuality is perceived differently at varying points of history, and it seems that the growing complexity of modern society has facilitated an extended range of possible sexual identities (Weeks, 1991, p. 92). The biological, the 'essence' of the so-called human nature (the sexual identity?), cannot be disentangled from social meanings. Weeks argues that:

> ... the meanings we give to sexuality in general, and homosexuality in particular, are socially organised, but contradictory, sustained by a variety of languages, which seek to tell us what sex is, what it ought to be, and what it could be. (Weeks, 1991, pp. 95–6)

We have to see gay and lesbian identities as both constructed and essential; they are historically shaped and prone to change, although inescapable in the final analysis (Weeks, 1991, p. 98). Biologically reducing a woman or sexual nature to 'body' poses a fundamental problem. An alternative perspective, as reflected in the literature, is to see woman's psyche as her nature.

To conclude this section, radical feminism's conceptualisation of women's nature as body and sexuality constitutes a distinctly biological model which rationalises the patriarchal social relationships and the historical panoply of the 'battle of the sexes'. Yet the sociobiological model up to a point serves the radical feminist purpose by establishing violence and aggression as naturally male, although such oppression may be subverted by new reproductive technology. The whole problem with the radical ecofeminist position is that it is uncritical of 'woman as body and earth', a position which accepts the Cartesian dualism and also implies that human nature must be *either* masculine or feminine, an unreal distinction given that *all* humans are rooted in nature. What is certainly required is the recognition that gender's social mutability is to be differentiated from sex. Without such fine discrimination, the biological school in feminist theory is sucked into an uncritical acquiescence of the conventional 'naturalist' evocation of sexual preference.

Woman Nature as Psyche

Freudianism, whilst still not severed from the biological, nevertheless engages more with the psychological, leaning towards *interpretation* by the child of the sexual attributes and the relationship surrounding them. Once more, of course, the picture of women's nature as 'psyche' is far from simple in considering the plurality of critiques and revisions. We need to examine more closely the significance of Freud and Freudian theory for women; the particular relationships between psychoanalysis and biological essentialism; specific criticisms of Freud; the singular reinterpretations of the Freudian Oedipus complex; postFreudian attempts to debiologise Freud; and the project of synthesising Freud's underlying theory of human nature with social constructionism.

In spite of his concentration on penis envy as a crucial explanatory factor underlying human behaviour, and his assumption of male superiority, Freud's ideas act as a catalyst to the feminist versions of the psyche. One may detect in Freudianism liberating as well as oppressive modes of thought. Freud interprets sexual variance experienced during the course of 'normal' psychosexual development as the determinant of gender roles, in effect a predetermined heterosexual genital sexuality.

The impact of the Oedipus complex among girls, suggests Freud, leads them to be more ambiguous and emotionally driven than boys. Lacking a penis bestows upon them a more or less permanent Oedipus complex, so that as women they want for a strong superego, moved more by their intrinsic affections or hostile feelings than by the committed abstract precepts and moral codes of conduct males would tend to follow.

Motivation in the direction of obedience is more prominent among males. Girls are less prepared for submission to the 'great exigencies of life' (Freud, 1905, pp. 257–8) and thus are destined to moral inferiority. Therefore, the male role lies in the rational work of civilisation, whilst females are motivated towards maternity. Such explicit divergences only emerge in the course of development. During the early stages there are no clear differences, and no *mechanistically* determined innate masculine or feminine features of a biological kind. Any behavioural sex distinctions are actually developed as the child begins to interpret her or his biography. Discrepancies will occur in female psychology with respect to passivity and feminity or activity and maculinity, although psychological feminity will be highly likely.

Sayers (1982) observes that Freud himself clearly distanced his own account of biology's influence on masculinity and femininity from biological essentialism and biological determinism, whereas the postFreudians such as Ernest Jones, Melanie Klein and Karen Horney, arguing that male and female psychologies are biologically determined from birth, challenge Freud's theory of the significance of the penis and its associated assumptions of male supremacy (Mitchell, 1974, pp. 121–31). Horney (1926) rejects Freud for his male bias, substituting her own analysis of femininity in a special, biological woman nature which simultaneously marginalises the role of penis envy. Simone de Beauvoir (1949), too, finds the psychological insights of Freudianism valuable, but counters his assumption of original superiority in the male with her own philosophy of woman's alienation (discussed later in this chapter). In de Beauvoir's eyes, Freud has not accounted for the ways in which *patriarchal culture* makes a girl aware of her real *social* inferiority.

During the 1970s the Freudian obsession with penis envy became a target of the women's movement's leading theorists. Friedan (1963) argues that psychoanalysis is just one more social science which regards the world through a cultural lens. The identity of a universal characteristic is passed off as essential human nature but really reflects cultural traits. She construes 'anatomy as destiny' as nothing but biological determinism, and rejects Freud's convergence on sex in defining woman's nature as an added device to justify the exclusion of women from the male preserve of public affairs, a 'natural' justification of patriarchy.

Consistent emphasis on sex and sexuality may be seen as ignoring power relationships and political domination, both in society generally and within the institution of the family (Firestone, 1972). Firestone deems psychoanalytic theories to be ideological in that they reconcile women to existing structures by normalising the belief that women are somehow intrinsically defective. Millett (1970) also attacks Freud's followers in searching *everywhere* for proof of 'natural' biological male aggression, arguing that there is scant support for the theory that women are naturally fated to play an inferior role to males (Millett, 1970, p. 109).

There are, however, feminists who have accepted some of the central tenets of *Freud's* ideas (rather than those of the neoFreudians). Sayers (1988, pp. 97–8) captures the ambivalence of psychoanalysis in feminism's resurgence:

> On the one hand feminists, like social workers, are wary of psychoanalysis. It all too often seeks to adjust people to the social inequalities that oppress them rather than help them to question

and change the social conditions producing these inequalities ... On the other hand some ... also see in psychoanalysis a means of understanding and undoing people's acquiescence in their oppression so that they might better deal with the conditions causing it.

Psychoanalysis may be viewed as a way of bringing to the surface what is *not* an immoveable facet of human nature; woman's nature is the unconscious internalisation of a patriarchal society's negative *images* of femininity reflecting and reinforcing women's social subordination, resembling Fanon's psychoanalytic application to explain blacks' internalisation of colonial images of themselves (Sayers, 1988, p. 98; and discussed further in Chapter 9).

Juliet Mitchell, most influential of modern feminists to positively build upon psychoanalytic insights pertaining to women's nature and condition, argues in *Psychoanalysis and Feminism* (1974) that Freud's own theorising amounts to more than a biological determinist statement that 'anatomy is destiny'. It does show how social beings emerge from biological ones; Freud's discourse on the social interpretation of sexuality was clearly anti-deterministic. Mitchell's critique is an endeavour to debiologise Freud through a synthesising of earlier theorists such as Reich and Laing, as well as Firestone. Reich's work in particular is motivated by a concern with sexual instincts and the social conditions within which sexual needs have to be expressed. Mitchell's synthesis of the psychoanalytical and the social – patriarchal moves in an opposite direction towards earlier psychoanalytic theorists who saw the psyche in need of the social for explanation. Biology and economic exploitation provide inadequate explanations of oppression:

> It is illusory to see women as the pure who are purely put upon: the status of women is held in the heart and the head as well as the home: oppression has not been trivial or historically transitory – to maintain itself so effectively it courses through the mental and emotional bloodstream. (Mitchell, 1975, p. 362)

Social and symbolic roles lodge deep in the psyche. Mitchell admits that the Freudian Oedipus complex is universal and inhabits the unconscious of human history. Nevertheless it becomes manifest and expresses itself differently under different economic social systems. In modern capitalism it is communicated via the nuclear family which, by encouraging the search for a partner *outside* the biological family, avoids the Oedipal situation (incest) and thus ensures the continued expansion of society. Consequently, with the dissolution of the Oedipus complex, 'man enters finally into his humanity (always a precarious business)'. However, 'it seems that the definition of that humanity – the differentiating instance between man and beast, i.e. the development of exchange relationships, may have become "unsuitable" for the particular social form in which it is today expressed' (Mitchell, 1974, p. 380).

We may characterise the unconscious as an integral 'eternal' component of human nature, embracing the way humans live their human-ness and 'the accidental experiences of the subjects and their particular culture'. This accounts for the persistence of ideology through changing cultures and economic modes, transforming itself along the way. It is 'why women are everywhere within civilization the second sex, but everywhere differently so' (Mitchell, 1974, p. 381). As such, the Oedipus complex is a vehicle of patriarchy which must be destroyed if women are to be made free. Women's consciousness can be significantly changed only by revolution.

There are difficulties in modifying Freud or conflating Freudian insights with socially grounded feminist theory. At one level, which we have already considered, Freud's antifeminist bias leads to a series of negative images characterising women's nature. At another level, one encounters a serious problem in Freud's underlying theory of human nature (Chapter 2) which appears irreconcilable with, for example, a historical materialist perspective, an enigma posed for the earlier Frankfurt School's Freudian–Marxian synthesis (Chapter 2). Freud's manifestation of human nature as unchanging, ahistorical and antisocial implicitly projects a profoundly pessimistic philosophy of the potential for communal consciousness and freedom.

In sum, Freud's model of human nature which converges on the psyche lends a basis to feminist theory's critical appraisal of crude bodily essentialism. The ambivalence of his Oedipal and the concern with child development creates liberatory possibilities for certain feminist strains, although his preoccupation with sex and sexuality is considered overly restrictive by others. Focus on the psyche may lead to an improved understanding of how oppression is filtered through the mind and the psychic world of the human being, so that women see themselves as inferior. On the other hand, such focus may well substitute one brand of mind:body dualism with another. Although Freud's insights are immediately problematical in the context of feminism (not least for their male bias and deep pessimism) nevertheless, as we shall see later in the chapter, their fusion with social constructionism renders them potentially explosive. Before analysing the feminist social constructionist model of human nature, however, we will examine the existentialist approach in feminist theory which interprets woman's nature as human potential.

Women's Nature and Potential: Existentialism

Earlier in this chapter we encountered positions that attribute to the biological a distinctly *female* significance culled from nature. In Simone de Beauvoir's feminist existential approach to woman and human nature we meet a world view which not only castigates the idea of woman nature for being totally biology laden, but which *accepts* the ideal of man as rationality and in the final analysis views woman's nature as 'becoming'. Her perspective combines a number of features. It is lodged within an anti-essentialist philosophy and derives its key insights from existentialism. Also, it radiates a political commitment to human potentiality and the human need for self-realisation.

De Beauvoir's *Second Sex* (1949) generates a plethora of ideas about the female condition, but the central insight on woman's nature is the concept of 'other', one half of the human conflict with its rival consciousnesses, the self. Albeit influenced by Sartrean theoretical distinctions of 'being-in-itself', 'being-for-itself' and 'being-for-others', de Beauvoir transposes the self into male and the 'other' into female, demonstrating the female's assimilation of the belief that man equates with essential and woman with inessential. She also adopts the existentialist position that human nature does not really exist. All that exists in all persons equally is a human condition without any self-definition. Females, like males, have to *make* their humanity; they forge their own nature.

The biological body of the woman is the obverse of her nature; it is her burden. It is the biological fact that weighs her down, 'it is the instrument of our grasp upon the world, a limiting factor for our project' (de Beauvoir, 1972, p. 66). In this existentialist thesis, the body is clearly oppressive for women. Pregnancy oppresses woman; in a male-dominated world which places a premium upon life *saving*, woman is banished to the spheres of otherness by *giving* life. She is pushed into the territory of the immanence of the body, but in a social context woman's bondage to the species is more or less severe depending upon the availability of hygiene and childcare facilities (de Beauvoir, 1972, p. 67). The female is able to achieve her own nature and truly develop only by escaping from biology, from 'mother' and the family. Neither Freud, who demarcates sexuality, nor Marx, who favours the centrality of class exploitation in capitalist societies, can satisfactorily explain for de Beauvoir the otherness of women, although she feels that one of the ways women may liberate themselves is *economically*. The other significant angle to de Beauvoir's model of 'human nature' as it affects women is the stress placed upon self-realisation and human potentialities, so that females may become fully human after the domestic imprisonment in immanence. They contain the capacity to attain the transcendence that males already possess; the journey into the realms of freedom and subjectivity. 'I shall place woman in a world of values and give her behaviour a dimension of liberty,' de Beauvoir declares.

> I believe that she has the power to choose between the assertion of her transcendence and her alienation as object ... For us woman is defined as a human being in quest of values in a world of values, a world of which it is indispensable to know the economic and social structure. (de Beauvoir, 1972, pp. 82–3)

Friedan (1965) also argues that woman's potential for self-development has met great physiological barriers, and that a crucial realm of non-biological needs inhabits the sphere of self-realisation. She propagates her ideas in relation to women's needs from the standpoint of humanistic psychology, and Maslow's ideas in particular (Chapter 9). Friedan justifies her stand in the following terms:

> There is something less than fully human in those who have never known a commitment to an idea, who have never risked an exploration of the unknown, who have never attempted the kind of creativity of which men are potentially capable. (Friedan, 1965, p. 274)

The really human needs are to be found at a distance, less dependent upon the material environment and physiological needs. Socially defined 'women's work', essentially stultifying, unrewarding and 'infantilising', stands inviolably opposed to the creation of a human identity. Millett (1972) similarly claims that all activities considered as human achievement beyond the level of biological experience are the preserve of the male (Millett, p. 26).

Each of these humanistic theorists expresses the disjuncture between biology or 'nature' on the one hand and culture on the other, with culture *transcending* the ordinary life. But the singular conception as expounded within de Beauvoir's philosophical framework is diametrically opposite to certain basic feminist needs. Transcendence by *definition* may be considered a *male* idea because it insinuates limitations *of* the feminine. '... [The] male perspective has left its marks on the very concept of "transcendence" and "immanence",' concludes Lloyd (1983, p. 9).

Again, the thought of becoming fully human outside of the body is totally idealist, and ends up by privileging the mind over the body, the epitome of western dualistic thinking. But as McMillan (1982, pp. 1–15) observes, these are unreal disparities between reason and feeling, and between the biological and the specifically human. They create misconceptions and ultimately lead to a devaluation of women, primarily because woman's sexual and domestic practices are socially grounded; they occur against a backcloth of beliefs and practices which are assuredly not 'natural' (in the sense of being biologically determined). Furthermore, 'reason' is more than some entity superimposed on animal nature. Feelings are intimately bound up with our knowledge and understanding of each other. Rationality involves not simply abstract theorising but also skills including childcare which McMillan mistakenly assumes is *necessarily* the primary responsibility of women, that is, the biological mother (Grimshaw, 1983, pp. 33–4).

A final criticism of de Beauvoir's argument suggests that the account, notwithstanding her intention, results in the ethnocentric portrayal of oppressed woman reflecting a narrow group of 'namely, white middle-class, heterosexual Christian women in Western countries' (Spelman, 1991, p. 199). Spelman notes that de Beauvoir:

> almost always describes relations between men and women as if the class or race or ethnic identity of the men and women made no difference to the truth of statements about 'men and women'. This poses some very serious difficulties for her attempt to give a general account of 'woman'. (Spelman, 1991, p. 204)

De Beauvoir recognises that existentialist insights into human nature must be connected to a social constructionist analysis. But that does not negate the dynamic impetus towards a liberated being, even within cultural and social constraints. '... woman lives beyond as well as in her complicity with man. She is both determined by and free of patriarchy,' Tong (1989, p. 214) states. The importance of de Beauvoir's work within the human nature debate dwells in the juxtaposition between woman as socially constructed and woman as achieving liberation by expressing 'a female way of being' (Tong, 1989, p. 214).

To summarise, the existentialist model of 'woman nature', the philosophical disjuncture between self and other, constitutes the foundations of female oppression as othered by the male. De Beauvoir's focus on the construction of self represents a direct assault on the biological school and its eulogising of woman as body. The thrust of the existentialist non-biological perspective in effect becomes explicitly antibiological, an *escape* from biology into the realms of intellectual self-realisation which renders the model overly idealist. Such a position which prioritises the mind must fall foul of any reservations we may also have of Cartesian dualism. (The practical difficulties of the latter are analysed in Chapter 8.) On the other hand, de Beauvoir's commitment to economic liberation for women is far from idealist, as is her final recognition that the liberation of the 'othered' female needs to overcome *social* and *cultural* barriers.

Woman's Nature as Socially Constructed

There is no way we can admit the discourse on the nature of human nature as being confined to the body, the psyche or the mind. Of course, no monolithic theory of the social construction of 'woman nature' exists. In this section we will focus on those ideas that treat the female as totally or almost totally culturally constructed, such as the sexual division of labour as institution; social constructions of gender identity; and those socialist feminist models which take as their starting point the Marxian dialectical relationship between biology, human society and the physical environment.

The sex–gender distinction has facilitated an impressive corpus of writing exploring the ways in which women's behaviour is structured in society, culturally formed by a process of gender roles and gender differentiation, but rationalised as natural sex difference. Women's role in diverse cultures means that sex has *no* significance in characterising woman's nature, in explaining her cognition, behaviour, activities and functions. The explanation is seen to fall entirely in the institutional and structural realms. Anthropology is a particularly fertile area of enquiry in producing evidence for the tremendous diversity of socialisation patterns and gender differences (Chapter 3). Oakley (1972) argues that the elision of such gender distinctions into natural sex differences is a means of oppressing women and making them dependent in social role and inferior in status. She founds her position upon a clear separation between 'nature' and 'culture', and between the 'biological' and the 'cultural', so that sex = biological and gender = cultural (Grimshaw, 1986, p. 114) are unhelpful distinctions in constructing a detached comprehensive theory of woman's 'nature'.

One school of feminist theory has gone so far as to repudiate completely the role of biology, arguing from a cultural determinist frame of reference that discounts even the naturalness of childbirth, female body and sex difference *per se* under the banner 'one is not born a woman' (Wittig, 1979). Approaching birth as a biological given means, for Wittig, 'forgetting that in our societies births are planned ... forgetting that we ourselves are programmed to produce children' (cited in Jaggar, 1983, p. 98).

Cultural determinists characterise the institution of patriarchy as the creator of women and men. Woman as a category becomes not much more than an artificially produced social fact, negating the idea of women as a 'natural group'. Categories of 'man' and 'woman' are condemned as cultural constructs or caricatures. The same rationale is applied to sexual preference, which has been viewed differently through time (Chapter 3). Dworkin (1974) contends that sexuality travels along a continuum, but that gendered society is actually based on the belief, clearly in the interests of males, of bipolar sexual opposites; biological theory is in the social interests of men, and human biological reality is socially constructed (Dworkin, 1974, cited in Jaggar, 1983, p. 99).

Social structure's centrality for women requires closer examination of patriarchy as a social construction, even though it has existed in almost all societies, and to be sure in those which have achieved 'high' levels of civilisation. 'Unrooted in necessity, patriarchy is structural*ism*, and its structures are therefore grounded in ideology rather than necessity, in male interests rather than universal masculine historicity' (O'Brien, 1989, p. 49).

Nevertheless, the nature–nurture, nature–culture, biology–society dichotomies are extremely tenuous and questionable. Biological determinism's alternative is not a wholesale refutation of human nature which substitutes its own determinism with a wholly socially constructed scenario. Neither is it that the male–female difference is a social construction (Levitas, 1983, p. 123). A more dialectical approach to human biology and social constructionism is appropriate for characterising woman nature. The Marxist model of human nature (Chapter 2) is germane to this task, in spite of classical Marxism's failure to address the woman question directly. With its focus on the reciprocal interrelationships of human biology, society and environment, the model proffers a suitable entrée to a socialist feminist narrative of woman nature. The feminist perspective, however, is more concerned with integrating psychological understandings into historical materialism (Firestone, 1972; Holmstrom, 1984; Jaggar, 1983). Engels's *The Origin of the Family, Private Property and the State* (1972) is a major inspiration for socialist feminists, positing that the social organisation under which people live from society to society and historically is determined by both kinds of production: 'by the state of development of labor on the one hand and of the family on the other' (Engels, 1972, pp. 71–2). Firestone (1972) extends and redirects Engels's definition of historical materialism so that it becomes:

> ... that view of the course of history which seeks the ultimate cause and the great moving power of all historic events in the dialectic of sex: the division of society into two distinct biological classes for procreative reproduction, and the struggles of these classes with one another. (Firestone, p. 20)

The theory of alienation expresses Marx's conception of human nature in capitalist society: freedom to eat, drink and procreate, whereas in their human functions humans are reduced to an animal. Socialist feminists, interpreting this as a male version of 'freedom', expand the orthodox category to formulate alienation from the body and feminity *per se* as an alienated condition. Superimposed upon industrial alienation, they insist, woman is also relegated to an instrument of man's sexual pleasure inside the family (Jaggar, 1983, pp. 131–2). As discussed later (Chapter 7) this familialism entailing reproduction and childcare is indeed a central plank in the ideology of the new right both in Britain and the United States, as a rationale for government social welfare policies aimed at keeping women to the confines of the home for caring purposes; the state's role 'supports' the 'natural, God-given unit' (Abbott and Wallace, 1992, pp. 5–21). What are justified as biologically necessary divisions are in fact *socially constructed* state policies involving gender separation and discrimination.

In answer to the question 'what is human nature?', the socialist feminist responds that all differences, including class *and* sex, make up the constituent elements of contemporary human nature. Biology is partially socially constructed; it is *itself* gendered, and not just sexed. To avoid cultural reductionism, the method (as we saw earlier) harnesses the social to the psychological, a teasing out of the correspondence between feminine and masculine psychology through a reworking of Freud (a methodological revision following in the wake of Reich, the radical Freudian who suggests that the emotional history of individuals is located in the body's muscular structure). Socialist feminism's angle on human nature indicates the error of simply deleting the biological dimension of human activity, as is the wont of those clinging to the sex–gender tradition. Sexual difference itself is not a characteristic which is merely given; it is a disposition conditioned by culture and subject to historical change.

Yet this orientation to human nature is not problem free. Freud's underlying pessimism in his portrayal of a human nature locked into the province of the unconscious begs the whole question of whether a psychological:social constructionist synthesis makes sense. However, the socialist feminist theorists utilising psychoanalysis refute a political fatalism; early established character structure in the human being remains sensitive to change, and the sexual division of labour that has subjugated character (although so far universal) may in principle be transformed. Whilst a new conceptual language is still required, Jaggar states, socialist feminism 'does not stand or fall according to its success in reconstructing psychoanalytic theory' (Jaggar, 1983, p. 151).

To summarise, so many facets of gender distinction have little to do with biological sex, or with biological mind, but (as anthropology shows) with the structuring capacities of social institutions and practices. However, in characterising biological determinism as a reflection of male interests, the cultural theorists substitute their own cultural reductionism. Nevertheless, patriarchy, despite its universality, may be better comprehended as a socially fashioned institution which erects its own mystificatory ideology, whilst understanding female nature requires a synthesis of biological, sociological, Marxist and psychoanalytical insights – thereby overcoming dualistic thinking.

Summary and Conclusions

To conclude, models of human nature differ historically, but all have been unerringly male oriented in their assumptions and conclusions. Feminism's rejoinders are exhilarating in their very diversity. Biological feminist models may well have rejected the male-oriented sociobiological paradigm, but they nevertheless offer qualitatively distinctive responses to the status of the female body. Ironically, the dangers of an essentialist view of human nature for women reside in their submission to patriarchy's alienating body:mind dichotomy. The treatment of woman's nature in terms of psyche illustrates the power of internalised and manipulable forms of behaviour and beliefs, but also signals the ambivalence of sexuality in psychoanalysis and Freudianism. Woman nature viewed as human potential, rooted in a philosophical humanism, represents a robust alternative to the preoccupation with body, in one respect seemingly idealist, yet in another galvanising women's economic and political potential. But it becomes revolutionary only within a social context. The evidence in support of social constructionist theory is strong, but the latter remains susceptible to social or cultural reductionism. What social constructionist models *do* make clear, when fused with insights from other models, is that 'woman nature' no less than 'human nature' is neither fixed nor consistently pliable. In the following chapters, beginning with broad governmental strategies, we consider how particular social policy areas, in their theory and practice, assume specific models of human nature.

Further Reading

General Surveys
Valerie Bryson, *Feminist Political Theory* (Macmillan, 1992).
Helen Crowley and Susan Himmelweit (eds.), *Knowing Women: Feminism and Knowledge* (Polity Press, 1992). A useful new reader.
Jean Grimshaw, *Feminist Philosophy* (Harvester, 1986). Includes section on human nature.
Alison M. Jaggar, *Feminist Politics and Human Nature* (Rowman and Littlefield, 1983). Whole of Part 2 on 'Feminist Theories of Human Nature'.

Rosemary Tong, *Feminist Thought* (Routledge, 1989). A systematic approach to the discrete perspectives.

Woman's Nature and Sexuality
Don Milligan, *Sex-Life: A Critical Commentary on the History of Sexuality* (Pluto Press, 1993). Covers mind:body and biology:culture debates within a historical framework.
Janet Sayers, *Biological Politics: Feminist and Anti-Feminist Perspectives* (Tavistock, 1982). Has tended to be the key text in this area.
Jeffrey Weeks, *Against Nature* (Oram Press, 1991). Analyses historical and cultural constructions of sexual identity.

Women's Nature as Psyche
Juliet Mitchell, *Psychoanalysis and Feminism* (Penguin, 1975).
Kate Millett, *Sexual Politics* (Abacus, 1972). An early contemporary classic; see Part II for attack on Freud.

Woman's Nature and Existentialism
Simone de Beauvoir, *The Second Sex* (Penguin, 1972). The real postwar pathbreaker in thinking about human nature.
Genevieve Lloyd, *The Man of Reason* 2nd edn. (Methuen, 1993).

Feminism and Social Constructionism
Ann Oakley, *Sex, Gender and Society* (Temple Smith, 1972). Still a useful illustration of the sex–gender distinction.
Rosalind Sydie, *Natural Woman:Cultured Man: A Feminist Perspective on Sociological Theory* (Open University Press, 1987). Develops a feminist social theory; includes chapters on nature:nurture, Freud, Durkheim, Weber and Marx.

7

Social Policy and Human Nature

Introduction

We have seen how human nature theories inextricably connect with social, cultural and political conditions. Their special quality is to focus upon particular human attributes such as individual autonomy or collective symbolism with their ideological antennae for social action. The social nature of our being means that our images of ourselves, the identity of our particular groups and those of 'others' are socially constructed. In acting as social animals, usually in a political way, we express our humanity. Models of human nature we adopt serve to orientate our vision of future possibilities which may come to fruition or founder according to state policies. This is why the human nature debate is of immediate interest for social policy analysis.

Social policy entails categorising people and social groups in the process of planning, formulating strategies and decision making in areas such as social security, housing, education, social service provision and health. Whilst its *modus operandi* has necessarily revolved around the idea of a social collectivity, the extent to which this collectivity is active or passive is much debated on the political left. Approaches to social welfare (which by definition entails the interpretation of need, decision making, 'scientific' policy analysis, judgements on matters of equality and inequality, the efficacy of state intervention and the status of individual privacy), reflect underlying perspectives on human nature. The choice of policy direction is necessarily ideological, especially at the broader strategic level. Thus social policy is necessarily a human *political* activity founded on respective models of human purpose.

In formulating and implementing social policies, governments respond to what they perceive to be particular sets of *needs* and attendant problems. In the course of policy formulation they must engage, albeit implicitly, in the assessment of such needs and problems. At the same time, the study of social policy should concern itself with evaluating how far policy makers are actually tendering to human needs and, perhaps most significantly, *whose* needs are being met by allocating resources. How far does the categorisation process effected by decision makers further marginalise and 'other' already disadvantaged social groupings?

Social welfare policies in this respect have drawn much of their strength from traditional political perspectives which act as a bridge between theories of human nature and strategic social policy. These traditions have also been crucial in charting directions in social change which effectively express human possibilities. And this very process of prescription suggests that social policy embodies an inbuilt ethical notion of purpose; there has to be a *politics* of social policy, which itself presupposes a philosophy of social policy. We can now more readily understand this view, although its ramifications may be unsettling for those who claim that analysis may be separated from prescription. The new paradigm affecting the way we see the world (Chapter 4) is exerting a profound impact on social policies and strategies, not only in the advanced capitalist sector but also in the former communist and state socialist societies. The essential feature of this postmodernistic re-evaluation is the rejection of collectivist models of human nature and the reshaping of the market individualism model. It is against this global backdrop that the chapter will investigate the interface between policies, ideology, power and human nature; the inviolable connection between human needs and the evaluation of social policy in meeting these needs; the significance of political traditions for social policy and their underpinnings in theories of human nature; the totalising nature of the new right project of the 1980s; and an assessment of the impact of technological determinism upon our perceived abilities and confidence to effect substantial social change in the face of fatalistic thought.

Political Traditions, Social Welfare and Human Nature

Understanding social welfare policies and how they are structured according to respective models of human nature requires an analysis of how they are mediated by political philosophical traditions. Political perspectives and key values addressing human relationships and implied notions of the 'good' have driven social welfare policies. This section examines the categorisation of political approaches to social welfare, the espousal of central values, and the ways in which those political perspectives rest upon discrete models of human nature. Traditions of political thought (Chapter 1) represent the 'working through' of basic assumptions concerning human nature and knowledge. Lee and Raban (1983) sketch the range of approaches which relate to key human values and assessments of what it is to be human. Different political perspectives place varying emphasis on specific values such as equality or inequality, collectivism or anticollectivism or individualism, individual or state. Each is founded on some *Weltanschauung* or overarching world view as to whether one believes, for instance, that humans are innately unequal or naturally equal, or whether humans are naturally atomistic or basically communal and co-operative. The juxtaposition of such values structures the debates between the prime political positions on social welfare: conservatism, liberalism, Marxism and social reformism (George and Wilding, 1976; Anderson, 1991).

However, as Lee and Raban (1983) note, there is no *automatic* correspondence between the value base and actual policies advanced. British Conservative beliefs in the primacy of the individual have not prevented the party from using the state to intervene profoundly in citizens' lives. The postwar period up to the 1970s was marked in Britain by a broad political consensus as to the necessity of a welfare state. This is why the Conservative government's unbroken period of office since 1979 has been so radical in its dismembering of the postwar consensus paradigm (Sullivan, 1992). As we shall see later, the Thatcherite world view of individualised society conditioned the whole direction and pace of social change and policy making. Despite the ambiguities and contradictions of Thatcherism in the 1980s and the disparity between strategies and official party doctrine, the *overt* advocacy of the party's revamped pivotal values has nevertheless set the tone for its social welfare policies. During 1993 keynote speeches from Major's Conservative government reverberated with emphatic proclamations of a 'return to basic values' embracing ideals of familial authority.

Thus we find that each set of political perspectives is underpinned by assumptions concerning human nature. Conservatism lays stress on instincts regarding family bonding, tempered with custom and continuity, instincts deemed to be an integral part of the body politic. But the nature is viewed as varying from person to person; humans are naturally imperfect, they sort themselves out hierarchically and they display a natural antipathy to radical change (Berry, 1983). Honderich (1990) on the other hand argues that in fact there is little to distinguish conservatism from socialism, except the former's selfish qualities. No consistent set of rational principles making up conservatism's picture of human nature exists, according to Honderich. However, Magill (1991) points out that conservatism as an ideology may not be governed by any overall rationale or principle (pragmatism has been a long-standing feature of English conservatism), but should be seen as a collection of positions and attitudes 'deriving some cohesiveness from certain key elements in the collection, including an on-going attitude towards equality, change, methods of political decision-making, the Family and, perhaps, the Nation' (1991, p. 46).

Anderson (1991) highlights a reluctance to theorise, a wariness of excessive rationalism and the conscious dangers of radical social engineering as the foundations of Conservative thought. Conservatism must be recognised as a philosophy of imperfection emphasising the limits on human capacities and the inequality between human beings.

What of political liberalism? It begins from the premise of self-interest; individuals are considered free and equal, although the stress falls upon liberty. The world dissects into the private and the public, with a predisposition towards the market as a self-regulating body which reflects the self-interest of individuals. The other side of the coin is liberalism's bias against the state, which liberals take to be interference with the individual's inborn rights. To this end, liberal policy strategy calls for the liberalisation of markets. Social change is to be welcomed, but the rewards ought to accrue to individuals for their initiative; correspondingly, individual failure should be subject to penalties. Clearly, however, the liberal picture of the human individual is flawed. A number of theorists (Taylor, 1985; Sandel, 1982; MacIntyre, 1981) view the idea of the self and self-interest as inadequate. It ignores how deeply human existence is entrenched in community and community practices, how far individual judgements are confirmed by social others, and thus how the precept of freedom to choose and make decisions is empty of content. Human values have to be *about* something. They indicate how humans decide to live their lives in a communal context within a history of those communities from which they derive their identities and their definition of 'goods' (that is, positive values). Liberal individualism's 'I am what I myself choose to be' erroneously ignores the many contingent external factors bearing down upon our social existence.

Social reformism, or social democracy, expresses a greater sense of the collectivist tradition in recognition of human beings' social nature, the idea of shared values and the political necessity for clear state involvement in social provision, but does not exclude market individualism. Social reformism adopts a moral position against inequality among human beings. It believes that human nature is a variant of social situations, and thus amenable to change by the improvement of better social conditions. As distinct from the conservative position which cedes an important role to the individual's biological, innate defects, social reformism perceives social problems as caused by 'the complex and changing nature of modern society and inadequate institutional arrangements' (Anderson, 1991, p. 13). In other words, as we saw in Chapter 4, social problems are socially constructed and not a function of a fixed human nature. Logically, change gradually managed and controlled by the democratic state can change the person.

Marxists (Chapter 2) and communitarians characterise humans as able to change their nature depending upon social circumstances and human action. Acceptance of communitarian assumptions about human nature invariably leads to the definition of the just society as one where the ideals of sharing, co-operation and altruism govern members' interrelationships. This leads in turn to a sharing in wealth, key decisions, opportunities to develop full potential, and an antagonism to class domination and individualistic self-aggrandisement. Only in this kind of a society, communitarians submit, may humans realise their full nature.

The 'capitalism or socialism' debate encapsulates conflicting perspectives on human nature. The individualist model resents intervention, whereas the communitarian model *expects* state intervention (for instance its influence upon taxation views) (Berry, 1986, p. 9). Communitarianism is explicitly committed to radical change (Duncan, 1983). The problem of interpreting change in purely Marxist terms is the proclivity to view economic classes as the exclusive agents of change, whereas radical strategies embrace a variety of change agents such as youth, black liberationists and feminists. By the same token, it would be naive to take all radical change as necessarily socialist centred or even politically progressive. As we will explore in greater depth, the British Conservative government's strategy towards welfare state services has been unarguably radical, as has its speed of implementation.

Approaches in social welfare, then, whilst intrinsically political, reflect competing models of human nature. A traditional Conservative position, built upon ostensibly *basic* instincts and custom, justifies social inequality, hierarchies and the exercise of historical caution in altering policy; it places family values uppermost, and in diametrical opposition to state distributive justice. Liberalism's championing of the market and its juxtaposition of individual liberty with state interference de-emphasises human social needs and communal moral constraints. Social reformism's support for a balance of market forces and state provision in the meeting of human needs survived as the social policy paradigm in Britain from 1946 until the late 1970s. Finally, the Marxist objectives of community, equality and radical social change based upon a model of human co-operation have influenced local British social policy in times of economic boom and labourist control. Sea changes in central European and global politics have brought Marxist strategies, too, into serious question.

Human Nature, Welfare and Human Needs

In this section we consider the relationship between human nature models and ideas of what our human needs are; the importance of human needs in social welfare policy; the debate between relativistic and universalistic approaches to human needs; and ways in which we may utilise a form of 'needs analysis' in social policy evaluation. Philosophical traditions have argued strongly that human beings' needs represent an integral part of our very nature (Thomson, 1987, pp. 23–34). The argument that needs are natural suggests they are *innately* rather than environmentally or socially determined. However, this has been disputed just as innate theories of human nature *per se* have been challenged (see the critique of Chomsky's theory in Chapter 3). Biological theories are suggestive of physical needs and drives, including the Freudian model of sexual drives. But whilst the behaviourist model focuses on needs as products of the external environment, the sociobiological focus on genetic drives still relates them to the environment.

Existentialist models of human need stress the exercise of autonomy, a thrust for liberty, a *need* to choose in the formation of one's own nature, implying for Sartre a human *commitment*. The Marxist model, more than other human nature models, addresses the question of human needs in the context of society. Debates within Marxism raise issues of wider concern, for example how much weight ought we to place on furnishing material requirements, and thus what are the *real* needs social policy must satisfy? Marxism's tendency to predicate tenets of need in relativistic social constructionist terms has fallen into disrepute especially since the 1989 events leading to the collapse of officially Marxist-oriented political regimes. We now find ourselves in the midst of a dramatic shift in the socialist discourse reflecting Marx's more humanistic articulation of basic human needs.

Tensions have long existed between relativist and universalistic interpretations of Marx's own work (Soper, 1981). Among the modern interpretations and commentaries, the relativist has gained the upper hand (Geras, 1983; Soper, 1981). Soper argues that:

> anti-humanism ... simply evaded discussion of any of the questions about needs that are implicitly raised by the Marxist critique of capitalism and its advocacy of the socialist/communist alternative. In its feverish anxiety to purge the science of historical materialism of any normative content, it has refused to countenance any but a positivistic definition of needs in terms of actual consumption. (Soper, 1981, pp. 31–2)

Postmodernist relativism characterised by philosophical pragmatism (Rorty, 1982), the advocacy of difference and the diversity of cultural groups, emphasis on market economic needs and the new right's insistence on individual choice, is fashionable in social theory. Doyal and Gough's *Theory of Human Need* (1991) is, however, a timely reaffirmation of the universalistic approach to human needs and welfare strategy which argues that *basic* physiological and biological needs, namely physical health and rational autonomy, *do* exist and must be *met* by policy. Basic needs are not reducible to the question of individual wants or preferences. Without these needs being met, participation in life's decision making and policy making is evidently untenable. There is no power *to choose*. Government in society has to meet such basics, along with other essential goods known as 'intermediate needs', namely shelter, food, water, physical and economic security, all shared, universal needs requiring provision by public policy makers.

Absence from disease, Doyal and Gough contend, is an insufficient goal. Individual autonomy, defined by a human being's understanding of oneself, one's culture and what is expected of one as an individual within it, is indispensable. Autonomy connotes the need for cognitive skills and hence the social need for teachers and the need for mental health (the individual's cognitive and emotional capacity to formulate personal options). Although powerful critiques of the western approach to mental illness exist, these should not rule out the possibility of culture-free identification of emotional as distinguished from physical or cognitive disabilities, since the overall impact is to reduce the individual's autonomy (Doyal and Gough, 1991, p. 62). Without the requisite self-esteem, human beings may find it extremely difficult to display altruistic attitudes. Furthermore, their ability to challenge social and political oppression is impaired with diminished autonomy (Moore, 1978). A range of available choices is a prerequisite for the human exploitation of a critical autonomy, equipped to deal with high-order preferences and values and so define one's nature in giving *meaning* to one's life. If freedom is to remain there must be no institutional restriction.

In the process of optimising need-satisfaction in theory, fundamental disagreements will continue to arise over the implications of choices in practice. There may well be disputes over the effectiveness of specific technologies, for instance genetic engineering, the efficacy of implementing preventive or curative policies, the merits of individual techniques for income and wealth distribution, or solving further dilemmas concerned with the precise meaning of optimising need-satisfaction in the context of resource constraints.

Doyal and Gough assess social policy practice against the theory and principles of satisfying needs (1991, pp. 247–73), charting human welfare need-satisfaction in the nations of the 'three worlds'. Their findings indicate that given that need-satisfaction generally varies with *per capita* incomes and levels of economic development, the third world countries stand *lowest* on need-satisfaction; state socialist societies are mixed in meeting basic needs, and advanced capitalist societies in the west display the highest individual and societal levels (1991, p. 288), but nevertheless the differentials between societies are wide. They conclude that state intervention is still a necessity: 'The market requires a strong set of normative underpinnings' (1991, p. 292). A nation's competitiveness demands some form of *state* development. Collective mobilisation of citizens, though, is also vital to optimise need-satisfaction when the state is constrained to act (1991, pp. 292–3).

A further project into the application of needs criteria is the 'needs audit' conducted by Leeds Metropolitan University, whereby a discrete local community was surveyed on its needs requirements. Coote (1993) justifies extending the use of such audits to satisfy local needs in advocation of the universalistic approach: '[In] a democracy there is no dodging the importance of involving citizens in decisions of this kind.'

To sum up, human needs are an essential component of 'human nature', but exactly *how* we characterise them has practical consequences for the implementation of social policies and our ability to evaluate their efficacy and egalitarianism. Although modern social theory, postmodernist philosophy and prominent Marxist interpretations have emphasised the social relativism of needs, it is a powerful proposition that the needs for health and autonomy, and intermediate needs are universal. The fact that few economies cater for such demands is a matter for action; policies which aim at minimal state intervention must be seen as highly questionable.

Individualism in Action and Human Nature: UK Social Policy in the 1980s

This section deals with how individualism has manifested itself politically in the 1980s, identifying the key philosophical underpinnings of the Reagan/Thatcher political epoch; the significance of the ideas of Hayek and Friedman in recreating the age of the entrepreneur; the new right's specific assumptions regarding human nature which lead them to undermine the basis of the welfare state; the ideological importance of the creation of an enterprise culture, and the hazards for future social policy of the revitalised version of an atomised 'human nature'. Western capitalism's current trajectory, measured by Doyal and Gough's thesis of binding human needs, casts serious doubt on whether social policies in the advanced economies *are* capable of meeting basic and intermediate human needs. Ascendancy of the atomistic individualistic model of human nature has paralleled an estimated breakdown in human beings' expressed need for social solidarity and community (Ignatieff, 1984). New right market policies in Britain and the United States have been greatly influenced by the work of two economists, Hayek (Chapter 5) and Milton Friedman.

Much of Hayek's writing has been directed against the rationalism of socialism and planning, which he replaces by the market, the product of a *natural* social evolution. State intervention by definition can only be unnatural, an offence to the idea of a natural spontaneous order in society. Correspondingly, the socialist ideals of equality, solidarity, altruism and co-operation in fact threaten the whole population (Hayek, 1988). Hayek's discourse on instinct and reason makes it obvious that such naturalness is not a *pure* biologism, but one based on cultural evolution and tradition – a tradition 'lying between instinct and reason' (Hayek, 1988, p. 21).

Assuming the naturalness of such individual behaviour, Hayek not only impresses the need for individual responsibility but harnesses his philosophy to the right's political attack upon a welfare state which has allegedly *eroded* individual responsibility and succoured dependency (although this has *not* actually happened). Available evidence demonstrates that the cessation of state welfare causes dependence upon families, dependence of a much more arbitrary nature, instead of inspiring the exercise of 'individual responsibility' (Goodin, cited in Tomlinson, 1990).

Friedman's formal consultative advice and mode of economic analysis (Friedman, 1962; Friedman and Friedman, 1980) lie behind British and American governmental economic policies during the 1980s. Yet his avowed *economic* critique of optimal state intervention is posited on his assumptions concerning human nature. Interventionist activities, he reasons, contradict human action's *natural* motivation towards self-interest, whilst the free market truly reflects and encourages natural human self-interest. Friedman's philosophy replicates the eighteenth-century market individualism, although the policies of the new right have pragmatically absorbed additional features.

The new right's assumptions appeal to nature and to intuition, and to the conservative ideal of family and private life. They imply indissoluble connections between the 'natural' family and the primacy of individual property, fused by human nature. The economic rationality of the self-calculating human is a basic assumption of individualistic liberal economics. Levitas (1985, p. 7) notes that the 'rationality of the economic competition favoured by neo-liberals and the genetic competition posited by sociobiologists is remarkably similar'. From this ideological base, the new right launches its major attack on the welfare state, based on the following rationale. The welfare state, they argue, has damaged traditional values and economically endangered the market system, but it has also challenged the *family's* autonomy through an invidious authoritarianism and growing intrusion into the realms of private life. The welfare state is attacked as irresponsibly increasing social benefits largely to maintain jobs for public-sector liberals.

Consequently, government and welfare state institutions must be displaced in the interest of effective welfare provision by *other* social institutions like the family and the voluntary, independent and commercial sectors (Stoesz and Midgley, 1991, pp. 24–42).

However, the denigration of the welfare state is more than an intellectual exercise and is aimed beyond welfare statism *per se*, given its assumed interconnection with collectivist and socialist values. It is also one part of a comprehensive programme of privatisation of services and an all-pervasive enterprise culture.

Privatisation of huge areas of the UK public sector during the 1980s and 1990s (Edgell and Duke, 1991; Loney et al., 1991; Kingdom, 1992) is a major tool of Thatcherite social policies. But ideologically the broad programme stands as an unambiguous experiment in the social reconstruction of human nature, a return to its *natural* home! Entrepreneurial capitalism does not merely inhabit the economic realm of production. Rather it is designed to nurture 'Thacherite values' in other avenues of life, to change 'how people think and what they value. Fundamentally, it is to do with changing how all of us understand ourselves' (Heelas and Morris, 1992, p. 2; Morris, 1991, p. 34).

The new human creature objectifies possession of individual enterprising *qualities*, such as initiative, the spirit of independence, boldness, energy, self-reliance and self-responsibility (Keat, 1991, p. 3). Hence, a whole enterprise *culture* has been formed for creating a new human being, with new modes of behaviour; it is a socio-political regime where the *individual* instead of the state is able to flourish. Its mission was announced early on: 'We want to work with human nature, helping people to help themselves and others' (Conservative Manifesto, 1977, cited in Morris, 1991, p. 33). The philosophy was reinforced in 1987: 'There is no such thing as society. There are individual men and women and there are families' (Margaret Thatcher, cited in Kingdom, 1992).

The nature of their individuality is defined by the new culture, so that human nature is about consuming. The human individual is an economic individual no less. The enterprise culture has prioritised the 'autonomous self' which is an 'enterprising self'; it is ambitious, takes initiative, and is steeped in a new consumerism (Rose, 1992, pp. 141–64). Enterprise production is consumer led, so that the inhabitants of the culture *define* themselves by their patterns of consumption. These assumed modes of 'natural' human behaviour bear close resemblance to the 'consumer sovereignty' of classical economics which invests the self-calculating consumer with control (Keat, 1991, pp. 216–30).

Clearly, the clutch of values comprising the enterprise culture does not cover the 'dependency culture' of the welfare state. The whole concept of enterprise tends to enhance inequality, indeed encourages it and so widens the gap between rich and poor, advantaged and disadvantaged. A further criticism of enterprise 'values' lies in their impracticability. The enterprise culture may set a frame of mind, but it does not necessarily deliver the material goods (jobs, for example). Again, it is argued that the functioning of enterprise behaviour and the standard of the market as a panacea for distributive justice lack a public morality. There must be moral boundaries, says Plant (1992, pp. 85–99). Primary goods commonly held in a society are basic needs without which fulfilment in life is an impossibility. The enterprise model for social policy spurns a complete set of human needs which may be properly served only by appeal to distributive justice. Yet new right policies have predominantly injured the weakest. Enterprise culture impoverishes the quality of personal life, in that it creates workaholics, encourages suspicion of one's fellow beings and downgrades the bedrock ethos of co-operation. Self in the present climate is one defined in terms of consumer items, representing a diminution of the richness of life and a reduction in our human nature.

Although media pundits may label the 1990s as a decade in which such values have been supplanted by greater community consciousness and citizenship awareness, the initial readiness of countries of the former Soviet bloc to adopt the enterprise culture out of a belief that it offers new grounds for hope (Sayers, 1992, pp. 120–38) has already produced the social danger signals of severe dislocation, human distress, civil political conflict and rising levels of poverty in societies such as Russia, Georgia and Rumania. Arising out of this mayhem has emerged the substantial electoral power of fascist parties with explicit racist and antisemitic platforms.

The policy turn of the 1980s has engendered a powerful programmatic radicalism; founded upon a revitalised Hobbesian model of the human as acquisitive atomistic individual, it has dislodged both the structural and philosophical supports of Britain's welfare state. But the framing of an enterprise culture, with its 'new' brand of consumerist human being, is exerting deleterious social consequences.

Sexism, Racism and Social Policy: Meeting Needs Unequally

This section will cover central issues of gender and racial discrimination as they have manifested themselves in social policy; the significance of 'natural' roles for females in the context of the welfare state, and the ramifications of the public man:private woman dichotomy; the marginalisation of black experience and the 'othering' of black and ethnic minorities in the formulation and implementation of policy. Social policy has been described as 'a set of structures created by men to shape the lives of women' (Wilson, 1983, p. 33). And certainly the human need for autonomy, meaning an active exercise of choice, is frequently denied to women. 'Public' and 'private' imperatives have proliferated throughout history, forming the basis of western political theory. But such a public:private split has occasioned serious repercussions for women and politics. Maleness has been articulated through political speech in the public realm. Historically, women were confined to the private domain, a silenced population, their views assigned inferior significance compared to the public, political activities of males ('political man'). As Elshtain explains:

> Women were silenced in part because that which defines them and to which they are inescapably linked – sexuality, natality, the human body (images of uncleanliness and taboo, visions of dependency, helplessness, vulnerability) was omitted from political speech. Why? Because politics is in part an elaborate defence against the tug of the private, against the lure of the familial, against evocations of female power. (Elshtain, 1993, pp. 15–16)

This socially constructed marginalising of women to the private spheres has distanced women from public life; they have wanted for a public voice and subsequently a place in the decision-making arena. Males have formulated social policies for females based on the male concept of woman's natural role. The design of the welfare state has sustained the subservient position of women in society (Wilson, 1977) and in particular has failed to challenge the patriarchal nuclear family, assumed as 'natural' despite anthropological evidence to the contrary (Chapter 3; and Edholm, 1991, pp. 141–52). The attributed role of woman was unequivocal in the underlying assumptions made by Lord Beveridge, architect of the British welfare state. According to Beveridge in his major governmental report (Beveridge, 1942) a woman is identified by and tied to marriage and family, an appendage to the male. Such premises once more reflect the unchallenged notions of 'female' human nature equated with family, bonding, the natural reproducer but also the natural nurturer. Not surprisingly, then, women have come to be viewed socially as the 'natural' carers within a basically patriarchal welfare framework. This model has underpinned social services policies, although institutional care has also been considered an essential constituent of the welfare state. However, the British Conservative government's key social policy of the 1990s, its community care strategy, lends a renewed importance to the assumed model of woman as natural carer, since the closure of public-sector institutions under the privatisation programme means an increased burden for informal carers in the community; such carers are overwhelmingly female, imprisoned in their 'natural' private role (Wicks, 1991, pp. 173–5; Langan, 1990; Dalley, 1988, pp. 13–19; Baldwin and Twigg, 1991).

Furthermore, we may see the familialist ideology (a stress on family) as tightly harnessed to the model of possessive individualism (Abbott and Wallace, 1990) whereby the *individual* is male but the 'owned' are women and children. According to Dalley (1988) this ideological familialism 'links the individual's circumstances of caring with society's organisation of welfare. The familial model of care, encouraged and depended upon at the level of the individual, becomes the model for social provision as a whole' (Dalley, p. 138).

It is through social policy that the 'othering' of different cultures may occur. Britain's black, Asian and other minority ethnic communities have been marginalised in a number of policy areas involving the provision of community services (Skellington and Morris, 1992). The IPPR local needs audit findings (discussed earlier) reveal that the social needs of these communities are not being met. The recently identified 'underclass' in modern capitalist social structures includes a large proportion of people from the black and minority ethnic groups. But it is also the case that certain interpretations of the concept hold the underclass to be a natural category, a familiar 'blame the victim' proposition (Westergaard, 1992) echoing the earlier biological and psychological explanations of educational inequality advanced by Jensen in the US and Eysenck in the UK, and then easily applied to black and Asian groups as well as to the white poor working classes.

The black experience has not only been marginalised in practice but has tended to be invisible in much of the social policy analysis literature (Williams, 1989). Solomos (1989) and Williams, among others, have opened up the issue of racism in social policy, articulating the process of marginalisation of minority ethnic groups from welfare services and decision-making frameworks. Welfare policies have to acknowledge the existence of racism, Williams (1989) states, whilst social policy evaluation must question whether welfare policies do challenge the 'pathologising' of blacks. Such pathologies imply the idea of black people and their cultures as 'problems', 'scroungers', unhealthy and nothing but 'victims'. Welfare policies and practices rarely confront ideas of white British cultural superiority. The traditional Fabian approach to social policy which handles policies as a social administrative matter accepted *de facto* the eugenics' movement's belief in imperial supremacy. And, of course, the black communities have fared no better in the wake of the new right welfare policies.

Chapter 5 indicated how the racist emphasis has shifted from a dependence on biological differences towards a remoulding of the conservative ideologies of Family, Nation and Culture. Cultural difference has replaced biological difference as a predominant rationale for inequality in social provision. Black people are severely disadvantaged by anticollectivist and privatisation policies. Though the new right clearly shares welfare statist assumptions that women and black people are naturally subordinate to whites and males, its use of familialist and nationalist ideologies justifies *less* state intervention, the market's supremacy and the existence of inequalities (Williams, 1989, p. 176).

To summarise, modern British social policy has served human needs unequally between social groups, such as women and members of minority ethnic communities. It is a logical product of patriarchal and ethnocentric models of human nature which assign primacy to male and white and inferiority to female and black, finally transmuted into white male autonomy in public decision making, in contrast to disempowered females and blacks inhabiting the 'dependency' sectors. Both groups have been subjected to naturalistic depictions of roles which separate them from the loci of power. New right policies which emphasise the 'natural' equation of family and caring and cultural difference magnify the 'othering' of female and black.

Despite the seeming proactivity of Thatcherite and new right perspectives, there reigns among communitarians and collectivists, who traditionally believe in the natural co-operativeness of humans (and indeed of animals), a mood of despondency and a sense of ineffectiveness. Strategies of dissent against injustice, racism or the like appear to be swimming against the tide. Community action and organisations are either on the defensive or they literally disappear. Simultaneously, conservative new right policies invoke market *forces* as if they were inviolable laws of nature brooking no opposition. It is a form of determinism originating in the Enlightenment economist Adam Smith's concept of a 'hidden hand' (*Wealth of Nations*, 1776) which mysteriously guides capitalism to a state of equilibrium. But another more recent version of fatalism has been forwarded by theorists who do not support the virtues of capitalism as a system. They raise again the crucial Weberian question as to whether pessimism is destined to be our predominant stance in an age of mass technology and economic rationality, a question to which we now turn.

Optimism Versus Pessimism: Technological Determinism, Social Policies and Change

Technology and its consequences are major issues at the close of this century, affecting perceptions of what is possible in social policy and how human collectivist values may be preserved rather than crushed. An earlier form of the debate revolved around the notion of the end of ideology and the technological determinism thesis of the 1960s; the later pessimistic prognoses relating to the consequences of modernism again raise the question of whether human subjects have a role to play in the shaping of their society.

The belief that technology and technical knowledge virtually bury the necessity for values and human purpose was intensely held in the 1960s but is again a focal concern of social theory and policy in the 1990s. Technological determinism suggests that technology irons out the differences in all advanced industrial societies (Aron, 1967; Lipset and Bendix, 1959), a revisiting of the principles of technical rationality (Bell, 1962). Ideology is deemed to have expired under the dynamo of technical requirements. Accordingly, the human being of the polis is no more, as essential differences disappear. Indeed, such is technology's manipulative force that changes in technology transform consciousness *per se*; electronics, media and the automobile *make* the modern human and the human condition.

Marcuse's *One Dimensional Man* (1964) articulates the political significance of the all-powerful technicism of modern industrial society, advancing the thesis that the system produces a one-dimensional thought capable only of discerning what *is*, and not what can be, thus producing a person who envisages no alternative to the immediate social system. Conflict and thus criticism are stymied. Only the technicist policies of systems maintenance are feasible. Marshall McLuhan's *Understanding Media* (1964) renders human intentions irrelevant under the domination of 'electronic media'. But in such a theory of media humans are no longer human beings but reified into things, 'robots dominated by environmental forces' (Fekete, 1977, p. 180). This theory (contrary to that of Marcuse) is divorced from the realities of social institutions and power, and thus ignores the way humans attempt to dominate others by technical means. McLuhan's abstracted technologism takes on a spiritual transcendental force in human life (Fekete, 1977, p. 182) yet it also resembles Weber's iron cage of instrumental rationality.

In the arena of social policy analysis, the fashionable field of futurology has claimed scientific status in its formulation of a predictive science comprising conjecture (speculation), forecasting and predicting. Policy makers, especially with the development of information technology and computerisation, have utilised the technique as a diagnostic tool. Popularised futurology (for example, Toffler, 1970; Robertson, 1983) proliferates. Typically, Toffler's vision of a super industrial society casts new technology in a major role, 'leading the way', posing whether or not we are able to *adapt* ourselves to the challenges brought by the new technologies as the prime question for human beings. The fact that humans by nature possess consciousness, can plan and deny as well as affirm, becomes an aside. Reports and forecasts of the 1970s, many on the environment (Bailey, 1988, pp. 77–95), portend almost imminent catastrophe. More recently, in the sphere of international affairs, historian Paul Kennedy (1993) outlines a scenario of global disaster signposting the likelihood of political *inaction* rather than the obverse, seeming to presage a twenty-first century of technicism, an iron cage and the spirit of pessimism.

In Chapter 4 we saw how Weber explained the tendencies for humans to rationalise their existence, best characterised by the formal bureaucratic structures of modern society, embodying instrumental reason and efficiency leading to a 'technological civilisation' of atomised individuals which imprisons us in the iron cage. Current social theory literature is preoccupied with the idea of instrumental rationality and modernism. Bauman's fusion of untold evil and modern rational structures (Chapter 5) communicates a powerful case for inescapable pessimism over any prospect for progressive change. But Bailey (1988) notes how pessimism was weaker during the 1970s whereas the possibilities of material social advance remained ebullient, along with a belief in strategic *controls* and planning.

However, models in which humans consciously steer their society have suffered a serious setback under the political new right's idea of a spontaneous social order and 'pure technologism as a compulsive restatement of an already failed faith' (Bailey, 1988, p. 54). The new pessimism, because it is infused with scientific argument and empirical detail, 'is so all-knowing and complacent in its confidence and its pretence to rationality that it seems to paralyse the will' (Bailey, 1988, p. 152); it creates a numbness from exposure to constant risk (Giddens, 1990; Beck, 1992) or evinces an immobilism in the face of constant social failure (Blackwell and Seabrook, 1993).

Blackwell and Seabrook retreat one step backwards and show how the fixed human nature thesis itself nurtures fatalism. They suggest that the classic conservative position that 'you can't change human nature' constitutes probably the greatest significant bulwark to developing new policy directions. This tenacious clinging on to such an assessment suggests that it is an *ideological* construct concealing interests of social power and privilege:

> An extraordinarily powerful society has produced, and then legitimated, certain restricted forms of behaviour, and has then declared them to be both unalterable and quintessentially human. No higher degree of social perfection could be imagined. (Blackwell and Seabrook, 1993, p. 111)

The catalogue of social problems, for example crime, explained in terms of an irredeemable fixed human nature, constitutes ideology that accepts and then reinforces things as they are. Statements that human nature cannot be changed are more a disguised prescription that human nature *must* not be changed (Blackwell and Seabrook, 1993, p. 122) in order for the capitalist system to operate. Hence, human nature is incarcerated by its own impotence.

Nevertheless, such an immobilism does *not* necessarily mean an inertness of action. A nagging anxiety for Blackwell and Seabrook is the tendency to see human nature as one thing or the other. It is far more complex than that. 'All that we can say is that human nature is indeed ambiguous, capable of great good and great evil' (1993, p. 139). Taylor (1991) echoes their sentiments and refutes the view of technological society as a kind of iron fate on the grounds of its ultra simplicity which forgets the essential. Whilst modern society tends to edge human beings towards atomism and instrumentalism, the connection between the latter and technological civilisation is not purely unidirectional. No one theory can cover the complexity of human beings and societies (Taylor, 1991, pp. 98–9).

In summary, the end of ideology thesis reinforces the propensity towards technological determinism and technicism. This belief has fostered the elimination of the human subject in social affairs and social policy, contributing to a fatalistic support of the status quo and a cynical pessimistic view of social change. However, such a stance derives from one-dimensional models of human nature which disregard the complexity of human beings and their responsive capacities. In reality, possibilities for social change remain fluid; 'you can't change human nature' is a prescription, not a truth.

Summary and Conclusions

To conclude, social policies assume particular theories of human nature which incorporate values and statements of human purpose. Thus social policy in theory and practice is intrinsically political. Perspectives in advanced social democratic economies during the mid twentieth century have not been so sharply delineated in practice as to reject change or collectivism out of hand. In fact, the social policy paradigm of the post World War Two epoch was a recognition of the interconnection between individual and collective needs (although certain social categories were differentially treated). But a new policy paradigm based on the social reconstruction of the 'old' and 'natural' individualistic predispositions has displaced the socialist principles of equality and social justice. Ironically, the new right's ideological pedigree regarding *natural* human attributes is an openly radical *social* behaviourist experiment to alter the human self, a mass project for the dismantling of collectivist welfare state institutions. The economic privatisation of public social services represents an aspiration to privatise the human subject no less. The negation of welfare state collectivism also reinforces patriarchal assumptions of women's 'natural' position, and confines minority ethnic groups to the boundaries by a *de facto* refusal of full community and participatory rights. Finally, technological determinism has been instrumental in the denial that all humans possess the potential power to change or transform their societies. Indeed, a major bulwark to effective strategic social change is the holding on to a set of assumptions that humans are naturally greedy, or lazy, or conservative. The following chapter investigates the specific policy area of health and how models of human nature inform particular approaches and practices within healthcare.

Further Reading

General Surveys

Ian Forbes and Steve Smith (eds.), *Politics and Human Nature* (Francis Pinter, 1983).

Paul Spicker, *Principles of Welfare* (RKP, 1986).

Vic George and Paul Wilding, *Ideology and Social Welfare* 2nd edn. (RKP, 1985).

Political Traditions, Social Welfare and Human Nature

Gillian Dalley, *Ideologies in Caring: Rethinking Community and Collectivism* (Macmillan, 1988).

Martin Loney et al. (ed.), *Social Policy and Social Welfare* (Open University Press, 1983). A valuable reader; see Lee and Raban's matrix of ideologies.

Michael Sullivan, *The Politics of Social Policy* (Harvester Wheatsheaf, 1992).

Human Nature, Welfare and Human Needs

Len Doyal and Ian Gough, *A Theory of Human Need* (Macmillan, 1991). Opens out the human needs debate in social welfare.

Individualism and UK Social Policy

Paul Heelas and Paul Morris (eds.), *The Values of the Enterprise Culture* (Routledge, 1992).

Sexism, Racism and Social Policy

Jean Bethke Elshtain, *Public Man: Private Woman* 2nd edn. (Princeton University Press, 1993). See Part II.

Elizabeth Wilson, *Women and the Welfare State* (Tavistock, 1977). Women defined by welfare policies.

Richard Skellington with Paulette Morris, *'Race' in Britain Today* (Sage, 1992). A recent introduction to ethnicity and social policy.

Optimism, Pessimism and Technological Determinism
Joe Bailey, *Pessimism* (RKP, 1988).

Trevor Blackwell and Jeremy Seabrook, *The Revolt Against Change* (Vintage, 1993). How our belief in a static human nature prevents us changing our social conditions.

8

Health Professions, Policies and Human Nature

Introduction

Our mode of approach to the social and economic fabric of life is important, and we observed in the last chapter how social welfare strategies are guided by the recognition accorded to specific human needs, potential for change and the significance we place on community and individual respectively. The reduced status of the NHS resulting from the privatisation of services is, for Britain certainly, a paradigm policy shift of the late century, crucial because physical health needs and mental autonomy are basic to life. Hence, ideas of health and sickness are integral to classical formulations of human nature. The twentieth century's particular understanding of health and illness remains wedded to western rationalist philosophy's major assumption, the Cartesian dualism propounded by René Descartes (1591–1650) which implies the separability of body and mind. Health is a universally accepted tenet of our nature, the absence of which hinders our capacity to enjoy being human and the related ability to participate socially. Our methods of recognising this absence of health are historically as well as culturally located. Twentieth-century perceptions of health have been shaped by the century's philosophising on the nature of human beings, and in this process behaviourism, Freudianism, existentialism, Marxism and biologism (Chapter 2) have all played their part.

By studying the health professions we may grasp the shifts in status accorded to these models of human nature, particularly the struggle between the scientific and the existential and the biological and the cultural. Accordingly, this chapter covers the questions of basic human needs and health and their relationship to culturally created social needs; the Cartesian discourse concerning human nature and the impact of the mind:body dualism upon western medicine; the significance of the recent moves from adoption of the medical model to the holistic; models of human nature as they inform ideas on mental health and the competing models of mental illness; the ethnocentric bias of western psychiatry; and an analysis of the individualistic, sexist and racist assumptions built into government health campaigns.

Society and Health Needs

Health literally rests at the heart of human needs. The very concept of health, however, is historically rooted, possessing facets relating to both the physical (body) and mind (mental), yet defining humans' *social* existence and their interrelationships. The idea of health has been traditionally linked with notions of the human being's *natural* condition, and indeed with the idea of ontological perfection and harmony. Witness the writers of the Old Testament and Ancient Greece, and the common belief in civilised societies that an ideal state of health and happiness (a body:mind equilibrium) is possible. Similarly, one may point to the Rousseauan 'return to nature' school's thesis that nature and goodness are synonymous. They define illness as the breaking of the natural bond. The Darwinian biologism of the nineteenth century questions this rather abstract philosophical approach with a more sophisticated exposition of the specific interaction between human fitness and the external environment. The scientific temper *is* to control disease rather than return to nature. But as Dubos (1984, p. 8) notes the urge to control the diseases of rampant nineteenth-century industrialisation sprang from a humanitarianism aimed at recapturing harmony with nature's ways. However, diagnoses of health and illness are socially and historically constructed. Even medicine cannot simply be 'medical' and traditional medicine is no better equipped to apprehend health and sickness than are other cognate spheres of knowledge.

Definitions of health have tended to be classified negatively, for instance as the absence of disease or pain, or positively such as in the World Health Organisation's definition (1946) of attaining a state of complete physical, mental and social well-being, or as in Talcott Parsons' notion of the capacity to fit into society (Aggleton, 1990).

We have already encountered the positive definition (Chapter 7) with Doyal and Gough's (1991) Marxist precept of health as the basis for human potential, a basic human need *per se*. Both physical and mental health are necessary to ensure the participation in full social being; the exercise of a Kantian autonomy demands 'a body which is alive' and 'the mental competence to deliberate and to choose' (Doyal and Gough, p. 52). This takes us closer to lay definitions which have countered the more official definitions, more holistic than biomedical and which revolve around the idea of human beings' wholeness and the ability to handle life. Being healthy is the paradigm of the competent social being. Yet certain health professions view with suspicion lay beliefs on health which loosely attribute causes of illness or disease either to external environmental effects or to internally determined dispositions (Aggleton, 1990, p. 16). Such cynicism is unfounded, Agggleton argues, since lay beliefs, like medical knowledge, are attempts to make sense out of our human condition. The diagnostic results do not differ greatly from the 'professional', although travelling from different starting points. Below we consider the reorientation of health professional practices in recent years away from a biomedical emphasis and towards holistic approaches.

As we saw earlier (Chapter 3), perspectives on facets of humanness such as the state of babyhood are culturally relative. The same applies to assessments of health and sickness. But *within* a society conceptions of health and illness differ along lines of age, social class and gender (Calnan, 1987; Miles, 1991). In other words, our techniques for monitoring or evaluating our personal well-being or ill-being are socially relative. Not all groups are accorded equal weight, especially in the context of a white, male, middle-class dominated medical profession. Brown and Harris's investigation into women and the social origins of depression (1978) illustrates that background social factors, for example property and poor housing, plus the intrusion of particular life events, intensify vulnerability to illness such as clinical depression, and hence affect the basic need for emotional autonomy (Doyal and Gough, 1991, p. 192).

Our conceptualisations of health, then, whilst universally valued have varied historically, socially and culturally. Although the health professions, and especially medicine, have seen health according to the independent realms of body and mind as either bodily health or mental health, competing definitions signal an increasing interest outside the medical profession with wholeness. But as we shall see below, the medical profession's *Weltanschauung* (world view) has tended to monopolise how we define our self-identity and state of health; such authority is firmly ensconsed in western philosophical dualism.

Human Nature, Cartesian Dualism and Western Medicine

Behind western medical approaches and practice is a cluster of assumptions concerning human nature and biology. Understanding their impact requires further examination of the significance of western Renaissance science and the ascendancy of the mechanical model of human beings; the primary importance of Cartesian dualistic philosophy in theorising the mind:body relationship; the social significance of the body in terms of social policy; and the predominance of medical perspectives in approaching illness.

The tradition of Renaissance science has given rise to a mechanical characterisation of human beings, exemplified by Hobbes's model of human nature (Chapter 1) and that of Descartes. The latter claims that the human body functions in the same way as a machine, arguing that one can explain processes like human growth, reproduction and the digestive system mechanically. But at the same time, human behaviour has to be seen in terms of mind as well as body, a feature not possessed by animals. This Cartesian dualism, implying the independence of mind (consciousness) has exerted a profound influence upon the way we perceive ourselves, and in the case of medicine and the health professions how we are treated in health and sickness. Descartes's mind:body dichotomy demands at this point some further explanation. His 'Meditation on the Existence of Material Things' elucidates the distinction of body and mind as corporeal and incorporeal substances, or body and 'soul' (Descartes, 1642, ed. Anscombe and Geach, 1970, pp. 59–124). Western medicine concentrated upon the corporeal element of the human, displacing Aristotle's concern with the organic unity of living beings, and thus facilitating the successful prevention or cure of disease by the acquisition of detailed anatomical knowledge (Doyal and Pennell, 1979, p. 29). Nevertheless, adoption of the mechanistic model *did* produce limitations for medicine: scientific medicine 'ultimately became curative, individualistic and interventionist, objectifying patients and denying their status as social beings' (Doyal and Pennell, p. 30). It is still the case with western medicine today, the result of refocusing 'from a person-oriented to an object-oriented cosmology' (Jewson, cited in Doyal and Pennell, p. 34). Scientific dualistic thought has also facilitated specialist treatment for body and mind, consequentially divorcing mental health from physical health. Specialised knowledge of each has invested the medical professions with hegemonic social power.

This social power draws its strength from western dualism's inherent hierarchy. Eldridge Cleaver's *Soul on Ice* (1968) is a black radical writer's protest against dualistic philosophy. Cleaver regards the mind:body duality as integral to the hierarchical class structure of western societies, reflecting the life of the body and the life of the mind. Modern western capitalistic society rates mind superior to body. The labourer is equated with the body, the administrator with the mind. Descartes has paved the way for modern thinking not simply by his 'proof' of the independent spheres of body and mind, but by the role he assigns to rational thought as opposed to bodily senses, which makes knowledge of the physical universe entirely reliant on mental processes and non-physical existence. The implied superiority leading to the power of an intellectual ruling class over a working class, given the position of blacks in the occupational hierarchy (filling the menial positions) becomes the rule of white over black, the hegemony of white intellect over the mythologised sensuous black body, and indeed becomes a rationalised racism (Hodge et al., 1975, p. 156).

Another sociological manifestation of western dualism discussed at a later stage (Chapter 6) is the male:female dichotomy which attributes a superiority to mind (for decision making in the public domain) and an inferiority to the body and the universe of biological childbearing (extended to childrearing). Freudianism has played a considerable part in the persistence of the western dualistic tradition; its powerful biological orientation in the theory of drives was instrumental in the development of psychiatry as a medical discipline. Freud's characterisation of the conflict between id, ego and superego is an extension of the traditional western perspective that reason stands above passion and instinct, and culture is superior to the natural. The sexuality of the body (id) he equated with nature and unregulated passions; he linked the morality of reason to the superego. Not only implicitly but explicitly the dichotomies are to be seen in terms of male superiority.

Due to the stress placed on sexuality, the female's mental development is hampered. She is unable to attain a full superego, wedded to the Oedipus complex with its ambiguous sexual emotions. Given that the superego is the transmitter of cultural values and civilisation, it is the male who is capable of exerting rationality and moral control; female nature is to be *controlled* through the focus on body. Having drawn attention to the biological facets of Freud's theory in inspiring psychiatry, the role of the Freudian model of human nature as a whole has been more complex and equivocal. In modern western culture the mind has been in the ascendant; the body has been the subject for control through the manipulation of knowledge and this has manifested itself in the social *institutionalisation* of knowledge and control.

Foucault's biopolitics demonstrates the historical and social significance of biology and the relationship of the body to social power. Social power has been essentially *disciplinary* power ever since the eighteenth century, entailing control and surveillance of the body by professional administrators through the institution of prison, clinic or the asylum (Foucault, 1973; 1975; 1977). *Birth of the Clinic* (Foucault, 1973) demonstrates how the eighteenth and nineteenth centuries augured in the 'medicalisation' of society and the birth of modern medicine. With the increase of empiricist methods of diagnosis (anatomo-clinical medicine) and the greater emphasis on training and theoretical knowledge, the status of medical doctors grew. Their diagnostic methods of 'gazing at the human anatomy lent them a quasi-mystical authority, and in the process objectified the passive body, lumps of flesh to be manipulated by the doctor' (Armstrong, 1987, p. 70).

To summarise, the Cartesian philosophical dualism and the mechanical model of human nature have proved crucial in characterising how we think of ourselves and in defining the key components of our being. The scientific paradigm of mind:body facilitates the growth of specialisation and medicalisation, so that the person comes to be viewed as body/object. A similar dualism in psychoanalysis has led to biologising the workings of the human psyche. At the same time the mind:body split has become subject to a Platonic hierarchy in which manual workers are subjugated by professionals, females by males and blacks by white. In the next section we look at the medical model's position in modern healthcare and nursing and the changing approaches which have developed as concepts of health have altered.

From Medical Model to Holistic Change

The medical model enjoys an enhanced status in the health professions. In this section we shall look at the question of the medical model in healthcare; its domination in this century and Illich's classic critique; the alternative models developed in recent years by healthcare groups striving for their own professionalisation; and the impacts of government policy upon the traditional models. The medical or biomedical model of care constitutes a process based on the natural sciences for viewing illness in terms of bodily disorder, and is adopted by 'experts' on health and illness. Given its adopted individualistic and functionalist orientation to health, medical practice has been essentially curative. Its physiological orientation supports the negative definition of health which means you are healthy if you do *not* possess any incapacities or disease that may be *externally* pathologically verified. Expressed differently, health is defined functionally as 'fitness' to perform normal socially designated tasks. Thus ill health represents a malfunctioning of the human machine, treated by surgical, chemical or electrolytic methods. Under a capitalist system, emphasis falls on the sick individual; disease is comprehended as some 'failure' internal to the individual's physiological machine.

The model may be criticised largely on the grounds of its narrow focus which devalues the broader social and environmental context which often constitutes the initial causes of sickness, pain and disease. Its exclusive concern with the biological is reductionist and mechanistic. Intensive promotion of high technology has led to a dehumanisation of the patient and a reduction in direct human care. Marxist critiques in the political economy of health argue that the scientific claims behind the medical model do in fact reinforce the hierarchical division of labour between professional doctor and other health workers. The unequal relationship between doctor and patient means that medical care comes to serve the purpose of socialisation and social control (Doyal and Pennell, 1979). People as patients experience the loss of autonomy and feel they have no control over their own bodies in the same way as they believe they have no power over their everyday social and economic conditions (Doyal and Pennell, p. 43). Hence, a human need central to our nature is denied.

Ivan Illich's humanistically inspired *Medical Nemesis* (1975) is a compelling thesis that the west has been overtaken by a medicalisation of culture leading to a retrograde change in people's lives. Three types of human damage are perpetrated by medicine: clinical iatrogenesis; social iatrogenesis and structural iatrogenesis. Hi-tech treatment is actually useless and exerts harmful effects, Illich claims; medical drugs and pills result in prolonged dependency and care needs and in reduced human self-activity. Health cultures that accept pain, suffering and death as the natural constituents of being human have been destroyed. A new medical culture has created a new human condition of life without limits, socially engineered by an all-powerful uninhibited medical profession.

Ironically, Illich's critique suffers from the ferocity of its own attack, blinding him to medicine's positive achievements in curing and offering immediate pain relief (Doyal and Pennell, 1979, p. 19). As well, it bears the marks of a technological determinism (Chapter 7) which weakens the powers of human social intervention. Medicine in the United States is part of a much wider capitalist system. Similarly, the British government's restructuring policies and consumerist ideology upon welfare services (Chapter 7) heavily impinge upon a medical profession under intense pressure to alter traditional practices.

But we must consider added dimensions to the debate over the medical model's credibility, and examine perspectives held by health professionals other than medical doctors and specialists. The nursing profession finally saw fit to question the medical model in the 1980s. Work on the nursing process exhibits a turn towards alternative socially and environmentally oriented models, to prevention instead of cure. Government policies and commissions, for example 'Project 2000', aim at an intensified retraining of nurses capable of handling the multifarious social transmutations (including permanent unemployment) affecting people's health; they may have been instrumental in reorientating the theoretical basis for practice away from the traditional medical model (Fahey, 1988, pp. 33–5). We may also discern in this movement an attempt by nurses to establish themselves as an autonomous profession. Their lack of power may be viewed as a function of their inability so far to create a framework of autonomous knowledge for supporting an occupational area where they can be seen as experts (Abbott and Wallace, 1990, p. 24).

Competing nursing models shed light on how nursing practice is invariably underpinned by philosophical assumptions concerning the human being's composition or 'nature'. The American *Illustrated Manual of Nursing Practice* (IMNP) (1991, pp. 5–6) lists eight models of nursing which differ in respect to the definition and purpose of nursing, and definitions of health and environment and of person. Pearson and Vaughan (1986) analyse six nursing models according to goals of nursing practice, required knowledge and skills, and the beliefs and values upon which the model is based. Luker and Orr (1985, pp. 92–3) outline six nursing theories in terms of their goals, activities and view of the individual. In each of the typologies the biological and behaviourist models lie at one end of the spectrum. Henderson's (1966) functionalist nursing model approaches the human as 'a biological being with inseparable mind and body'; health is the ability to function independently using 14 components of nursing care as a gauge to health (IMNP, 1991, p. 5). Johnson's behavioural model encapsulates the human individual as a behavioural system comprising eight subsystems: affiliative; achievement; dependency; aggressive; eliminative; ingestive; restorative and sexual. The nursing goal is to ensure the behavioural stability of the individual. However, in neither case do we encounter social situations.

Most of the other models on the other hand are founded on explicit holistic and humanistic existential attitudes to the human being which conceptualise the individual as a wholeness and in constant interaction with the external environment. Neuman's stress model (1982) defines the individual as a physiological, psychological, sociocultural and developmental being who must always be seen as a whole. Each of the components is subject to stressors including those in the external environment. Nursing's aim is to offer a 'unifying focus for examining the individual, group or community's relationship to stress' (IMNP, 1991, p. 5; Luker and Orr, 1985, p. 93).

Holism and humanistic existentialism underscore changing general social attitudes to health and medicine, illustrated by the growth in holistic medicine's popularity and in the growing number of challenges to medical professional power by patients and health workers (Pearson and Vaughan, 1986). Existentialism's emphasis upon personal autonomy and individual responsibility is understandable against a historical backcloth of control by the 'superior' omnipotent others. Humanism's underlying belief is that patients should own the power to make decisions for themselves and define their needs (including psychosocial needs such as sense of security, maintaining identity and searching for opportunities to develop and utilise one's human potential) as basically autonomous human beings. Royle and Walsh (1992, p. 1) suggest that a consensus exists among nursing theorists recognising that the individual client should actively engage in decisions about their care.

In this respect, Maslow's hierarchy of needs (1968), originating from humanistic, existentialist precepts of the individual, is commonly used in nursing theory for decision making and care planning and for diagnostic categorisation. Maslow's hierarchy classifies human needs on the assumption that basic biological and physiological essentials require prioritisation over the higher needs of self-actualisation. (The application of Maslow's humanistic psychology in counselling and theory is discussed further in Chapter 9.)

The reorientation of nursing's traditional approach to the patient is reflected in the restructuring of the district nurse's role towards *community* nursing, in response to the UK Conservative government's *Care in the Community* (1989) strategy. The sharper profile of the individual client's wider social network necessitates more interdisciplinary and interprofessional team work with social and community workers, affecting in turn the education and training of nurses, health visitors and other healthcare professionals. Curriculum has become more geared to the social construction of health and illness (Black, 1991).

Sceptics speculate that this diversion from the medical model is little more than a pragmatic lending of some academic aura to nursing; it may even be practically dangerous given the untried and unresearched nature of the nursing models. McCaugherty (1992) comments that 'concepts of pathology, signs and symptoms and diseases that people possess are not going to disappear overnight. How a nursing model can be independent of them is unclear ...' Considering the community care strategy's ostensibly broadening effects, however, the holistic perspective and the use of theoretical nursing models in health professional education may yet be forced into retreat, as entrepreneurial and budgetary constraints allow no room in practice for non-medical treatments.

To summarise, the physiologically oriented medical model has held sway with the medical profession, but has met with strongly argued critiques defending the autonomy of the person under assault from an over-medicalised culture. We have argued that the biomedical model is about social power founded on a constricting version of human nature. Nursing models, too, adopting holistic and existential definitions of humanness, signify important alternative modes of treatment. Nevertheless, these face barriers in the form of a managerialism which in the end limits the scope of care.

Human Nature, Mental Health and Mental Illness

As with issues of the body and physical health, models of healthy and unhealthy nature compete for acceptability in the arena of mind and mental health. At certain times the conflicts are sharp, since the adopted model may determine the nature of treatments, some of which may have profound consequences for an individual's life, such as personality transformation or the denial of personal liberty by incarceration or by labelling. Below we shall consider the concepts of mental health and mental illness; the organic medical model and the associated dominance of psychiatry; psycho-dynamic or psychotherapeutic applications; the sociotherapeutic perspectives; the significance of anti-psychiatry and social labelling.

Definitions of mental health and illness are crucial to the debate in that universal agreement is so much more difficult to achieve taking into account the complexities of cultural relativism. Heather (1976, p. 67) proffers that a diagnosis of mental *illness* by psychiatry is invalid, since the profession is completely unlike legitimate medicine as an activity. Psychiatry's concept of mental illness renders it a disease of the mind or brain affecting behaviour which represents a deviance from the normal; that is, abnormal thinking and abnormal behaviour. But within psychiatry the distinctions in approach commence with the definition. Thomas Szasz (1967; 1970) argues that because disease is something that attacks the body, and mind is not an organ or part of the body, it cannot be 'diseased' in the same way. He suggests that most 'mental illness' cases are about the problems of living and malfunctioning in the network of social relationships. Mental illness is thus a totally social construct (Szasz, 1967).

Clearly, difficulties abound in establishing the 'normal' state of mental health against which mental illness is assessed. Although psychiatry is about medical treatment, its definitions of mental health are nebulous but distinctly moral, social and by extension, political. For instance, mental health is:

> ... an adjustment of human beings to the world and to each other with a maximum of effectiveness and happiness ... the ability to live ... happily, productively, without being a nuisance. (Barbara Wootton, 1959, cited in Clare, 1990, p. 15)

Britain's Mental Health Act 1983 defines mental disorder as: 'mental illness'; 'arrested or incomplete development of mind'; 'psychopathic disorder'; 'any other disorder or disability of mind'. As with its predecessor, the Mental Health Act 1959, the term 'mental illness' itself stays undefined, its operational definition considered 'a matter for clinical judgment' (MHA, 1983, Section 1). But whether it is in effect a *clinical* judgement is of course under dispute. A number of competing theories of mental illness exist which we may classify in accordance with organic, psychodynamic (including psychotherapeutic methods of treatment), anti-psychiatric and social constructionist models.

Through the auspices of the psychiatry profession, the organic medical model has dominated the diagnosis and practice of mental illness, reflecting a neurobiological and behaviouristic view of the human being, preoccupied with genetic, physiological and neuro-biological factors affecting human behaviour. The model distinguishes between immediately organic and functional conditions. The former diagnoses physical causes for symptoms embracing brain damage from injury, drug induced and brain degenerative disorders. Functional conditions such as manic-depression and schizophrenia (a disorder of the thought processes) are classed as serious psychotic disorders to be equated with physical disease; neurotic disorders are portrayed as a human reaction to stress (for instance, anxiety, hysteria, various phobias and obsessions). This distinction is significant, in that it ascribes biological causes to psychoses, whereas psychological factors figure prominently in explanations of neuroticism.

The psychodynamic approach does not question the existence of mental illness, but interprets it as an illness of the mind which has its source in history; it is about relationships with others, not about organic disorders. Freudianism treats the presence of hysteria as partially psychopathological conjoined with the person's early experiences, like disturbing autobiographical memories culminat-ing in a range of physical symptoms. Here Freud breaks with the neurological to adopt psychological explanation (internal psychic conflict between id, ego and superego) of neurotic symptoms in patients. Freud comes to view hysterical behaviour as a network or pattern of significant signs, reflecting the individual's repressed unconscious sexual history which transcends a biological pathology. As a psychotherapeutic method of treatment, psychoanalysis aims at freeing the tortured individual's repressed, unconscious memories. (As a form of therapy or treatment it is discussed further in Chapter 9.) Indeed, the disjuncture between Freud's explanatory model of mental illness and his treatment of it may be interpreted as para-doxical. Hirst and Woolley (1982, pp. 140–63) support Freud's attempt to retain contact with the evolutionary biology of the nervous system whilst differentiating his approach from a directly biological theory. On the other hand, Heather (1976, p. 62) construes the potential *liberating* force of psychoanalysis as an antidote to the positivism of Freud's instincts theory, implying a humanising influence in practitioners' interpretations of Freudianism as a therapeutic tool.

Whereas Freudianism has often steered a course between the biological and the psychological, anti-psychiatric models have condemned outright the psychiatric organicist model of mental illness. There are nevertheless variations within the anti-psychiatry position. Szasz (1967) questions the validity of the mental illness concept *per se*; it is nothing more than a myth comparable to witchcraft, manufactured to advance psychiatry's scientific standing and to control the individual's liberty. Individuals, however, argues Szasz, are rational autonomous creatures who choose freely (and consequently antisocial behaviour should be ignored or punished if illegal). Alternatively R.D. Laing, from a basis in Sartrean existentialism, turns to the territory of social interrelationships.

Unlike Szasz, Laing recognises mental illness as a phenomenon. Laing and Esterson (1964) diagnose seemingly irrational symptoms as rational behaviour in response to irrational social institutions, particularly the family. Genetic and organic explanations of schizophrenia and the institutionalised forms of mental treatment are rejected. The school interprets schizophrenia as a metaphor for persons not conforming to the accepted model of social reality. Laing's main ideas are essentially a refashioning and development of Sartre's existential model of human nature (Chapter 2; and Laing and Cooper, 1971). Sartre's own existential psychoanalysis refined in studies of Baudelaire (1950) and Genet (1963) is grounded in the principle that the human being's only choice lies in the revelation of oneself, a process by which 'each living person makes himself a person' (Sartre, 1958, p. 574). In *Divided Self* (1959), an examination of the essential self exists which acts as a fulcrum of the individual's experience, Laing applies existentialism to the analysis of schizophrenia. The schizophrenic experiences a split with the world and within herself, fragmentations including the divorce of self from body and of outer self from inner self, a sense of 'ontological insecurity' which leads to a petrified state of depersonalisation. Later work (Laing and Esterson, 1964) focuses on the role of 'others' in the family (Sartre's 'hell is other people'). Diagnosis of schizophrenia is discovered neither in internal clinical or existential causes, but in terms of social phenomenonology. The later Laing (1967) characterises schizophrenia as the authentic voice against the social 'others' (family and experts) who conspire to incarcerate, control and degrade them.

This eventual inversion of values and 'normality' with its denial of pathology, and its designation of all social relations and institutions as inauthenticity, alienation and ill health has been attacked by Marxist critics for its extreme antisociality and mystical utopianism character. Sedgwick (1974; 1982) and Hirst and Woolley (1982) note the antiwelfarist implications of the philosophy; people most adept at utilising alternative therapies and personal philosphies do not usually have need of the remedies that institutional psychiatry *can* offer. At the same time, such people have personally benefited from welfare state institutions and interventionist political philosophies.

The Laingian-Sartrean perspective of human beings has also been criticised by an existential psychiatry which affirms a personal freedom but recognises the validity of a scientific determinism. Ledermann (1984) construes mental illness as a reality that strips humans of their essential freedom and distorts their personal self-image. Self-liberation is not possible if one accepts the determinism of the social nexus (Ledermann, p. 40).

The fourth model of mental illness, however, concentrates exclusively upon the social construction of mental health and illness, conceptualising the latter as a labelling process which controls those who break society's implicit, 'residual rules' (Scheff, 1966), a reply of the eccentric or odd 'deviant' behaviour of rule breaking citizens. Kesey's *One Flew Over The Cuckoo's Nest* (1962), dramatised in film, provides a tragic example of such labelling. Becker (1963) claims that the labelling process is usually in defence of middle-class values applied to the working-class patients who comprise the majority in mental institutions. The latter, acting as social control agents, are hence able to 'justify' the medical treatments in psychiatry like the administration of drugs, ECT and psychosurgery, all involving the control of human personality which replaces abnormal with normal behaviour, and moulds individual identity.

Foucault's work on the role of madness in society (1965) serves as a more historically situated and sophisticated account of socially constructed perspectives on mental health, reaching beyond the analysis of stigmatisation. He documents the functions of psychiatry and institutional confinement in exluding the mad from society. Psychiatry needs to be seen as a historical development in the categorisation of insanity and treatment, with its new 'moral methods' and more enlightened techniques for ensuring the maintenance of social discipline; a medicalisation of the *knowledge* of madness conducted from within the scientific paradigm. Hence, psychiatry and the birth of the clinic in the nineteenth century were practices embodying social power as expressed through prevailing discourses of the epoch (Foucault, 1973). Turner (1987, p. 80) suggests that *all* human societies are thus 'characterised by a certain dynamic of exclusion which is defined by a certain set of practices and beliefs'.

The precise way in which the mentally ill human subject arrives at an identity which is no longer a threat to the modern social order is demonstrated in the celebrated case studies of Erving Goffman. *Asylums* (1961) portrays the contemporary mental hospital as expressing order, control, acceptance of authority; it aims at modifying patients' view of their own selves and others, collapsing the human individual's former identity and remodelling it to fit institutional definitions – in effect, the institutionalisation and stigmatisation of human behaviour which is a feature of all total institutions. Goffman's thesis is that human beings become skilled in surviving this process of adaptation. Whilst they approach socially constructed knowledge in similar fashion, Goffman (as discussed in Chapter 4), unlike Foucault, founds his interpretation upon the model of human beings as autonomous, rational and self-calculating manipulators of their self-image.

To sum up, no real consensual definition of mental health and illness is on hand. Most prominent among definitions of mental illness is the biomedical/neurological, but existential and sociological critiques are more pluralistic. The biological organic model of disease dominates within the psychiatry profession, reflecting the acceptance of a biologically reductive model of human nature. However, the psychodynamic model, notably psychoanalysis, has acted as a bridge from biological theory to the psychological treatment of obsessive and hysterical human behaviour. Existentially based models, duly critical of psychiatry's theoretical and institutional base, are nevertheless ideologically suspect in their intense subjectivism and implicit antipathy to collectivism. Sociological models stressing social interaction between patient and the threatening 'others' signify an alternative to medical and atomistic models, yet too easily lose sight of the human subject's inner experience of mental disorientation.

Western Psychiatry, Mental Health and Racism

Given the prominence of the psychiatric medical model in characterising and diagnosing the state of health of human beings' minds, and the substantial evidence that institutional psychiatry reflects hierarchically tiered social power, we will focus below on those specific ideological impacts in treating people from other than western cultures or from non-white ethnic backgrounds, which stem from western psychiatry's categorisations and diagnoses of the mental condition. The section confronts the basic assumptions of western psychiatry; the practical racist consequences emanating from implicit evaluations of black human beings and assumptions of their alleged sicknesses, and the political nature of psychiatry's assumptions and approach.

Psychiatry's assumptions are western, white and ethnocentric. Even the white critiques of the profession have not really addressed the issue of *racism* in western psychiatry. Clare's seemingly comprehensive survey of the psychiatric profession in dissent (1980) scarcely discusses the issues of racism and psychiatry. Yet western psychiatry, which treats many people migrating from other cultures and meets with a host of different cultural assumptions over the specification of mentally ill behaviour, employs diagnostic methods based upon western cultural assumptions and norms, not least acceptance of the Cartesian belief in an independent mind requiring compartmentalised treatment. The question of culture cannot be eliminated from models of 'natural' mental health. Various cultures conceptualise the life span and life events in a variety of ways (Chapter 3).

With respect to conceptualising mental illness, one encounters great inconsistencies in recognising symptoms or manifestations of suffering. Such variations are highly consequential for the psychiatrist's diagnosis. For instance attitudes to 'eccentric behaviour' differ. Persons possessed by spirits in parts of Africa will not necessarily be considered ill; in Britain, they would be transported to the psychiatrist (Rack, 1982, pp. 97–112). Psychiatry's reading of a 'mental state' whereby patients' reports of experiences are taken to depict their inner state of mind characterises schizophrenia in a culture-bound way. Frequent misreadings of cultural nonconformity and the misconstructed 'nature' of, for example, black Afro-Caribbeans have spawned practical racist repercussions, namely in admission rates and quality of service received.

Empirical statistical evidence is sparse due to lack of data on health by ethnic origin, the complicating factor of the philosophical debate itself, and the absence of a common framework (Grimsley and Bhat, 1988). Nevertheless, a clear picture does emerge from available material. Relatively high numbers of black inpatients in the United States were assessed as psychotic in the late nineteenth and early twentieth centuries. Reports in the 1970s demonstrated a higher rate of schizophrenic diagnoses among American blacks relative to whites (Fernando, 1991). British empirical studies carried out on disparities in diagnosis during the1970s and 1980s in Britain draw attention to the greater tendency for Afro-Caribbeans and Asians to be labelled schizophrenic (Fernando, 1991; Sashidharan, 1989). Younger Afro-Caribbeans are especially prone to be thus diagnosed by psychiatrists who, inclined to see these youths as the culprits of modern social ills, conflate social and medical pathologies in their diagnosis (Knowles, 1991). A parallel picture emerges for admittance to detention (Littlewood and Lipsedge, 1989).

Knowles (1991) argues that psychiatry is racist in its effects because of the *nature* of the activity *per se*; it happens in a private context with patients divorced from their normal everyday social setting, hence strengthening the chances of an uninformed prognosis especially in a multicultural society, and given the set of racist preconceptions the western psychiatrist brings to the interview (Fernando, 1991, pp. 116–17). The profession's medical scientific training is also not well suited to the philosophical and artistic approach demanded for understanding the many aspects of the human condition affecting a patient's mental disposition.

Psychiatry's knowledge base in the biological sciences has tended to attach biological/racial categories to socially constructed behaviour, a biological racism institutionalised through diagnostic procedures. Inappropriate diagnosis is taken for genetic or constitutional inferiority (Fernando, 1991, p. 121). The consequences of misdiagnosis and biological racism determine the types of treatment administered, which again exhibit disparities as between black and white; greater proportions of blacks receive ECT, are incarcerated in high-security institutions (Littlewood and Cross, 1980) and experience higher levels of compulsory detention (Cope, 1989; Cochrane, 1977).

Change is exceedingly slow in the 1990s. An Italian official visitor to a London psychiatric hospital in 1992 found only Jamaican people in the hospital's one special closed ward explained away by the resident psychiatrist as 'the aggression of people from Jamaica' (Asylum, 1993). No UK enquiry has been set up to investigate the series of deaths by black people in psychiatric institutions over the past eight years. Fanon (1970) in the earlier colonial context assessed the ideological and political significance of doctor–patient relationships within a colonialism where practices of 'racial' oppression in themselves generate forms of psychic and emotional distress among the oppressed. It is an oppression which mirrors the psychiatric treatments of the colonised, basically a treatment of the 'alien'. Mercer (1986) suggests that the black psyche continues to be a key site of struggle in the health and illness debate in post-colonial Britain, and calls for a black critique of psychiatry's spurious scientific 'objectivity'.

We have seen in this section that white, western and racist assumptions underpin the dominant organic model of mental health. Thus, western psychiatry is ill prepared to deal transculturally with culturally related human actions. Psychiatrists evaluate eccentric behaviour as symptomatic of disease and psychotic mental illness. Trained from within the scientific medical paradigm, psychiatry is liable to classify inaccurately subjects as schizophrenic, with all its attendant consequences for members of the black and Asian communities. Erected upon a questionable model of human normality and mental functions, psychiatric diagnosis has become a highly charged ideological and political issue.

Individualism, Human Nature and Health Policies

In Chapter 7 we studied the underpinnings of social policy by assumed models of human nature. Health education campaigns offer interesting case material on the connections between theory and practice. Below we discuss the principles underlying health strategies and particular campaigns supported by the 'free choice' model of classical economics; analyse the cultural and ethnocentric notions supporting health education practice; locate the implied sexism of health education campaigns; and identify the ideological dimensions of current British health policy. Conventional health education offers a pertinent instance of strategies driven by unique perspectives of human beings and their behaviour. Traditional health education has in practice been determined by the medical model, adopting behaviouristic and individualistic principles. Rodmell and Watt (1986) suggest that the latter may be discerned in the amount of attention granted to 'lifestyle' or doing things the 'right way', such as healthy eating. This again implies acceptance of the polarities of adequacy and inadequacy, ideological in its pathologising of typical conduct and in the packaging and labelling of social behaviour.

Lifestylism and individualistic models presume that human behaviour is tantamount to that of the rational economic *consumer* (Chapter 7). It is a simplistic and highly conservative proposition which devalues the impacts of social institutional power. The 'Look After Yourself' Campaign during the later 1970s in Britain stressed the *individual* as the maker of healthy choices. More recently, the strategy has been broadened to the idea of health promotion. Occasionally this has meant an improvement in transcending a purely individualistic, medical model. Campaigns for non-smoking, sport, fitness, child safety and the counteraction of coronary heart disease have publicised more the social context and avoidance of 'blame the victim' expositions. Generally, however, individualism has informed health education's paternalistic attitude which ignores social inequalities as a reason for ill health; the medical model has provided the behaviouristic and individualist framework for health campaigns.

A close examination (Naidoo, 1986) of selected campaigns on safety and fitness reveals antipathy to state intervention, the imputation of *parental* responsibility for safety, and an adoption of 'lifestylist' promotion and marketing that tacitly blame the victim whilst turning the human individual into consumer. Focus on education and persuasion evidently assumes a rational, calculating atomistic consumer as the purveyor of natural behaviour. But such a conceptualisation of the problems directs us inexorably towards solutions which disregard those structural barriers that may inhibit the free play of choice. By so doing, it serves to reinforce the operation of a free market capitalism and the continuation of social class inequalities.

Health education campaigns, by appealing to medical models that assign causes of ill health to individuals or to cultures also tend to reinforce racist ideology by pathologising minority group lifestyles and cultural differences. White practices are perceived as the norm;

white health education professionals define black people as a problem, in *special* need and thus requiring special attention rather than simply possessing universal human health needs (Pearson, 1986). British public campaigns such as the Rickets Campaign (Pearson, 1986) and the Asian Mother and Baby Campaign (Pearson, 1986; Rocheron, 1991) have misguidedly depicted minority groups as from 'alien' and inferior cultures responsible for their own sickness and for their apparent unresponsiveness.

Health education food campaigns have also evinced a patriarchal approach to the needs of the female psyche in defining woman's 'natural' domestic role, implicitly 'othering' the female, whilst falsely representing her as an autonomous, rational choice consumer freely able to select from available alternatives. Strategies in persuading women to change family food consumption patterns have been shown to be ideological in their disregard of the male's power to lead family food preferences, and political in their failure to challenge the strength of the profit-motivated food manufacturers. Such a challenge demands a collective response. Health education campaigns target the *woman* of the domestic family, resulting in individual women experiencing a heightened sense of guilt rather than effecting any real change in family diet which entails an added financial burden (Charles and Kerr, 1986).

The view of human beings as individuals who consume health in the same way as we consume cars is not exclusive to health education programmes. For many years health service delivery in the United States has been based upon the idea of individuals as consumers of health services and medical products. Britain's restructuring of its welfare state since 1979 (Chapter 7) has involved a radical overhaul of the National Health Service through the privatisation of services reinforced by the notion of market individualism and managerial objectives. Enterprise culture's very language is intrinsic to corporate goals and political strategies. The UK government's NHS and Community Care Act 1990 talks of 'consumer care packages' and the individual consumer client as the prime unit of cost. By pursuing a strategy to de-emphasise collective provision, the government has ideologically justified its closure of many large regional mental hospitals in 'efficiency' financial savings by appeals to aspirations of individual independence through living out in the community. Yet many individuals who have been released have been institutionalised for so long that they *cannot* behave in an independent manner. Independence, as with dependence, is a socially learned condition and hence may be unlearned. The numbers of reported incidents of accident, neglect, homelessness or even suicide bear testimony to this. 'In the community' is not necessarily *of* the community and indeed the enterprise culture's admiration of individualistic behaviour sits uneasily alongside recognition of community and associated models of collective social life.

We have seen, then, how health and promotion policies are essentially behaviouristic and individualistic, oriented to the medical model yet disseminating the belief that the consumer in singleminded pursuit of health does possess the wherewithal to choose an appropriate lifestyle. These perspectives are class based, culturally relative and sexist, treating working-class people, blacks and females as 'other'; they maintain the *status quo* by imputing to *individuals* the responsibility for unhealthy practices which are socially rooted. Finally, these tendencies must be seen as part of a comprehensive health policy strategy aimed at the atomisation and fetishisation of human health needs.

Summary and Conclusions

In conclusion, the medical model may have maintained its dominance in practice, but it is apparent that health needs are not just bodily needs, something more readily recognised by lay definitions than by medical professionals. Medical practitioners have generally relied on the philosophical mind:body duality to preserve their professional authority, but the challenge from holistic, humanistic and socially oriented nursing models is a strong antidote to philosophical dualism. The current climate is one of equivocation. Shifting community care policies, exerting pressures to break down traditional specialised practice on the one hand, are simultaneously reinforcing an individualised consumerism which may eventually hamper more liberal holistic approaches. Perspectives on mental health and illness bring home to us the implications of adopting particular models of human nature, and display the pitfalls of biologism and scientism in the psychiatric treatment of *mental* illness. Humanistic existentialism is significant (its limitations are discussed in Chapter 9) in countering monolithic organic approaches, whilst Marxist structural and sociological accounts offer greater insight into how mental illness is socially constructed and how western psychiatry demonstrates not merely a weakness in dealing with the whole person, but inherently represents an institutionalised racism. Finally, government health and education policies too easily adopt behaviouristic and individualistic models of the human being, reflecting consumerist policies which do not undermine prevalent class, patriarchal and racist stereotypes. In Chapter 9, the final discussion of the caring professions, we consider the significance of human nature models and the consequences of government policies for social work.

Further Reading

General Surveys
Peter Aggleton, *Health* (Routledge, 1990).
Len Doyal and Ian Gough, *A Theory of Human Need* (Macmillan, 1991).

The Mind:Body Split and Western Medicine
Graham Scambler (ed.), *Sociological Theory and Medical Sociology* (Tavistock, 1987). Includes exposition of Goffman and Foucault.
Bryan Turner, *Medical Power and Social Knowledge* (Sage, 1987).

Models of Health
Lesley Doyal with Imogen Pennell, *Political Economy of Health* (Pluto Press, 1979). Largely a Marxist approach.
Ivan Illich, *Medical Nemesis: The Expropriation of Health* (Calder and Boyars, 1975). An unshackled attack on the medical model.
Alan Pearson and Barbara Vaughan, *Nursing Models For Practice* (Heinemann, 1986).

Mental Health and Illness
George W. Brown and Tyrrell Harris, *Social Origins of Depression: A Study of Psychiatric Disorder in Women* (Tavistock, 1978).
Anthony Clare, *Psychiatry in Dissent* 2nd edn. (Routledge, 1980).
Michel Foucault, *Madness and Civilisation* (Mentor, 1965). The classic structuralist interpretation.
Ronald D. Laing, *The Divided Self* (Tavistock, 1960; Penguin, 1965).

Psychiatry and Racism
Suman Fernando, *Mental Health, Race and Culture* (Macmillan, 1991).
Philip Rack, *Race, Culture, and Mental Disorder* (Tavistock, 1982).

Individualism, Racism and Health Education
Sue Rodmell and Angela Watt, *The Politics of Health Education* (RKP, 1986).
I.U. Ahmad Waquar (ed.), *'Race' and Health in Contemporary Britain* (Open University Press, 1993).

9

Social Work and Human Nature

Introduction

The discussion in Chapter 8 intimated that the traditional doyen of the caring professions, healthcare, has been dominated by the prestigious medical profession's way of working, tied to a biological perspective of human nature. Yet its microscopic focus on the body, coupled with the medicalisation of the mind, has meant the development of a separate profession for meeting people's social care needs; it is a development accordingly less impelled by the biological. As such, social work theory is more eclectic, drawn to a range of models of human nature. Like many interventionist disciplines, such as urban planning, it has borrowed its major insights and paradigms from other disciplines, predominantly in the social sciences. Nevertheless, its practice base and face-to-face casework orientation has attracted social workers to psychological methodology and the adoption of mechanistic views of human nature. Social work as a relatively new profession, lacking a theoretical position of its own, has chosen models fitting the dominant practice, in this instance one-to-one casework. Hence, social workers have inclined towards models of human nature derived from psychology, either the portrayal of the individually autonomous human being in a constant state of flux, or to a lesser degree the individual subject to external modification.

Whereas organisationally British social services have moved in the direction of systems and structures management, driven by the policy initiatives of the 1980s and the 1990s (Chapter 7), individual social workers themselves have attempted to retain a professional autonomy by a reassertion of the client–social worker style, based on more personal responses to the human being. This chapter examines a range of key methods reflecting seminal, but not always compatible, models of human nature. What is the role played by the key twentieth-century models of human nature in social activity? To answer this question means looking first of all at social workers' attitudes towards behaviourism and behavioural modification. The chapter then analyses social workers' applications of the Freudian model and the latter's somewhat ambivalent reception in the profession. Thirdly, we discuss the ways in which the existential model as applied in psychotherapies has offered considerable scope for the prevalent client–social worker casework mode. Influences of the Marxist perspective on human action in social work are analysed before the chapter finally considers major aspects of disadvantage and disempowerment in the light of socially constructed images of self.

Behaviourial Social Work

Behaviourism has played an equivocal role in social work. Learning theory has been applied in specific areas of the profession, but tensions arise between expressed professional desire for a form of 'scientific' status (implying deterministic methodology) and social workers' humanistic aspirations. Application of such methods also raises the question of whether social workers as opposed to health professionals may authentically adopt the medical model without medical credentials and whether a strong directional impulse and social work values are mutually compatible. Each of these aspects is discussed below.

Positivistic psychology, particularly Skinner's ideas of operant conditioning, reinforcement and programmed learning and his assumptions on human nature, which justify changing the individual through control and manipulation of the environment (Chapter 2), has had a notable if not substantial effect upon British social work. Behavioural social work, based largely on learning theory principles which handle observable behaviour, concerns itself less with the mind or its thought processes than with the application of punishment and rewards. As with behaviourism *per se*, it assumes human nature to be subject to manipulation and control. Social learning theory underpins behavioural therapies. Bandura, (1977) advances the notion of role models who stimulate clients to imitate them. The learning process, embracing common features such as motivation, cues or discriminative stimuli, responses and reinforcement (Jehu, 1967), may well involve permanent changes in behaviour.

How do social learning theory insights relate, then, to social work? Of basic significance is the developed or learned perception of the self. A human being's self-concept bears heavily upon behaviour. How people view themselves is a key to understanding their own behaviour. The implications of this experience are sifted, assimilated and applied where experience accords with how a person views herself (Jourard, 1964). Yet in the case of the particular experience *not* according with self-image, the implications appear alarming and unacceptable and lead the individual to withdraw. The social worker is then cast in the role of facilitator, intervening and assisting in reshaping the client's self-concept and enabling her to come to terms with the behaviour (Sutton, 1979, pp. 159, 164).

Although the issue is equivocal, it is not easy to treat behavioural methods as compatible with a humanistic approach. On the one hand they recognise the enormous potential for change residing in human beings (Sheldon, 1982). On the other hand behavioural social work is highly deterministic. The stress upon external control collides with the conception of client empowerment (discussed below). Behavioural engineering must be considered ethically suspect for its *denial* of human autonomy.

A further major philosophical issue concerns the use of the medical model of behaviour. The traditional Cartesian version of the relationship between consciousness and behaviour, where the latter is held to be merely symptomatic, has monopolised social casework, as well as psychiatry and psychology. Its dominance has nevertheless led to arguments that non-specialists (like social workers) should avoid practical activities such as dealing with people with behavioural problems classified as sickness and thereby subject to medical solutions. Yet the practitioner or therapist remains in control and may often completely alter a previous diagnosis when taking over a case (Sheldon, pp. 33–4).

Behavioural approaches utilising such methods as the token economy are common in residential work, in child sexual abuse cases, and in handling a variety of children's problems (Herbert, 1986). Such techniques have been practised in schools and residential homes for young persons with behavioural difficulties (Sutton, 1979, pp. 167–8). But control is the underlying goal. Here, social workers monopolise the channels to reward and punishment. Positive effectiveness *has* been demonstrated but largely in the short term. Behaviourism has not been adopted generally in social work; certainly conventional behaviour modification techniques are now less in evidence in counselling.

Payne (1991) offers three main reasons to explain the lack of impact of these methods in social work. In the first place the open assault on traditional psychodynamic social work coupled with the behaviourists' positivist critique of social work's effectiveness has produced a defensive posture among social workers. Secondly, social workers feel uncomfortable with behaviourism's directive methods and behavioural social work's mechanistic terminology and mode of procedure. Thirdly, on ethical grounds social workers have been apprehensive of adopting a non-social work style of operating (CCETSW, 1976; Payne, 1991, pp. 132–3). Hence they may have gravitated professionally towards those methods that *do* empathise with the inner human being.

In sum, behaviouristic psychology, with its focus upon behaviour rather than mind, has received an ambivalent response from within the social work profession. Whilst social workers have found the individual centred psychological focus appropriate to the norm of casework, techniques involving manipulation of the environment, punishment and direct control over the client conflict with the more humanist inclinations implict in counselling activities and with the profession's ethical code emphasising free choice and respect for client autonomy.

Freudianism and Psychoanalytic Social Work

As we shall see below, psychoanalytic social work implies a focus on the unconscious. It also entails a certain acceptance of claims by traditional psychoanalysis to a scientific 'distance'; it includes diverse perspectives, but displays a continuing interest in the individual's inner, emotional state and in the experiential journey from childhood to adulthood. The limitations to the approach will also be examined. The work of Freud and the Freudian school's approach to human nature has attracted social workers attempting to achieve deeper insights into their clients' *subconscious* and into explanations of the effects of personality upon behaviour, pain and emotional suffering. But historically its acceptance has varied, depending upon the institutional alignment of social work as a profession. The high point was from the 1930s to the 1960s, when social work was organised in close proximity to psychiatry; the medical model remained relatively unchallenged, which meant that mental abnormality instead of social problems was viewed as social work's *raison d'être*.

Chapter 2 showed that the ideas of psychoanalysis are based on a rationalist approach of understanding in its quest to be 'objective', distant and analytical, adopting the classical tenets of scientific methodology. To this extent, psychoanalysis has lacked personal engagement. But the psychoanalytic approach towards the human being has been far from monolithic. Jungian-derived models have placed greater weight on commitment, engagement and creativity. Psychodynamic models and the practice of psychotherapy have influenced social work's resolute non-judgemental strain and the recognition it accords to psychological and *emotional* factors. They have also been instrumental in the continued emphasis upon casework and treatment in social work. The underlying goal is to improve self-knowledge, which contrasts with the behavioural approach in that it administers to the human's *inner* state in order to change external behaviour.

In psychodynamics, the social worker's role is to draw out the client's feelings of anger, hatred, grief and guilt (Hollis and Woods, 1981). The theory analyses clients' interactions with the outside world, while the casework relationship serves them in their personal growth. Social work is treated as a *process* rather than a series of one-off procedures (the latter a feature of psychosocial casework). Winnicott's *Human Nature* (1988) represents an immediate application of a Freudian model of human nature to understand and treat childhood problems, analysing emotional development, charting the child's development of the inner world, the development of interpersonal relations, how the child establishes a relationship with external reality, and the functioning of the intellect (that is, the place of the mind in human nature). It is the therapist's role to exert the creative act in the understanding of barriers preventing maturation (Winnicott, 1988, p. 8).

However, Winnicott's theory is tightly bound by the notion of psychic unity and the idea of perfect development in the child so that in effect the external environment fulfils merely a passive supportive role which, suggests Frosh (1987), assists 'the unfolding of an integral, unified ego that is genetically preordained' (p. 107). The environment unobtrusively supports the *natural* process of the child's evolving ego; any fragmentation of the child's ego is due to environmental *failure*. But Winnicott is also guilty of blind gender assumptions. Crucial to the 'natural' process he identifies is the interconnection with the mother, who sets up the image expectation of 'self' for the child. Winnicott's interpretation of the therapeutic relationship in social work is that the therapist/analyst plays the part of the mother figure. The 'good mother' uses an 'intuitive' personal knowledge of the patient's needs that ostensibly imitates the 'natural' responses of a mother towards her child. Such an assumption of the 'natural' caring relationship and the idea of analyst as mother is intrinsically patriarchal. Thus, Winnicott's account of child development in the end attributes the failures of ego development to women (the child's environment) for not performing well enough as good mothers (Sayers, 1988, p. 102).

Transactional analysis (TA), based on the writings of Eric Berne (1961; 1964; 1974), straddles the psychoanalytic tradition and humanistic therapy and views the person as an autonomous being. 'Each person defines his own life,' states Berne (1974, p. 4). People *do* possess the capacity to act and decide responsibly through their patterns of communication. In this respect, the method posits a rather different version of human nature from the more deterministic psychoanalytic theory, and has produced an independent system of specialist therapy, with its own training programmes. TA charts the interactions of one person's ego state with another's, and the exchanges which may contain dangerously *hidden* messages. The therapeutic social worker utilises the transactional analysis to discover clients' particular ego states, thus facilitating their improved communication.

Any assessment of the psychoanalytic social work approach must rest at least partially on earlier comments made *vis-à-vis* the Freudian perspective of human nature. Its claims to scientific status, its implicit ethnocentric, class and sexist assumptions, plus the marginalisation of environmental factors and indeed of any social policy framework are all problematical (Payne, 1991, pp. 81–3). Freudianism's pretensions scientifically to explain human behaviour have been shown as flawed by behaviourists who place emphasis upon *testable* experiments rather than theoretical reasoning and unprovable assertions. Such attacks question the value and effectiveness of analysis and consequently its appropriateness for social work practice. But at a deeper philosophical level, the aspiration to be empirically scientific in the sphere of personal problems is suspect, leaving no scope for human self-determination (an issue tackled more seriously by the existentialist school of practitioners discussed below).

The adoption of the medical model by practitioners in psychodynamic social work embodies a hierarchical power relationship of 'expert' and patient which does not easily coexist with the more equal client–social worker relationship. Furthermore, the underlying white middle-class assumptions of psychoanalysis have encouraged the interpretation of black ethnic behavioural and personality differences as abnormal, which results in serious misdiagnoses of sickness experienced by people from Afro-Caribbean and Asian backgrounds (Chapter 8). With respect to gender, the classical Freudian model identified earlier was severely male oriented. But its applications and reinterpretations have offered a springboard for female resistance to male oppression. Later discussion in this chapter considers the formation of an explicitly anti-Freudian feminist psychotherapy.

The class bias particularly emerges in psychoanalytic social work's requirements for a specific type of skill in the exercise of self-examination. Such a requirement downgrades the practical problems of less articulate working-class clients. Problems of this kind often reside in the domain of social and environmental factors demanding policy intervention and collective responses (challenging the non-directive social work style). Psychoanalytic social work's preoccupation with the human being's emotional state tends to preclude responsibility for solutions. But as we noted in Chapters 4 and 7, policies and social institutions often fashion a client's emotional condition in the first instance.

In summary, the focus on the human's inner state has appealed to individualistic casework-oriented social work. The scientific analytical methods have been attractive to specialist social workers seeking special professional recognition and a professional 'distance', but this aspiration of 'value-free' analysis is a cause for concern among those who see human beings as social, committed beings. The marginalisation of the external social environment leaves psychodynamic casework dependent upon the client achieving personal insight, but there is then nowhere else to go. Before discussing a more collectivist, Marxist-based position in social work, the following section examines the overtly antiscientific orientation of existential therapy and humanistic psychology.

Existential Therapy and Humanistic Psychology

Ironically, the existential model of human nature, rooted historically in a nihilistic and despairing philosophy of life, has in its application appealed to casework-oriented social workers not least due to its optimism. In this section we look at how existential and humanist therapies entail optimistic visions of freedom; examine the nature of non-directional counselling and the significance attributed to human potential, self-awareness and non-material sources of human tension; and finally a specific therapy born out of personal suffering in the Jewish Holocaust.

Existentialist and humanistic therapies focus on the individual client, and hence lend themselves to client-centred therapy in social work. Existentialist models of human nature of both the secular and the spiritual variety sustain existentialist therapy. Availability of choice and the capacity for change are considered key values among social workers, but the existentialist route has also offered them greater *practical* guidance than have other more academic ideas.

Applied as therapy, existentialism challenges the Freudian psychoanalytic model's pessimistic prognosis of human nature. Although one may locate the humanism of the humanistic psychologists within the rationalist Enlightenment tradition reflecting a secular optimism, it is nevertheless trained on the individual's inner subjectivity; it encompasses spiritual and mystical experiences and highlights individual autonomy (Royce and Mos, 1981, p. 76).

The human psychology school, led by Carl Rogers (1902-87), arguably the leading humanist therapist for social work theory and practice by way of counselling, generally assumes a positive outlook on human nature. Counselling has become the accepted method for providing individuals with the *freedom* to make choices. Its practitioners perceive human beings as intrinsically motivated to change, to seek personal fulfilment and to love their fellow beings, a profoundly *optimistic* depiction of the human condition. They argue that such a position does not discount environmental impact. Rather, given a sympathetic environment, any person possesses the capacity to flourish. This perspective on human nature invests trust in individuals to make decisions dependent upon their personal inner experiences; it contradicts the Freudian preoccupation with factors of control and sublimation in both explanation and treatment.

Rogers's formulations stand in stark contrast to Skinner's behaviourist conceptualisation of human nature rendering the human being little more than a blank piece of paper. The role of counselling is aimed at clients discovering their own cures. It accords considerable weight to the relationship between therapist and client: hence its draw for social workers. Counselling as a practice in social work necessitates the acceptance of values of unconditional positive regard and empathy towards the client in a non-directional manner, reinforcing the notion of a non-judgemental, non-directive social work which encourages development of the 'self'.

Carl Rogers's position on human nature is reflected in the significance he attaches to therapy, which reveals the organic nature of the human always in the process of becoming (Rogers, 1961). To quote:

> When man's unique capacity of awareness is thus functioning freely and fully, we find that we have, not an animal whom we must fear, not a beast who must be controlled, but an organism able to achieve, through the remarkable integrative capacity of its central nervous system, a balanced, realistic, self-enhancing, other-enhancing behavior as a resultant of all these elements of awareness. (Rogers, 1961, p. 105)

His argument that human beings are able to achieve a constant and enhanced awareness of themselves eschews the notion of discrete stages in personality development. The experience of unconditional positive regard is equated with the potential for a flexible and adaptable personality. Therapy's function is the production of an authentic and acceptable climate which removes any necessity for the client to act in a defensive manner, thus allowing a full exploration of inner experience (Nye, 1992, pp. 105–8).

Rogerian therapy prioritises the individual's *conscious* capacities, in contrast to a Freudian methodology more designed to unearth the intricacies of the unconscious. Rogers is not concerned with the modification of the individual as 'object' (*pace* the behaviourist perspective) but with subjective self-knowledge. The initial task is to empathise and to know the other, although the objective method is not entirely rejected. Rogers treats humans as conscious and rational beings – a holistic position which places value on the whole person, unlike the Freudian focus on unconscious and irrational forces inside the human being, or the Skinnerian methodology of studying the human as object.

Abraham Maslow's self-actualisation thesis revolves around the achievement of human potential. *Towards a Psychology of Being* (1968) makes explicit connections between psychology and existentialism, mainly through the concept of personal identity. According to the model, our nature incorporates the spur to change ourselves. The basic motives for self-development support our actions and behaviour, part of a hierarchy from the physiological to the higher needs including the acceptance of self and others, spontaneity in living, the search for privacy, the possession of autonomy, enjoyment of peak experiences, the possession of creativity and being well adjusted (Shaw, 1972, pp. 131–2).

Concepts of psychotherapy and individuation represent an extension of mainstream Freudian psychoanalytic perspectives (as discussed in Chapter 2). Carl Jung calls for religions to be viewed as psychotherapeutic systems because they offer form and expression to deep psychological needs. Due to the inappropriateness of traditional religions now perceived as archaic and unacceptable, he attempts to derive 'a method for the modern individual of giving form and expression to these needs' (Shaw, 1972, p. 135).

Existential psychotherapy, emanating directly from an existential model of human nature, has engendered the practice of counselling. Existentialist psychotherapist and counsellor Rollo May (1992) suggests that the effectiveness of counselling depends on our 'understanding of what human beings are' (May, 1992, p. 13) as expressed through personality (basic nature). Personality in this case is characterised by four essential features: freedom, individuality, social integration and religious tension. Counsellors, it is contended, assist the human being in the search for the self, but counselling too involves grappling with 'the spiritual tension inherent in human nature'. May (1992, p. 40) notes that '[it] is the counselor's function, while aiding the counselee to free himself or herself from morbid guilt feelings, to assist the counselee courageously to accept and affirm the spiritual tension inherent in human nature'.

A group of analysts, among them Bettelheim and Frankl, felt compelled and qualified to apply their immediate experience of the Holocaust's horrors and the lower depths of human behaviour to assist suffering people by means of therapy. Victor Frankl presents a specific method of logotherapy for analysis and therapy (Frankl, 1959) which affirms the need for us to discover our own meaning in life. Based on an explicitly declared philosophy of life, logotherapy as a method makes three fundamental assumptions forming a series of interrelated links: freedom of will; will to meaning; and the meaning of life (Frankl, 1967, pp. 13–14). In *Man's Search For Meaning* (1963, p. 167) he analyses 'the existential vacuum', a widespread twentieth-century phenomenon predominantly manifested in a state of boredom. People must take responsibility for identifiable tasks (responsibleness) as a way of overcoming this condition. But where Frankl's thesis differs from Maslow's self-actualisation concept is in the argument that 'human existence is essentially self-transcendence rather than self-actualisation ... self-actualization cannot be attained if it is made an end in itself, but only as a side-effect of self-transcendence' (1963, p. 175).

Logotherapy concentrates on enabling people to discover meaning in life in three ways: by doing a deed, by experiencing a value, or by suffering (Frankl, 1963, p. 176). Performing a deed provides the sense of achievement that contributes to the sense of self-transcendence, making contact with the world, rendering an answer to the question of what is her/his nature with a specific, concrete response. Understanding the essence of others requires us to experience the value of love. What attitude we adopt to our suffering helps to form the potentiality for meaning in our existence. Therapy of this kind implicitly accepts a human nature embracing an intrinsic spirituality. Brandon's advocacy of Zen in social work (1976) adapts an eastern spiritual approach to the requirement for social workers to develop their own personality and to interact with the client. The goal is to aid people undergoing great suffering, a purpose set apart from the search for greater fulfilment.

Psychotherapeutic methods as a whole lack clarity and tend to obfuscate explanations of clients' particular behaviour difficulties. But there are deeper ideological problems. The location of psychotherapists in the private sector has meant an underlying commercialism and a predisposition towards clients' disempowerment; the therapist retains continuing and final control over the counselling situation and clients' efforts to interpret their own inner nature (Weldon, 1992). Finally, but by no means least, such techniques tend to underplay the forces and impacts of external change. Masson (1988; 1990) rejects the idea of psychotherapy in total. His critique of psychoanalysis and therapy *per se*, pursued on the grounds of its manipulative practices, produces an ironic twist, given therapy's own impassioned attack on behaviourism. A former practising psychotherapist, Masson berates therapists such as Freud, Jung and even Rogers (although in more muted fashion) for an avoidance of negative possibilities, including the evasion of the practice of abuse.

Rogers's very denial in his statements of being 'political' suggests political implications endemic in the nature of psychotherapy. With Jung's writings and therapeutic practices, the criticism is politically damning in the light of Jung's one-time Nazi affiliation. This real world is omitted from his therapy:

> What I find totally absent in Jung's accounts is any sense of all the tragedies that go on in people's lives. The real world is simply absent from his books ... [The] essence of the defect of Jungian psychotherapy is the attempt to avoid touching on those issues

> that are most concrete, most real, most relate to the body and
> to a specific moment in history ... Jung's psychotherapy was a
> screen behind which he could hide his own unpalatable past.
> (Masson, 1988, p. 164)

In short, existentialism's application in the counselling arena has ably fitted traditional social work's non-judgemental style. The Rogerian stress upon the natural human act of becoming and Maslow's model of the human journey towards self-realisation create a positive role for the practitioner and substantial autonomy for the client, a counter to the deterministic cast of Freudianism and behaviourism. The individual's ability finally to overcome even the most traumatic of human experiences, including the Holocaust, through engagement with social and spiritual tensions, is impressive. But the suggestion of uncontrolled client autonomy and freedom must be called into question, especially considering the control psychotherapists actually wield – a tacit power to exclude the material world whilst engaging with the spiritual realm. It is to the material world in particular that we turn in the next section.

Marxism and Radical Social Work

In the light of social work's client-led approach, the Marxist model of human nature has been less influential than other models in social work. Nevertheless, it has not been without influence, depending upon specific historical conditions. Below we shall look at the Marxist impact on the radical social work of the 1970s; the stress on collectivism, social change and community as an antidote to individualism; the attempt to develop a materialist perspective on the psychological domain; revolutionary social work's waning significance, and the shift in organisational focus.

The Marxist approach to human action, as we have seen, gives prominence to humans' *social* nature, is critical of an individualistic world view and argues that *collective* class-based activity leads to simultaneous change in the environment and oneself. This idea of a committed collectivism was generally inimical to traditional institutionalised British social work and to the more specialist therapeutic and behaviourist dominated models. However, a more buoyant capitalist economy, strong trades union organisation and the spread of socialist ideas in the 1960s encouraged a burgeoning radical social work movement, which challenged conventional social work's individualistic, pathologising preoccupations and its devaluation of collective action.

Radical social workers expressed a strong political commitment to forms of socialist action, and an antipathy towards treating unemployed persons, poor members of the working class or groups such as gays as the 'other', not truly human. Holding to an optimistic vision of human change, radicals called for a revolutionary transformation in the social system (embracing welfare benefits, housing and employment) so that victimised groups could achieve their full human potential. The view of change encompassed new participatory styles of decision making between social work agencies and between client and social worker. The social worker's professionalised framework was considered a 'distancing', which meant an unequal client–social worker relationship.

Radical social work gave greater credence to collective alliances with workers' organisations. At the same time, the concept of community, defined as the interaction of social equals, and a minimal concern with personal self-interest so as to break down class and other social divisions created by capitalism (Plant, 1974, pp. 16–22), figured high on the radical agenda. Through the late 1960s and the 1970s community development and community action were prominent in urban areas. Community workers were seen as the viable substitute for social workers. However, the community perspective became incorporated into social work practice with the promotion of community social work in the 1980s, more concerned with the decentralisation of formal social service structures than with organised self-activity or with a critique of the state. Hence, the orientation to alliances with the working-class labour movement meant that radical social work paid scant attention to the human individual.

Radical social work theory, largely built upon Marxian analyses of the oppressive role of the political state and the reproduction of social class relationships, reflects this relative disregard for the non-material human condition. In an attempt to rectify the imbalance from within the critical theory tradition (Chapter 2) Leonard's materialist theory of personality (1984) grafts an analysis of consciousness on to the sphere of material existence, relating collective action and the material world. His consideration is with the contradictory pressures in people's lives and the understanding of family conflict. Collective action, he reasons, assists in the individual's psychological growth involving the intimate relationship between consciousness, practice and change. Where the theory differs from the Freudian conception of consciousness raising is in the relevance of external change: a 'greater self-knowledge is dependent on engaging in the struggle, along with others, to change some aspect of the social relations through which the self is constructed' (Leonard, 1984, p. 207).

Notwithstanding Leonard's materialist psychological analysis, radical social work's influence has waned with the harsher economic climate of the 1980s and 1990s, the changing balance of political forces and the dominance of managerialist ideology in social service provision, so that few advocates of traditional revolutionary politics remain among radical social workers. But current radical social work has refocused its sights upon the problems of socially oppressed groups *per se* (rather than displaying an exclusive preoccupation with working-class affiliation) and the democratisation of existing structures. In these areas, as discussed later, there is a more pronounced tendency to engage with the emotional and the structural together. Even if the Marxist historical materialist approach has too often isolated the material, the radical perspective in social work is significant for the importation of power and ideological oppression into the analysis of human behaviour and the solution of social problems.

To summarise, the Marxist materialist thesis of human purpose, with its robust appeal to collective social action, self-activity and commitment to total systemic change, held sway over radical social work practice in an epoch of relative affluence and the spread of revolutionary ideas. The Marxist model is largely instrumental in the challenge to social work's individual orientation. Also, it has led to a questioning of social work's 'professional' mode of operation. Its economistic dominance, however, has displaced the concern for non-material individual suffering, although the adaptation of Marxist insights to social work issues suggests new avenues to be explored. Finally, the waning of radical social work's credence alongside the deepening economic recession may have led to disillusionment with the notion of complete structural change, but not to a rejection of optimism. The most important tendency has been radical social work's swing away from the Marxist revolutionary class perspective towards the issues of discrimination, empowerment and dependency. The following section examines these issues in the context of race, gender, age and disability.

Anti-discriminatory Perspectives in Social Work

The marginalisation of various social groups, explained not by class membership nor by material deprivation nor by psychological disposition, is of increasing concern. Social and political pressures can exert substantial effects in isolating human groups. Below we scrutinise the impacts of the process of 'othering', and the tensions between psychological and social models. This entails discussing the issue of self-image creation among black people and the social work response; the significance of women's emotional lives under male oppression; and the role of contemporary social work initiatives in forging change through a synthesis of the collective and the therapeutic.

In Chapter 5 we considered the ways in which biological theories have not only underscored but succoured racism. And as we have seen, ways of viewing different ethnic groups take on particular political and historical significance relating to the exertion of power in society. White social work, not least through its casework approach, has received uncritically the notions of black and Asian ethnic communities as 'other' and of white supremacy. Imagined boundaries are delineated by whites, creating a sense of inner community, implicitly excluding blacks as 'other' (Miles, 1989, p. 87). This influences black clients' self-image in the face of white domination, prefiguring their supposed 'essential' nature. Black 'nature' is sited on a lower plane, professedly bearing unique inferior capacities and potentialities. Integral to this self-effacing process is the internalisation of white values by blacks, a colonisation of the psyche. Indeed, a belief in the superiority of Anglo-Saxon culture has prevented black persons' behaviour and expectations from being taken seriously (Gilroy, 1987). White social workers have failed to understand the *psychological* damage caused to black people (Small, 1989, p. 289). The self-definition of blacks has been distorted, part of a disjuncture between the conception of self by black people and white society. Indeed, as we saw in the last chapter, the tension and contradictions lead to a disproportionate number of black people with psychiatric disorders originating in 'the struggle of the world constructed by white society'. Small (1989) suggests that the significant number of 'fall-outs' of blacks from mainstream society is a direct result of the failure of individuals to live up to the ambivalent demands of the white social worker and society (Small, 1989, p. 289).

The pathologising perspective which treats the problems as individually inspired is misplaced. Racism is more than the individualised aberration adopted by the casework style of operating. The major issue is institutional and cultural racism. Too great a psychologistic emphasis upon 'prejudice' and attitude falls prey to the view that racism is nothing more than an intrinsic human nature. Dominelli (1989) argues that racism 'permeates social work from its ideological underpinnings through to its practice and demonstrates how conceptualising racism as the irrational beliefs of an evil few is misguided' (pp. 21–2). Racism exacerbates the practice of social control in social work. Furthermore, social work's stance as an apolitical activity tends to hinder positive action, whilst the attitude of professionalism acts as an obstacle to antiracist organisation at the grass roots (Harris, 1991).

Empowerment strategies to dispel the marginalisation of black ethnic groups entail confronting negative evaluations. But social work is weak on changing institutional frameworks and operations so as to empower oppressed groups, because of its historical emphasis on changing individuals rather than the institutional practices. Concentration on the individual is too limiting; any individualising response demands a collectively orchestrated challenge. The upsurge of the new racism in Britain (analysed in Chapter 5) suggests that an 'ethnic sensitivity' is insufficient, and that antiracism needs to acknowledge the politics of race, and to recognise the material and collective struggles of black people (Husband, 1991).

As Chapter 4 has already discussed in detail, humans are social beings rather than isolated individual atoms. Self-images are socially constructed. Collectivism focuses more on the way in which racial discrimination expresses group or institutional power. Thus the collectivist response acts as an antidote to individualised pathology. It stresses the importance of the power relationships involved in racial discrimination in social work; further, it demands a critique of the British modern state.

> For social work, it means a breaking down of professional barriers and theoretical divisions between social work and other areas of the state ... This is not something which professional social workers, and the institutions of social work training and provision have in the past found compatible with their location within the state. (Husband, 1991, p. 70)

What of the significance of feminist portayals of human nature in social work? Chapter 6 studied the various ways in which strains of feminism have challenged the male-dominated theories of human nature, drawing attention to the social construction of images. At the same time, other positions suggested a differentiation from the male for biological reasons. Certainly, the differences may be located in terms of the importance attached to the *emotions* so far as women are concerned. Sections in social work practice have begun seriously to explore the depths of the emotional life in women's nature. Feminist social work represents a challenge to the male-defined priorities in goal- and task-oriented social work, building upon radical feminist thought which emphasises the link between the internal oppression felt by women and their external circumstances. It also involves drawing the connections between gender and oppression in women's lives. Most importantly, it presents an optimistic perspective on change.

The development of organised psychotherapies and mutual support groups within the feminist movement reflects the collectivist potential of human beings. Instead of a demoralising passivity, *change* of circumstances becomes a feasibility (Dominelli and McLeod, 1989). Female collective organisation is better equipped to counteract male-dominated constructions of identity. In this sense, feminist psychotherapy may be regarded as more of a perspective than a set of specialist techniques. Its predominant feature is that the feminist therapist is able to identify closely with a woman's way of seeing the world (Taylor, 1990). Hence, the woman is less likely to be treated as 'other'. Male therapists have been inclined to interpret differences in women's emotional response as instances of individual pathology, ignoring the social and cultural factors acting on the inner psyche. But work by feminist therapists and women's therapy centres has aimed at a practical denial of the Freudian paradigm which has dominated psychosexual psychology (see Chapters 2 and 6).

However, the feminist alternative is not unproblematic. Women's therapy and consciousness-raising groups have remained essentially class bound, so that one is predominantly dealing with the emotional needs of middle-class women. Another mode of 'othering' appears. Furthermore, the central body of the feminist therapy literature fails to incorporate a black perspective. 'For black women, the quality of their emotional well-being is mediated by their experience of racism and their responses to it, whilst that of white women is not,' suggest Dominelli and McLeod (1989, pp. 86–7).

To summarise the issue of ethnic and gender discrimination in social work, racist ideology infuses social work practice: its individualising casework *modus operandi* serves to pathologise and 'other' black people's problems and to redefine the black client's reality. Professional perspectives simply exacerbate the unequal ethnic relationship. Given the sprinkling of black or Asian social workers, oppositional collective organisation or radical critique has been weak. In the case of females, the recent history of women's social movements, feminist theorising and the much larger numbers of females employed in social work has led to more consciously produced collective initiatives which also connect with the construction of a positive self-image and the emotional life. The pertinent factor here is the *collectivising* of a traditionally individualistic, clinical or existentially based therapy which works towards environmental transformation.

Human Nature and Dependency in Social Work

Dependency relationships, too, may lead to discriminatory treatment in caring, emanating from distinctly ideological ways of viewing vulnerable groups. Constructed images of what these groups are set the agenda for their particular treatment. The discussion below analyses the impacts of socially constructed images of age upon old people themselves; the role of psychologistic models which indicate an irreversible biological determinism; the socially constructed interpretations of mental handicap reflecting a mechanistic model of human capacities; the implications of behaviourist methods for the disempowerment of such groups; and the efficacy of a 'normalisation' strategy for people with mental handicap.

Our view of age reflects an underlying image or model of human nature. The phenomenon of ageism involves the notion of self and images of self; it is a mirror for *socially constructed* identities. Dependency disempowers old people, but the state of dependency itself is constructed out of unequal power relationships and dominant ideas concerning human development. Physiological and psychological models have served as the predominant modes of explanation for the process of ageing. Again, the scientific perspective has presented the picture of *natural* processes of ageing (a determined human nature) which bears upon the socially constructed attitudes of what an old person actually *is*. In this way adverse treatments of old people are ideologically justified; older persons become politically disenfranchised, denied participation rights (Phillipson, 1982).

A host of psychological explanations exists to account for the treatment of old people; their dependency is interpreted as infantile, an invitation to treat them as if they *were* children:

> Infantilising the elderly eventually yields its own predictions – old people may be induced to accept a 'child-like' role as the only legitimate way in our society of being physically dependent upon another person. (Phillipson, 1982)

Conceptualisations of old people's condition as naturally fixed and biological serve as a theoretical prop for discriminatory policies. Psychology even boasts theories of becoming older which include the idea of a clock of ageing, focusing on a genetically determined mechanism. Ageing as a process is also tied to the decline of IQ and to cognitive changes in adulthood and old age (Gross, 1990). The rigidity of these psychological 'human nature' models reinforces a routinised allocation of old people to their 'natural' social space.

Erikson's deterministic model of the 'Eight Ages of Man' (1980) charts a series of psychosocial stages extending the process beyond Freud's concern with childhood. Most significantly, he sees it as *human nature* to pass through a *genetically predetermined* sequence of stages. However, this model is effectively ageist in laying too much emphasis on the *chronological* age of a 60 year old (for example) reinforcing obstructive attitudes towards older people in the labour market and their low priority in the area of community care. This fails to take into account the subjective age (basically the life of the self, discussed in Chapter 4) and indeed the social age, which may open up many more human possibilities for an older person.

Dependency and its ideological construction extends to other groups too. Mental handicap (people with learning difficulties) is an area of particular interest which reveals the very basic approaches to defining what people are – or what their nature is shown to be. Historical accounts of mental handicap chart the dehumanisation of idiots, a view of human nature excluding or 'othering' them from the social pale. Ideas of degeneracy persisted into the current century, reflecting human fears fuelled by findings in eugenics. The repressive notion of determined intelligence (analysed in Chapter 5) was also evident in psychological perspectives on mental 'deviants'. Burt's definition of mental deficiency as 'an innate deficiency in innate intellectual capacity, or briefly, a defect of intelligence' (cited in Ryan and Thomas, 1987, p. 110) suggested an IQ pessimism which holds serious policy implications. Social welfare resources are less likely to go towards social groups labelled unproductive and without potential.

More recent psychological research has challenged some of the cruder theories from an earlier period. Contemporary empirical work has shown that all human beings are capable of at least some learning. But the arrival of these 'new' insights has been tardy. Psychologists have taken 50 years to discover much of what was already known earlier but was simply repressed: 'that mentally handicapped people can display all kinds of skills if the conditions for acquiring and using them are appropriate' (Ryan and Thomas, 1987, p. 123). IQ fatalism has nevertheless been displaced by an equally crude environmentalism of the Skinner behaviourist mode:

> The assumption of this approach, as applied to the mentally handicapped, is that anybody's behaviour can be 'modified' (i.e. changed) if the required behaviour is broken down into sufficiently discrete units and if the correct system of rewards is used at each stage of learning. (Ryan and Thomas, 1987, p. 125)

Whilst this behaviourism has been welcomed by many hospitals, considerable apprehension has been expressed about such a powerful method of controlling behaviour, especially its implementation with people who do not understand what they are being subjected to. 'No choice is given on participation in programmes, nor on what aspects of behaviour are to be altered, nor on the kinds of rewards used' (Ryan and Thomas, 1987, p. 127).

Although the 'exploiting potential' approach has become more acceptable, emphasis remains on changing the individual's behaviour normatively according to the idea of normalisation (Wolfensberger, 1972; Wolfensberger, 1980; Tyne, 1991), defined as 'the utilization of the means which are as culturally normative as possible, in order to establish and/or maintain personal behaviors and characteristics which are as culturally normative as possible' (Wolfensberger, 1972, p. 28). The normalisation principle views handicapped persons' needs as the same as those of able bodied people at root (other than that their specific medical or therapeutic needs require aid and assistance). The principle, attributing great importance to the total environment and especially how institutions increase the burden of being handicapped and devoted to reproducing everyday living as closely as possible, now represents the accepted philosophy for the non-hospitalisation advocates. Nevertheless, an overt emphasis on 'culturally normative behaviors' begs the whole question of possibilities; it reinforces the tyranny of the status quo. Conformity and moral authoritarianism remain unchallenged. Normalisation as a culture-specific concept means in the last analysis that it supports individualism, the dominant ideology of the epoch and the prevailing individualised care ideology (Dalley, 1992).

The condition of dependency, then, is not necessarily natural. In the case of old people and mentally handicapped persons, socially constructed images and the 'human nature' models on which they are based have actually increased the groups' levels of dependency, thereby reducing their autonomy (a basic human need as discussed in Chapter 8). Psychological models of ageing, displaying a distinct rigidity in their genetic chronology, deny not only the vital life of the inner being but also the effects of social stimulation on older people's activity. Fatalistic models of human intelligence and potential have condemned mentally handicapped people to the status of lesser human for much of the century. The application of behaviouristic learning theory recognises learning potential but still leaves unanswered ethical issues of disempowerment. The 'normalisation' idea of reproducing learned 'normal' behaviour is certainly more socially liberating than subjection to the medical model of treatment; on the other hand, it is still subject to behaviourism's uncritical view of the social or cultural norm.

Summary and Conclusions

Freudianism and its attendant model of human nature has exerted considerable impact on psychodynamic theory and psychotherapy in social work. For specialist social workers its early medical orientation lent an authenticity to their professional credentials. The perspective becomes limited, in a dynamic activity, at the point where the client recognises the need for change. Where lie the means for change? Is a rational awareness sufficient? Behaviourism's answers to these questions, entailing positive psychological manipulation of the individual's learned responses to the social environment, are uncomfortable to many caring professionals concerned with emotional autonomy.

The apparent similarities between the existentialist-based psychotherapies and Freudian techniques are misleading, by dint of their focus on the inner being. The Freudian model's biology of the unconscious drives and practitioners' penchant for scientific 'distance' from the client contradict existential therapy's interest in human autonomy and the more accessible realms of conscious subjectivity. The latter's human *commitment* contrasts with the clinical value-freedom of psychoanalysis and the environmental determinism of the behaviourist school.

None of the above schools of thought, however, has treated clients (and themselves) as social beings tackling the social problems collectively. As we have discussed, the Marxist model of human nature is the fundamental philosophy of radical social work approaches. Yet radical social work has made uneven progress during the past decade, itself marginalised by a highly individualistic, entrepreneurial and anticommunitarian social policy climate. Following the restructuring of contemporary neoMarxist and socialist thought, radical theory and practice in social work has redirected its central thrust away from labour movement action towards a systematic critique of ideological, socially structured oppression. Attention has moved to the marginalisation and disempowerment of 'othered' social groups such as racially oppressed minority ethnic communities, old people, women and mentally handicapped persons.

To conclude, the adoption in social work of Freudian, behaviourist, existential or Marxist models of human nature reflects the plurality of interests and professional tensions. Most evident is the weight accorded to models from psychology. Significantly, however, a resistance remains to the adoption and application of scientific, biologically based theories, whereas historically they have dominated among health professionals. What this chapter and the preceding one have attempted to demonstrate is the dynamic relationship between models of human nature and the caring professions' contending theories and practices.

Further Reading

General Surveys

Malcolm Payne, *Modern Social Work Theory* (Macmillan, 1991). Analysis includes behaviourist, existential, psychoanalytic and Marxist approaches.

David Howe, *An Introduction to Social Work Theory* (Wildwood House, 1987). Shows how different theories lead to different practices.

Social Work and Behaviourism

Brian Sheldon, *Behaviour Modification* (Tavistock, 1978).

Social Work and Existentialism
Rollo May, *The Art of Counselling* 2nd edn. (Souvenir Press).
  Existentialism applied.

Social Work, Psychology and Psychoanalysis
Donald Winnicott, *Human Nature* (Free Association Books, 1988).
  Applies human nature theory to child development.
Geoffrey Pearson et al. (ed.), *Social Work and the Legacy of Freud*
  (Macmillan, 1988). Essays on Freudianism as social theory and
  a feminist critique.

Social Work and Marxism
Mary Langan and Phil Lee (eds.), *Radical Social Work Today*
  (Unwin Hyman, 1989). A re-evaluation of the Marxist per-
  spective as applied to social work.
Peter Leonard, *Personality and Ideology: Towards a Materialist
  Understanding of the Individual* (Macmillan, 1984). Attempts to
  develop a Marxist theory of the individual through focus on the
  interplay between personality and collectivism.

Discrimination and Social Work
H. Brown and H. Smith (eds.), *Normalisation: A Reader for the
  Nineties* (Routledge, 1992).
Lena Dominelli, *Anti-Racist Social Work* (Macmillan, 1989).
Lena Dominelli and Eileen McLeod, *Feminist Social Work*
  (Macmillan, 1989).
Michael Oliver, *The Politics of Disablement* (Macmillan, 1990).
  Analyses the ideological and social constructions of disability.

10

Conclusions

Models and theories of human nature, as I have attempted to demonstrate, inform our theory and practice. What we assume to be natural in human action and the world of public affairs signals to others in so many ways our predisposition towards the issue under debate. To invoke the natural means to imply a consensus about a phenomenon that we consider does not require explanation at all. Thus such a perspective tends to rationalise the status quo. The intrinsic power of the 'human nature' concept lies in its ability to galvanise people into action or the contrary, to leave them transfixed or impotent. Depending on the model selected, the invocation of human nature may stimulate a spirit of optimism and hope, a confidence in our possibilities for controlling the future, or alternatively it may imbue a stance of fatalism or pessimism, a sense of impending circumstance, a rigidity. It suggests to us a rightness or a wrongness in our activities, thoughts, arguments and human relationships. The concept implies that regardless of how we may appear on the surface in our everyday lives, there is nevertheless something nestling deep in all of us which accounts for what we do and why we do it.

This book has shown that because the idea of a human nature is so basic a concept as to *define* our humanness, then it necessarily generates a significance for social theorising pervading a vast area of debate in the various disciplines. Because of its relevance, the very fabric of creative art and literature tries to say something about it. Philosophical discourse wrestles to offer a coherent perspective in the process of definition. Given the enormity of such a task, there is no way in which one small volume can hope to elucidate the full complexity of the concept and the detailed implications of the human nature debate; to accomplish this entails conceptualising and carefully weighing the material of our existence. This seems to me a pretentious goal, and equally unfeasible. All that I feel is possible is to show *how* our theorising is founded upon what we consciously or implicitly assume about human thought and action. Furthermore, I hope that I have demonstrated that uncritically holding to a set of unexamined assumptions leads often to unacceptable consequences. A theory or a policy will be wrong-footed if its underlying suppositions are shaky.

Certainly, the precept of a fixed 'human nature' is untenable, yet it is the one notion so commonly expressed by all kinds of people, including leading functionaries on public platforms. As the concept is intended to provide explanation, it serves the purpose of justifying a set course of action, a strategy, a train of events; it frequently falls into the category of aggression, conflict, violence, warfare, cruelty, an ostensible absence of altruism or the prevalence of self-interested economic acquisitiveness. Aggression and war are popularly attributed to some wild animal nature and biological instincts. But how can this theory constitute a valid explanation for the protracted, strategically planned declaration of war by national states, or for the *systematic* cruelty of the Jewish Holocaust (Chapter 5)? However, any belief that there is *one* categorical human nature, some final indisputable causal factor underlying these seemingly inhuman symptoms, clearly meets the problem of the very plurality of available models. The general range of such theories through history (Chapters 1 and 2) ought to convince us that the debate is open rather than closed, and that a theory which claims a fixity in human nature is simply one among a number, and is likely to mirror the world view of a specific time or place or social group. The great classical models of human nature – the rationalism of Plato, Aristotle and Descartes, the spirituality of Christianity or Hinduism, the mechanical atomism of Hobbes, the organicism of Darwin and Durkheim, the environmentalism of Rousseau and Owen, the communitarianism of Kropotkin and Marx (Chapters 1, 2 and 4) – represent a mosaic of basic assumptions concerning human beings which are not always reconcilable. Even within the confines of our present century, no clearcut consensus reigns; there is no *one* self-evident model of human nature. If anything, contending theories serve to emphasise the differences in perspective, usually by selecting a discrete aspect of a human being. Empirical psychology for instance focuses on external visible behaviour; the Freudian model illuminates the dynamic interplay of psyche, sexual instinct and aggression; sociobiology stresses the human gene; existentialism portrays the conscious self; Marxism prioritises human sociality. Notwithstanding, we should remind ourselves that all possess a built-in dynamic of change. We even discover *within* a discipline such as anthropology a fundamental rift between proponents of contending human nature models, the one that focuses upon a universal mind, the other that concerns itself wholly with the weft and weave of disparate institutionalised cultural practices: the one impressed symbolically on the mind through the production of language, the other implemented through the acts of social ritual. Nor does the feminist challenge to patriarchy (Chapter 6) posit a unidimensional set of assumptions about 'male' or female nature; once more, the foci range from the body to the psyche to the cultural and the social. Hence, where is the fixed human nature? Where is the monolithic instinct or gene?

Support for the view that there is *one* human nature, a final unequivocal cause underlying symptoms such as aggressiveness or greed, clearly flies in the face of the plurality of available models of human nature. The historical range of theories and models discussed in this book ought to warn us that the issue is far from closed, and that a theory which claims fixity in human nature is simply one among a number. The ascendancy of one particular model reflects the particular time or place or group power. But what should also be transparent is that the alternatives are not necessarily those of static or changeability. As I have attempted to show, most theories project change, but the type and manner of change is still open to debate. The anticipated trajectories of change may depend on whether we adopt a collectivist or an individualist model of human nature. But it may also depend on a preparedness to explore the dialectic between these two polarities, which leads me on to a related issue.

The debate is frequently posed as between academic disciplines as an either/or debate. For example, do we accept that our biology determines all that we can make of ourselves binding us to our essentialism? Or, on the other hand, are we simply *tabula rasa* to be written upon with the real content of our lives? The behaviourist tenor leaves us with a strong sense of the manipulability of human beings, as does the contemporary ascendancy of cultural relativism and the seeming power of cultural imagery regarding the constructed self which suggests that the human body and its evolutionary journey are no longer significant – a crucial error. Continued destruction of the earth's ecological balance points up the futility of anthropomorphic models of human nature which place all emphasis on rationality and human distinctiveness. One needs a non-reductionist naturalism embodying the human–animal continuum to offset the socially dangerous models of plasticity at large not only in psychology but also in sociology. Ted Benton's *Natural Relations* (1993) adopts this position in relation to ecology, animal rights and social justice. By the same token, the biological contributions are reductionist and profoundly political. Unintentionally or not, they have reinforced a scientific determinism; the conflation of animal instinct biology and human social behaviour is a crude evasion of the significance of human consciousness. Sociobology's geneticism, despite the claims to incorporate cultural change, renders itself incapable of recognising a non-selfish altruism. Human nature cannot exclude the abilities of humans to contemplate facets of existence such as their own image or the template of social relationships. It is pointless to separate biology and culture, or nature and nurture, since the one implies the other. The nature of human existence is such that neither is autonomous. Posed in these terms, the debate becomes a non-debate or has to be reformulated.

At the same time, we must be wary of models or theories that on the surface appear to accept the inseparability but then make a *de facto* separation. Educational psychology's insistence on the presence of a *general* intelligence (the residual G-factor) as distinguishable from culturally constructed factors reflects just such a distinction. Yet psychologists argue that this 'general' factor is found in unequal measure as between different people and indeed different social groups, in the light of the categorising, measurement and grading consequent upon the dichotomy. This interpretation of innateness is a far cry from Chomsky's recognition of universal innate abilities that enable each of us to speak a language (Chapter 3). Hence, the kernel of the debate is intensely ideological; in the education sector, the 'difference' in children's general intelligence comes to justify differential treatment in the progression of schooling. Furthermore, I would argue that the ideological, in such cases, resides within these very categorising processes. The genetic pedigree of IQ is a sobering one (Chapter 5). Groups of human beings perceived as innately inferior receive inferior treatment. The Jewish Holocaust of course represents the ultimate in extending the logic of this argument (Chapter 5). But it is also a constituent generally of racism, sexism, nationalism and different forms of 'othering'. Cultural and social constructions, too, entail processes of inclusion and exclusion which lead to group 'othering'; the labelling of the social categories is then rationalised in naturalistic terms (effectively by adoption of essentialist models of human nature).

This book has concentrated on making connections between the human nature debate and social theories, because of the importance of assumptions behind theories. All of the major social theorists I have referred to earlier, for example Marx, Freud, Skinner, de Beauvoir, Sartre, Arendt, Foucault and Rogers, are engaged in addressing the precise issue of our human nature. The interface between social theory and human nature theory is a translucent one. Take the instance of psychology. As the century's archetypal social science discipline, it cultivates an explicit *scientific* methodology which assumes that humans can be studied objectively, observed and understood from a clinical distance. However, are we able to understand humans better by analysing their external behaviour, their bodily movements and their outward responses? We may well reply in the negative. But the answer cannot be divorced from the purpose to which the knowledge is being put. Insights gained may facilitiate control and a conscious manipulation of power over others. Another procedural point is also of relevance. Psychology's intrinsic focus upon the *individual* is an isolating process, yet humans are social animals. Findings in psychology treat the human as atomistic, yet collective processes play a major role in creating the human context. Positivistic psychology has performed a useful service for modern corporate managements in motivating their workforce, in organisational change strategies and in marketing of products. An empirical model of the atomistic respondent neatly fits a consumerist culture and a market-driven society. Even the human need to reflect upon one's self-development is soon subjected to market direction and consumer cultivation through the 'scientific' manipulation of human desires and wants. *Measurement* of expressed wants and desires justifies the measured *creation* of wants and desires, which come to be mistaken for human needs. Hence the centrality of empirical measurement under the banner of scientific procedure.

Some of the fiercest attacks on Freudianism on the grounds of its unscientific method have come from *within* the discipline of psychology, whilst some of the most fruitful efforts to develop Freudian insights have emanated from feminists whose whole frame of argument rejects the scientific paradigm (Chapter 6).

Social constructionist theories of human nature also have their problems, particularly the tendency to deny the significance of self and self-determination. Much of the debate in modern sociology has expressed this tension between the unconscious movement of structures, and the rationality of human agency. The Foucauldian dismissal of any self-conscious production of human existence is scarcely less deterministic in the final reckoning than scientific determinism.

The applicability of the human nature debate is clearly not confined to the realms of theory. As this book has shown, policy and applied social professional fields may be examined in a similar way. Unless we know what is being assumed about human beings, it is difficult critically to evaluate contending approaches in care or alternative policy strategies. Here is a somewhat different proposition from the cynical popular dismissal of human behaviour as 'just human nature'. Bringing a critical frame of mind to the analysis of practice entails consideration of the consequences of any action and of future possibilities. The caring professions of health (Chapter 8) and social work (Chapter 9) supply interesting cases in point, given their declared aims of 'caring', a significant facet of human relationships. When we then enquire as to *how* these professions actually care, we participate in the human nature debate by examining precisely how as professionals we treat our fellow humans. Do we categorise them as patients or clients in a clinical manner, or do we treat them equally in caring for others' health and welfare? *Because* they may require special care and attention, do we treat them as 'other' to be approached differently from the able bodied? Because a person may be old in years, do we automatically treat her or him as naturally, biologically dependent? And when people are being assessed for mental illness, do we 'other' those from other cultural backgrounds that we do not understand by deeming their actions 'unnatural' in accordance with narrow ethnocentric models of normal behaviour? Adoption in the health professions of the medical model implies an exclusivist concentration on sickness as sick 'body'. A closer inspection of basic human needs reveals that human well-being is both physical and mental (Chapter 7) and that the lack of autonomy and power may affect our whole bodily disposition and total health. In the arena of social policy, the fulfilment of needs is highly contentious and inextricably influenced by how these needs are conceptualised in the first place. So much of social policy, by definition formulated in a public decision-making context which usually excludes females, is based upon precepts of need which assume a male nature and thus marginalises women. Human needs are read as male needs (Chapter 6), with iniquitous social and political consequences. Models of human nature that 'other' the female are made explicit in social policy. The model of 'woman' as both reproducer and family carer is promoted as natural. Such an invocation of human nature is transparently ideological, although the consequences for women and especially working-class women are heavily economic; the fact that 'caring' as a concept is still effortlessly associated with 'female' indicates the continued strength of the idea that a female nature does exist. Women's movements have challenged these assumptions, but continue to meet powerful corporate and state resistance; for women to break the model in practice requires policy change imperatives in spheres such as communal care services. This in itself provides a cogent example of the longevity of intellectual traditions and patriarchal practices; the old ideas continue to be politically manipulated by those in power even when their plausibility is seriously brought into question.

There is sufficient empirical historical evidence to quash what are clearly myths about natural eternal female desires and their inability to perform what was considered to be 'men's work'. Traditional theories about women's 'natural' lack of viable skills in the worlds of private business, industry and public affairs have been overturned by the concrete practices of women in precisely these areas. Nevertheless, social *institutional* barriers such as the lack of crèche facilities and male-dominated promotion and appointment boards prevent women from expanding their gains; at the same time, male decision makers justify their policies by recourse to 'naturalistic' models. Along similar lines, white imperialist biological myths of black people as savage, sexual and generally racially inferior were dispelled during an era when black African nations achieved independence and black Afro-Americans began to enter a number of professional occupations. Despite these changes, white governments have discovered new ways to 'other' blacks, this time in the language of *cultural difference* symbolically translated into natural differences.

Within the professional health field the historical dominance of the biologically oriented medical model of the patient is because of general practitioners and consultants' professional power through the NHS. Contemporary restructuring of medical services on a commercial and competitive basis, however, has rendered their authority more ambivalent. The promotion of alternative models is also subject to such contingent developments. Any substantial challenges to the medical model have stemmed either from outside the formal health service, among private-sector holistic medicine practitioners unconstrained by the direct authority of medical consultants, or from organised non-medical health professionals and nurses intent on demonstrating their professional autonomy, but additionally pressurised to adopt a broader social approach towards clients in the community under the auspices of government community care legislation.

Whichever perspective is promoted as human nature, it cannot be disengaged from its historical context. The nature of 'human nature' is historical; the expression of social concern in defining human nature, as well as the terms of the debate itself, is historically contingent. During times of great flux the issue of human nature reappears on the social agenda. To cite sociologists Gerth and Mills (1954, p. xvii): 'Problems of the nature of human nature are raised most urgently when the life-routines of a society are disturbed.' At the present *fin-de-siècle*, novel formulations of the human nature debate are espoused in the eclectic language of postmodernism. Terms such as 'autonomy of self' and 'individual choice' converge with the discourse of market competition, entrepreneurialism and anticollectivist social strategies.

Yet we should not assume that the undisputed sea change constitutes a permanent, fatalistic transfiguration in communitarian world views, no matter how breathtaking its scope. A careful scrutiny of the philosophical contours of the Thatcherite epoch in Britain (Chapter 7) unearths a notable contradiction. Thatcherism's discourse (its ideological language) has projected a *naturally* atomistic, self-searching, acquisitive, entrepreneurial human being. Nevertheless, these behavioural attributes have been *consciously* engendered by a systematic programme to explicitly change people's behaviour, a major exercise in social engineering implemented by a cynical exertion of political and corporate economic power against a background of recession and fear. People are more easily thrown against each other in conditions of unemployment or other hardships.

The rapid creation in eastern Europe of the economically motivated competitive human is now one of western capitalism's priorities.

New ways of defining our nature certainly appear at particular historical moments (Chapter 1). Material advance can facilitiate the extension and restructuring of human *possibilities*. But a key point that needs to be made is that such a pespective does *not* imply that previous versions of human nature cease to hold currency and dissolve forever. A theory may briefly take cover and then re-emerge in more appropriate conditions, adopted by contending parties depending on social conditions. New right ideas and laissez-faire ideology, for example, reinforce Hobbes's seventeenth-century mechanical model of human nature.

In conclusion, changing ideas about our human nature are radicalising in their social impact, since human beings are not only products of their world, they also make it. To grasp this means to explore first of all the relationship of human nature theories to their specific intellectual traditions; secondly, the crucial moments of historical transformation; thirdly, the economic, cultural and social conditions; and finally their political and professional expression. Clearly, the human nature debate is no respecter of narrow academic specialisms. We cannot authentically stand outside of the debate, disengaged by the seemingly 'value-free' act of evaluation. Theories and models of human nature tell us what we are, and thus what we might become. Our own actions, however, are part and parcel of the process, so that our *commitments* always influence the future. Any evacuation of commitment is an evacuation of human purpose and a surrender to impersonal forces. 'Common sense' is the antithesis of critical values. The renewal of fascism, racism and anti-semitism across the whole of Europe based on spurious concepts of human nature should be positively countered rather than theorised into obscurity. Yet postmodernism's puerile obsession with fashion is blind to the realities of economic power and the power of dangerous and irrational ideas. Higher education is becoming less instead of more critical of commonly held assumptions. The state is now intent to downgrade and punish subjects that treat critical education as a greater human need than servile training. It does so at its peril.

Bibliography

Abbott, P. and Wallace, C. (1990) 'Social Work and Nursing: A History' in P. Abbott and C. Wallace (eds.) *The Sociology of the Caring Professions* (Basingstoke, Hants: Falmer Press), pp. 10–28.

Abbott, P. and Wallace, C. (1992) *The Family and the New Right* (London: Pluto Press).

Aboulafia, M. (1986) *The Mediating Self: Mead, Sartre and Self-Determination* (New Haven; London: Yale University Press).

Adorno, T.W., Frenkel-Brunswik, E., Levinson, D.F. and Sanford, R.N. (1950) *The Authoritarian Personality* (NY: Harper and Bros).

Aggleton, P. (1987) *Deviance* (London, Tavistock).

Aggleton, P. (1990) *Health* (London: Routledge).

Aitchison, J. (1976) *The Articulate Mammal: An Introduction to Psycholinguistics* (London: Hutchinson).

Alper, J., Beckwith, J. and Miller, L.G. (1978) 'Sociobiology is a Political Issue' in A. Caplan (ed.) *The Sociobiology Debate* (NY: Harper and Row), pp. 476–88.

Anderson, J. (1991) *Social Science and Society*, Block 7 Reader, D103 (Milton Keynes: Open University Press).

Ardener, E. (1975) 'Belief and the Problem of Women' and 'The Problem Revisited' in S. Ardener (ed.) *Perceiving Women* (London: Malaby), pp. 1–18, pp. 19–28.

Ardrey, R. (1966) *The Territorial Imperative* (NY: Atheneum; London: Collins, 1967).

Arendt, H. (1963) *Eichmann in Jerusalem* (Harmondsworth: Penguin).

Aries, P. (1965) *Centuries of Childhood: A Social History of Family Life* (NY: Random House; Harmondsworth: Penguin, 1979).

Armstrong, D. (1987) 'Bodies of Knowledge: Foucault and the Problem of the Human Anatomy' in G. Scambler (ed.) *Sociological Theory and Medical Sociology* (London: Tavistock), pp. 59–76.

Aron, R. (1967) *The Industrial Society* (London: Weidenfeld and Nicolson).

Asylum (1993) 'Report on Conference on European Philosophy and Psychiatry', Sheffield University, 18–20 September 1992, winter, vol. 7, no. 1.

Badcock, C.R. (1975) *Levi-Strauss: Structuralism and Sociological Theory* (London: Hutchinson).

Bailey, J. (1980) *Ideas and Intervention* (London: RKP).

Bailey, J. (1988) *Pessimism* (London: RKP).

Baldwin, S. and Twigg, J. (1991) 'Women and Community Care – Reflections on a Debate' in M. Maclean and D. Groves (eds.) *Women's Issues in Social Policy* (London: Routledge), pp. 117–35.

Bandura, A. (1977) *Social Learning Theory* (NJ: Prentice-Hall).

Barker, M. (1981) *The New Racism: Conservatives and the Ideology of the Tribe* (London: Junction Books).

Barrett, W. (1962) *Irrational Man* (NY: Doubleday).

Bauman, Z. (1989) *Modernity and the Holocaust* (Cambridge: Polity Press).

Baumann, B. (1969) 'George H. Mead and Luigi Pirandello: Some Parallels between the Theoretical and Artistic Presentation of the Social Role Concept' in P. Berger (ed.) *Marxism and Sociology: Views From Eastern Europe* (NY: Appleton Century-Crofts) pp. 202–46.

Beck, U. (1992) *Risk Society: Towards a New Modernity* (London: Sage).

Becker, H.S. (1963) *Outsiders: Studies in the Sociology of Deviance* (NY: Free Press).

Bell, D. (1962) *The End of Ideology* (NY: Free Press).

Benedict, R. (1935) *Patterns of Culture* (London: Routledge, Kegan and Paul).

Benoist, J-M. (1973) 'Classicism Revisited: Human Nature and Structure in Levi-Strauss and Chomsky' in J. Benthall (ed.) *The Limits of Human Nature* (London: Allen Lane Press), pp. 20–48.

Benthall, J. (ed.) (1973) *The Limits of Human Nature* (London: Allen Lane Press).

Benton, T. (1991) 'Biology and Social Science: Why the Return of the Repressed Should be Given a (Cautious) Welcome', *Sociology*, vol. 25, no. 1, pp. 1–29.

Benton, T. (1993) *Natural Relations: Ecology, Animal Rights and Social Justice* (London: Verso).

Berger, P. (ed.) (1969) *Marxism and Sociology: Views From Eastern Europe* (NY: Appleton Century-Crofts).

Berger, P. and Luckman, T. (1967) *The Social Construction of Reality* (NY: Anchor).

Berne, E. (1961) *Transactional Analysis in Psychotherapy* (NY: Grove Press).

Berne, E. (1964) *Games People Play* (NY: Grove Press).

Berne, E. (1974) *What Do You Say After You Say Hello?* (London: André Deutsch).

Berry, C.J. (1983) 'Conservatism and Human Nature' in I. Forbes and S. Smith (eds.) *Politics and Human Nature* (London: Francis Pinter), pp. 53–67.

Berry, C.J. (1986) *Human Nature* (London: Macmillan).

Bettelheim, B. (1986) *Surviving the Holocaust* (London: Fontana).

Bettelheim, B. and Janowitz, M. (1975) *Social Change and Prejudice* (New York: Free Press).

Beveridge, W. (1942) *Report of the Committee on Social Insurance and Allied Services: Beveridge Committee* (London: HMSO).

Biddiss, M. (1977) *The Age of the Masses* (Harmondsworth: Penguin).

Billig, M. (1979) *Psychology, Racism and Fascism* (Birmingham: Searchlight, cited in Seidel, 1986, p. 47).

Black, P. (1991) 'A Force for the Future: the Changing Role of the District Nurse', *Professional Nurse*, October, pp. 54–8.

Black, N., Boswell, D., Gray, A., Murphy, S. and Popay, J. (eds.) (1984) *Health and Disease: A Reader* (Milton Keynes: Open University Press).

Blackburn, R. (1969) *Student Power* (Harmondsworth: Penguin).

Blackwell, T. and Seabrook, J. (1993) *The Revolt Against Change: Conserving Radicalism* (London: Vintage).

Bottomore, T., Harris, L., Kiernan, V.G. and Miliband, R. (eds.) (1983) *A Dictionary of Marxist Thought* (Oxford: Blackwell).

Brandon, D. (1976) *Zen in the Art of Helping* (London: RKP).

Brown, D.E. (1991) *Human Universals* (Philadelphia: Temple University Press).

Brown, G.W. and Harris, T. (1978) *Social Origins of Depression: A Study of Psychiatric Disorder in Women* (London: Tavistock).

Brownmiller, S. (1975) *Against Our Will: Men, Women and Rape* (NY: Bantam).

Bruner, J. (1983) *Child's Talk: Learning to Use Language* (Oxford: Oxford University Press).

Bukharin, M. (1926) *The Theory of Historical Materialism: A Popular Manual of Marxist Sociology* (Ann Arbor, 1969).

Burleigh, M. and Wipperman, W. (1991) *The Racial State: Germany 1933–1945* (Cambridge: Cambridge University Press).

Callinicos, A. (1983) *The Revolutionary Ideas of Marx* (London: Bookmarks).

Calnan, M. (1987) *Health and Illness: The Lay Perspective* (London: Tavistock).

Campbell, T. (1981) *Seven Theories of Human Society* (Oxford: Oxford University Press).

Caplan, P. (ed.) (1987) *The Cultural Construction of Sexuality* (London: Tavistock).

Caplan, A.L. (ed.) (1978) *The Sociobiology Debate* (NY: Harper and Row).

Carrithers, M. (1992) *Why Humans Have Culture* (Oxford: Oxford University Press).

Caulfield, M.D. (1985) 'Sexuality in Human Evolution: What is Natural in Sex?' *Feminist Studies*, 11, 2, summer, pp. 343–64.

CCETSW (1976) *Values in Social Work: A Discussion Paper* (London: CCETSW).

Charles, N. and Kerr, M. (1986) 'Issues of Responsibility and Control in the Feeding of Families' in S. Rodmell and A. Watt (eds.) *The Politics of Health Education: Raising The Issues* (London: RKP), pp. 57–75.

Charny, I.W. et al. (1982) *How Can We Commit the Unthinkable? Genocide: The Human Cancer* (Boulder, Colorado: Westview Press).

Chomsky, N. (1968a) *Language and Mind*, selection in L. Stevenson (ed.) (1981) *The Study of Human Nature: Readings* (NY: Oxford University Press).

Chomsky, N. (1968b) *For Reasons of State* (London: Fontana).

Chomsky, N. (1974) 'Noam Chomsky and Michel Foucault: Human Nature: Justice Versus Power' in F. Elders (ed.) *Reflexive Water* (London: Souvenir Press), pp. 133–97.

Clare, A. (1980) *Psychiatry in Dissent: Controversial Issues in Thought and Practice* 2nd edn. (London; NY: Routledge).

Clark, C.L. and Asquith, S. (1985) *Social Work and Social Philosophy: A Guide for Practice* (London: RKP).

Cleaver, E. (1968) *Soul on Ice: Selected Essays* (London: Jonathan Cape).

Cochrane, R. (1977) 'Mental Illness in Immigrants in England and Wales: an Analysis of Mental Hospital Admissions 1971' *Social Psychiatry* , vol. 12, no.1, pp. 25–35.

Cohen, A.P. (1992) 'The Personal Right to Identity: A Polemic on the Self in the Enterprise Culture' in P. Heelas and P. Morris (eds.) *The Values of the Enterprise Culture: The Moral Debate* (London; NY: Routledge).

Cohn-Sherbok, D. (1992) *The Crucified Jew* (London: Harper Collins).

Coote, A. (1993) 'Social Needs Must' *Social Work Today*, 21 January, pp. 21–2.

Cope, R. (1989) 'The Compulsory Detention of Afro-Caribbeans Under the Mental Health Act' *New Community*, vol. 15, no. 3, pp. 343–56.

Craib, I. (1976) *Existentialism and Sociology: A Study of Jean-Paul Sartre* (Cambridge: Cambridge University Press).

Craib, I. (1989) *Psychoanalysis and Social Theory: The Limits of Sociology* (Hemel Hempstead: Harvester Wheatsheaf).

Craib, I. (1992) *Modern Social Theory: From Parsons to Habermas* 2nd edn. (Hemel Hempstead: Harvester Wheatsheaf).

Cuff, E.C., Sharrock, W.W. and Francis, D.W. (1990) *Perspectives in Sociology* 3rd edn. (London: Unwin Hyman).

Curtis, M. (ed.) (1986) *Antisemitism in the Contemporary World* (Boulder, Colorado: Westview Press).

Dalley, G. (1988) *Ideologies in Caring: Rethinking Community and Collectivism* (London: Macmillan).

Dalley, G. (1992) 'Social Welfare Ideologies and Normalisation: Links and conflicts' in H. Brown and H. Smith (eds.) *Normalisation: A Reader for the Nineties* (London: Routledge), pp. 100–11.

Daly, M. (1978) *Gyn/Ecology: The Metaethics of Radical Feminism* (Boston: Beacon Press).

Darwin, C. (1859) *The Origin of Species* ed. J. Burrow (Harmondsworth: Penguin, 1968).

Dawkins, R. (1976) *The Selfish Gene* (Oxford: Oxford University Press, 2nd ed. 1989).

De Beauvoir, S. (1949) *The Second Sex* (Harmondsworth: Penguin, 1972).

De George, R. and F. (eds.) (1972) *The Structuralists From Marx to Levi-Strauss* (NY: Anchor Doubleday).

Descartes, R. (1642) *Meditations On First Philosophy* trans. E. Anscombe and P.T. Geach (eds.) *Descartes: Philosophical Writings* (Milton Keynes: Open University Press, 1970).

Dews, P. (1989) 'The Return of the Subject in Late Foucault' *Radical Philosophy*, 51, spring, pp. 37–41.

Dickens, P. (1992) *Society and Nature: Towards a Green Social Theory* (Hemel Hempstead, Herts: Harvester Wheatsheaf).

Dominelli, L. (1989) *Anti-racist Social Work* (London: Macmillan).

Dominelli, L. and McLeod, E. (1989) *Feminist Social Work* (London: Macmillan).

Donald, M. (1991) *Origins of the Modern Mind: Three Stages in the Evolution of Culture and Cognition* (Cambridge, Mass; London: Harvard University Press).

Doyal, L. and Gough, I. (1991) *A Theory of Human Need* (London: Macmillan).

Doyal, L. with Pennell, I. (1979) *The Political Economy of Health* (London: Pluto Press).

Dubos, R. (1984) 'The Mirage of Health' in N. Black et al. (eds.) *Health and Disease: A Reader* (Milton Keynes: Open University Press).

Duncan, G. (1983) 'Human Nature and Radical Democratic Theory' in G. Duncan (ed.) *Democratic Theory and Practice* (Cambridge: Cambridge University Press).

Duncan, G. (ed.) (1983) *Democratic Theory and Practice* (Cambridge: Cambridge University Press).

Durkheim, E. (1933; 1893) *The Division of Labour in Society* (NY: Macmillan).

Durkheim, E. (1951; 1897) *Suicide: A Study in Sociology* (Glencoe: The Free Press; London: RKP, 1952).

Durkheim, E. (1915; 1912) *The Elementary Forms of Religious Life: A Study in Religious Sociology* (London: Allen and Unwin; NY: Macmillan).

Durkheim, E. (1964; 1914) 'The Dualism of Human Nature and its Social Conditions' in K.H. Wolff (ed.) *Emile Durkheim: Essays in Sociology and Philosophy* (NY: Harper and Row).

Dworkin, A. (1974) *Woman Hating* (NY: E.P. Dutton).

Eagleton, T. (1991) *Ideology: An Introduction* (London: Verso).

Easton, L.D. and Guddat, K.H. (1967) *Writings of the Young Marx: Philosophy and Society* (NY: Doubleday Anchor).

Edgell, S. and Duke, V. (1991) *A Measure of Thatcherism* (London: Harper Collins).

Edholm, F. (1981) ' The Unnatural Family' in M. Loney et al. (eds.) (1991) *The State or the Market: Politics and Welfare in Contemporary Britain* 2nd edn. (London: Sage), pp. 141–52.

Eisenstein, H. (1984) *Contemporary Feminist Thought* (London: Unwin).

Elders, F. (ed.) (1974) *Reflexive Water: The Basic Concerns of Mankind* (London: Souvenir Press).

Elshtain, J.B. (1993) *Public Man: Private Woman: Women in Social and Political Thought* 2nd edn. (Princeton, NJ: Princeton University Press).

Engels, F. (1972) *The Origin of the Family, Private Property and the State* (New York: International Publishers).

Erikson, E.H. (1980) *Identity and the Life Cycle* (NY: Norton).

Fahey, W. (1988) 'Models of Health and Ill-Health' in *Midwife, Health Visitor and Community Nurse,* January/February, pp. 33–5.

Fanon, F. (1967) *Black Skins, White Masks* (New York: Grove Press).

Fanon, F. (1970) *A Dying Colonialism* (NY: Grove Press; Harmondsworth: Penguin).

Fay, B. (1975) *Social Theory and Political Practice* (London: Allen and Unwin).

Fekete, J. (1977) *The Critical Twilight: Explorations in the Ideology of Anglo-American Literary Theory from Eliot to McLuhan* (London, Boston: RKP).

Fernando, S. (1991) *Mental Health, Race and Culture* (London: Macmillan).

Feuerbach, L. (1957) *Essence of Christianity* (NY: N. Evans).

Firestone, S. (1972) *The Dialectic of Sex* (London: Paladin).

Flory, W.S. (1986) 'The Psychology of Antisemitism: Conscience Proof Rationalization and the Deferring of Moral Choice' in

M. Curtis (ed.) *Antisemitism in the Contemporary World* (Boulder: Westview Press), pp. 238–50.

Ford, G. (ed.) (1992) *Fascist Europe: The Rise of Racism and Xenophobia* (London: Pluto Press).

Foucault, M. (1965) *Madness and Civilisation: a History of Insanity in the Age of Reason* (NY: Mentor Books).

Foucault, M. (1970) *The Order of Things: An Archaeology of the Human Sciences* (NY: Random House).

Foucault, M. (1973) *The Birth of the Clinic: An Archaeology of Medical Perception* (NY: Vintage Books).

Foucault, M. (1977) *Discipline and Punish:The Birth of the Prison* (NY: Pantheon; Harmondsworth: Penguin).

Foucault, M. and Noam Chomsky (1974) 'Human Nature: Justice Versus Power' in F. Elders (ed.) *Reflexive Water* (London: Souvenir Press), pp. 137–97.

Foucault, M. (1982) 'The Subject and Power' in H. Dreyfus and P. Rabinow (eds.) *Michel Foucault: Beyond Structuralism and Hermeneutics* (Chicago: University of Chicago Press).

Foucault, M. (1986) 'Interview: What is Enlightenment?' in P. Rabinow (ed.) *The Foucault Reader* (Harmondsworth: Penguin).

Frankl, V. (1963) *Man's Search For Meaning: An Introduction to Logotherapy* (NY: Washington Square Press).

Frankl, V. (1959) *Psychotherapy and Existentialism* (Harmondsworth: Penguin).

Freud, S. (1905) *Three Essays on the Theory of Sexuality*, J. Strachey (ed.) (London: Hogarth Press, 1955).

Freud, S. (1920) *Beyond The Pleasure Principle* (London: Hogarth Press).

Freud, S. (1923) *The Ego and the Id* (London: Hogarth Press).

Freud, S. (1930) *Civilisation and its Discontents* (London: Hogarth Press).

Friedan, B. (1963) *The Feminine Mystique* (NY: Norton; Harmondsworth: Penguin, 1965).

Friedman, M. (1962) *Capitalism and Freedom* (Chicago: University of Chicago Press).

Friedman, M. and Friedman, R. (1980) *Free to Choose* (Harmondsworth: Penguin).

Fromm, E. (1941) *Escape From Freedom* (NY: Holt, Rinehart and Winston).

Fromm, E. (1955) *The Sane Society* (NY: Holt, Rinehart and Winston; London: Routledge, 1970).

Fromm, E. (1957) *The Art of Loving* (London: Allen and Unwin).

Fromm, E. (1961) *Marx's Concept of Man* (NY: Ungar).

Fromm, E. and Xirau, R. (eds) (1968) *The Nature of Man* (NY: Macmillan).

Fromm, E. (1977) *The Anatomy of Human Destructiveness* (Harmondsworth: Penguin).

Frosh, S. (1987) *The Politics of Psycho-analysis : An Introduction to Freudian and Post-Freudian Theory* (London: Macmillan).

Geertz, C. (1965) 'The Impact of the Concept of Culture on the Concept of Man' in J.R. Platt (ed.) *New Views of the Nature of Man* (Chicago, London: University of Chicago Press); reprinted as Chapter 2 of Geertz, *The Interpretation of Cultures* (NY: Basic Books, 1973; London: Fontana Press, 1993).

Geertz, C. (1972) *The Interpretation of Cultures* (NY: Basic Books).

Gentner, D. and Stevens, A.L. (eds.) (1983) *Mental Models* (Lawrence Erlbaum Associates).

Geoghegan, V. (1987) *Utopianism and Marxism* (London; NY: Methuen).

George, V. and Wilding, P. (1985) *Ideology and Social Welfare* 2nd edn. (London: RKP).

Geras, N. (1983) *Marx and Human Nature: Refutation of a Legend* (London: Verso Press).

Gerth, H. and Mills, C.W. (1954) *Character and Social Structure* (London: RKP).

Giddens, A. (ed.) (1972) *Emile Durkheim: Selected Writings* (Cambridge: Cambridge University Press).

Giddens, A. (1991) *Modernity and Self-Identity: Self and Society in the Late Modern Age* (Cambridge: Polity Press).

Giddens, A. (1993) *Sociology* 2nd edn. (Oxford: Polity Press).

Giddens, A. (1990) *The Consequences of Modernity* (Cambridge: Polity Press).

Giddens, A. (1992) *The Transformation of Intimacy: Sexuality, Love and Eroticism in Modern Societies* (Cambridge: Polity Press).

Gillison, G. (1980) 'Images of Nature in Gimi Thought' in C. MacCormack and M. Strathern (eds.) *Nature, Culture and Gender* (Cambridge and New York: Cambridge University Press).

Gilman, S. (1991) *The Jew's Body* (NY; London: Routledge).

Gilroy, P. (1987) *There Aint No Black in the Union Jack* (London: Hutchinson).

Girard, R. (1972) *Violence and the Sacred* (London: Athlone Press).

Glennester, H. and Midgley, J. (eds.) (1991) *The Radical Right and the Welfare State: An International Assessment* (Hemel Hempstead: Harvester Wheatsheaf).

Glover, J. (1988) *I: The Philosophy and Psychology of Personal Identity* (Harmondsworth: Penguin).

Glucksmann, M. (1974) *Structural Analysis in Contemporary Thought* (London: RKP).

Goff, T.W. (1980) *Marx and Mead: Contributions to a Sociology of Knowledge* (London: RKP).

Goffman, E. (1958) *The Presentation of the Self in Everyday Life* (Harmondsworth: Penguin).

Goffman, E. (1961) *Asylums: Essays on the Social Situation of Mental Patients and Other Inmates* (NY: Anchor Doubleday).

Goffman, E. (1963) *Stigma* (NJ: Prentice-Hall; Harmondsworth: Penguin, 1968).

Goldberg, D.T. (1993) *Racist Culture: Philosophy and the Politics of Meaning* (Oxford: Blackwell).

Goldberg, S. (1977) *The Inevitability of Patriarchy* (London: Temple Smith).

Goldman, L. (1969) *The Human Sciences and Philosophy* (London: Jonathan Cape).

Goldstein, E.G. (1984) *Ego Psychology and Social Work Practice* (NY: Free Press).

Goodin, R.E. (1985) 'Self-Reliance versus the Welfare State' *Journal of Social Policy*, January, vol. 14, no. 1, pp. 25–48.

Goody, E. (1991) 'The Learning of Prosocial Behaviour in Small-scale Egalitarian Societies: An Anthropological View' in (eds.) R.A. Hinde and J. Groebel *Cooperation and Prosocial Behaviour* (Cambridge: Cambridge University Press).

Gordon, P. and Klug, F. (1986) *New Right: New Racism* (Birmingham: Searchlight Publications).

Gould, S.J. (1991) *Wonderful Life* (Harmondsworth: Penguin).

Griffin, S. (1980) *Woman and Nature: The Roaring Inside Her* (NY: Harper Colophon).

Grimshaw, J. (1983) 'Review of Carol McMillan, Women, Reason and Nature' *Radical Philosophy*, 34, summer, pp. 33–4.

Grimshaw, J. (1986) *Feminist Philosophy* (Brighton: Harvester).

Grimsley, M. and Bhat, A. (1988) 'Health' in A. Bhat, R. Carr-Hill and S. Ohri (eds.) *Britain's Black Population: A New Perspective* 2nd edn. (Aldershot; Brookfield, Vt: Gower).

Griscom, J.L. (1987) 'On Healing the Nature/History Split' in B.H. Andolsen, C.E. Lindorf, M.D. Pellauer (eds.) *Women's Consciousness, Women's Conscience: A Reader in Feminist Ethics* (San Francisco: Harper and Row).

Gross, R.D. (1987) *Psychology: The Science of Mind and Behaviour* (London: Edward Arnold).

Guillaumin, C. (1972) *L'Ideologie Raciste:Genese et Language Actuel* (The Hague: Mouton, cited in Seidel, 1988, p. 11).

Hardy, M. and Heyes, S. (1987) *Beginning Psychology* 3rd edn. (London: Weidenfeld and Nicolson).

Harris, V. (1991) 'Values of Social Work in the Context of British Society in Conflict with Racism' in (ed.) Northern Curriculum Development Project, *Setting the Context for Change* (London: CCETSW), pp. 128–52.

Hawkins, M.J. (1977) 'A Re-Examination of Durkheim's Theory of Human Nature' *The Sociological Review*, vol. 25, no. 2, New Series, May, pp. 229–51.

Hayek, F. (1988) *The Fatal Conceit: The Errors of Socialism* (ed.) W.W. Bartley III (London: Routledge).

Heather, N. (1976) *Radical Perspectives in Psychology* (London: Methuen).

Heelas, P. (1991) 'Reforming the Self: Enterprise and the characters of Thatcherism' in R. Keat and N. Abercrombie (eds.) *Enterprise Culture* (London: Routledge), pp. 72–92.

Heelas, P. and Morris, P. (1992) 'Enterprise Culture: its Values and Value' in P. Heelas and P. Morris (eds.) *The Values of the Enterprise Culture* (London: Routledge), pp. 1–25.

Heelas, P. and Morris, P. (eds.) (1992) *The Values of the Enterprise Culture* (London: Routledge).

Heidegger, M. (1962) *Being and Time* (NY: Harper Brothers).

Heller, A. (1979) *On Instinct* (Assen, Neths: Van Gorcum).

Henderson, V. (1966) *The Nature of Nursing* (London: Collier-Macmillan).

Herbert, M. (1986) *Psychology For Social Workers* 2nd edn. (London: Macmillan).

Herrnstein, R. (1971) *IQ in the Meritocracy* (Boston: Little, Brown).

Hinde, R.A. (ed.) (1991) *Cooperation and Prosocial Behaviour* (Cambridge: Cambridge University Press).

Hinde, R.A. (1982) *Ethology* (London: Fontana).

Hirst, P. and Woolley, P. (1982) *Social Relations and Human Attributes* (London; NY: Tavistock).

Hobbes, T. (1968) *Leviathan* (1651) ed. C.B. Macpherson (Harmondsworth: Penguin).

Hodge, J. (1987) 'Women and the Hegelian State' in E. Kennedy and S. Mendus (eds.) *Women in Western Political Philosophy* (Brighton: Harvester Wheatsheaf).

Hodge, J.L., Struckmann, D.K. and Trost, L.D. (1975) *Cultural Bases of Racism and Group Oppression: An Examination of Traditional 'Western' Concepts, Values and Institutional Structures which Support Racism, Sexism and Elitism* (Berkeley, Calif: Two Riders Press).

Hofstadter, R. (1960) *Social Darwinism in American Thought* (Boston: Beacon Press).

Hoggett, P. (1992) *Partisans in an Uncertain World: The Psychoanalysis of Engagement* (London: FA Books).

Hollis, M. (1977) *Models of Man* (Cambridge: Cambridge University Press).

Hollis, F. and Woods, M.E. (1981) *Casework: A Psychosocial Therapy* (NY: Random House).

Holmstrom, N. (1984) 'A Marxist Theory of Women's Nature' *Ethics*, 94, 3, pp. 456–73.

Honderich, T. (1990) *Conservatism* (London: Hamish Hamilton).

Honneth, A. and Joas, H. (1988) *Social Action and Human Nature* (Cambridge: Cambridge University Press).

Horney, K. (1926) 'Flight from Womanhood' *International Journal of Psychoanalysis*, vol. 7, pp. 324–39.

Howe, D. (1987) *An Introduction to Social Work Theory* (Aldershot, Hants: Wildwood House).

Hughes, H.S. (1958) *Consciousness and Society: The Re-orientation of European Social Thought, 1890–1930* (NY: Vintage).

Husband, C. (1991) ' "Race", Conflictual Politics and Anti-Racist Social Work: Lessons from the Past for Action in the 90s' in NCDP (ed.) *Setting the Context for Change* (London: CCETSW), pp. 46–73.

Ignatieff, M. (1984) *The Needs of Strangers* (Chatto and Windus).

Illich, I. (1975) *Medical Nemesis: The Expropriation of Health* (London: Calder and Boyars).

Illustrated Manual of Nursing Practice (1991) (Springhouse, Pennsylvania: Springhouse Corporation).

IPPR (1992) *Understanding Local Needs* (London: IPPR).

Jaggar, A. (1983) *Feminist Politics and Human Nature* (NJ: Rowman and Allenheld).

James, W. (1880) *The Principles of Psychology* (NY: Henry Holt).

Jehu, D. (1967) *Learning Theory and Social Work* (London: Routledge and Kegan Paul).

Jensen, A. (1969) *Harvard Educational Review*, 39,1.

Jordan, W. (1991) *Divorce Among The Gulls: An Uncommon Look at Human Nature* (London: Abacus, 1992).

Jourard (1964) *The Transparent Self: Self-Disclosure and Well-Being* (Princeton, NJ: Van Nostrand).

Jung, C. (1933) *Modern Man in Search of a Soul* transl. W.S. Dell and C.F. Baynes (NY: Harcourt, Brace and World).

Jung, C. (1958) *The Undiscovered Self* trans. R.F.C. Hull (London: RKP, 1974 paperback edn.).

Kamin, L. (1974) *The Science and Politics of IQ* (Harmondsworth: Penguin).

Kaye, H. (1986) *The Social Meaning of Modern Biology* (New Haven, Connecticut: Yale University Press).

Keat, R. (1991) 'Consumer Sovereignty and the Integrity of Practices' in R. Keat and N. Abercrombie (eds.) (1991) *Enterprise Culture* (London: Routledge), pp. 216–30.

Keat, R. and Abercrombie, N. (eds.) (1991) *Enterprise Culture* (London: Routledge).

Kennedy, P. (1993) *Preparing For The Twenty-First Century* (NY, London: Harper Collins).

Kennedy, E. and Mendus, S. (eds.) (1987) *Women in Western Political Philosophy: Kant to Nietzsche* (Brighton: Wheatsheaf Books).

Kesey, K. (1962) *One Flew Over The Cuckoo's Nest* (London: Abacus).

Kingdom, J. (1992) *There's No Such Thing as Society?: Individualism and Community* (Milton Keynes: Open University Press).

Knowles, C. (1991) 'Afro-Caribbeans and Schizophrenia' *Journal of Social Policy*, vol. 20, no. 2, pp. 173–90.

Koestler, A. (1973) 'The Limits of Man and His Predicament' in J. Benthall (ed.) *The Limits of Human Nature* (London: Allen Lane), pp. 49–58.

Koestler, A. (1973) 'The Limits of Man and His Predicament' in J. Benthall (ed.) *The Limits of Human Nature* (London: Allen Lane), pp. 49–58.

Kohn, M. (1992) 'Sex and the Brain' *New Statesman and Society*, 27 November.

Kolakowski, L. (1968) *The Alienation of Reason: A History of Positivist Thought* (NY: Doubleday).

Kolakowski, L. (1981) *Main Currents of Marxism Vol. 3: The Breakdown* (Oxford: Oxford University Press).

Kretschmer, E. (1951) *Physique and Character* (NY: Humanities Press).

Kropotkin, P. (1902) *Mutual Aid: A Factor of Evolution* (London: Heinemann).

Laing, R.D. (1959) *The Divided Self* (London: Tavistock; NY: Pantheon; Harmondsworth: Penguin, 1965).

Laing, R.D. (1961) *Self and Others* (London: Tavistock).

Laing, R.D. (1967) *The Politics of Experience* (Harmondsworth: Penguin).

Laing, R.D. and Cooper, D.G. (1964) *Reason and Violence: A Decade of Sartre's Philosophy* (London: Tavistock; NY: Vintage, 1971).

Laing, R.D. and Esterson, A. (1964) *Sanity, Madness and the Family* (London: Tavistock).

Langan, M. (1990) 'Community Care in the 1990s: The Community Care White Paper: "Caring for People" ' *Critical Social Policy*, autumn, vol. 10, no. 2, pp. 58–70.

Langan, M. and Lee, P. (ed.) (1989) *Radical Social Work Today* (London: Unwin Hyman).

Lasch, C. (1979) *The Culture of Narcissism* (NY: Norton).

Leach, E. (1970) *Levi-Strauss* (London: Fontana).

Leach, E. (1982) *Social Anthropology* (London: Fontana).

Leach, E. (1978) *New Society*, 12 October.

Ledermann, E.K. (1984) *Mental Health and Human Conscience: The True and False Self* (Amersham: Avebury).

Lee, D. and Newby, H. (1983) *The Problem of Sociology* (London: Hutchinson).

Lee, P. and Raban, C. (1983) 'Welfare and Ideology' in M. Loney et al. (eds.) *Social Policy and Social Welfare* (Milton Keynes: Open University Press), pp. 18–32.

Lenin, V.I. (1908) *Materialism and Empiriocriticism* – Collected Works (Moscow: Foreign Languages Publishing House, 1962).

Leonard, P. (1984) *Personality and Ideology: Towards a Materialist Understanding* (London: Macmillan).

Levi, P. (1988) *The Drowned and the Saved* (NY: Simon and Schuster).

Levi-Strauss, C. (1962)*The Savage Mind* (Chicago: University of Chicago Press; London: Weidenfeld and Nicolson, 1966).

Levitas, R. (1985) 'New Right Utopias' *Radical Philosophy*, 39, spring, pp. 2–9.

Levitas, R. (1983) 'Feminism and Human Nature' in I. Forbes and S. Smith (eds.) *Politics and Human Nature* (London: Francis Pinter).

Lewis, J. (1974) *The Uniqueness of Man* (London: Lawrence and Wishart).

Lifton, R.J. (1967) *Thought Reform and the Psychology of Totalism* (Harmondsworth: Penguin).

Lipset, S.M. and Bendix, R. (1959) *Social Mobility in Industrial Society* (Calif: California University Press, 1959)

Littlewood, R. and Lipsedge, M. (1989) *Aliens and Alienists: Ethnic Minorities and Psychiatry* (Harmondsworth: Penguin).

Littlewood, R. and Cross, S. (1980) 'Ethnic Minorities and Psychiatric Services' in *Sociology of Health and Illness*, vol. 2, no. 2, pp. 194–201.

Lloyd, G. (1983) 'Masters, Slaves and Others' *Radical Philosophy*, no. 34, spring.

Lloyd, G. (1984) *The Man of Reason* 2nd edn. 1993 (London: Methuen).

Lombroso, C. (1911) *Crime, Its Causes and Remedies* (Boston: Little, Brown).

Lombroso, C. and Ferrero, W. (1895) 'The Criminal as a Born Criminal Type' in E. Rubington and M.S. Weinberg (eds.) *The Study of Social Problems: Six Perspectives* 4th edn. (Oxford: Oxford University Press), pp. 23–7.

Loney, M., Bocock, R., Clarke, J., Cochrane, A., Graham, P. and Wilson, M. (eds.) (1991) *The State or the Market: Politics and Welfare in Contemporary Britain* 2nd edn. (London: Sage).

Loney, M., Boswell, D. and Clarke, J. (eds.) (1983) *Social Policy and Social Welfare* (Milton Keynes: Open University Press).

Lorenz, K. (1940) 'Angew. Psychol. Characterunde' 59, 2, cited in L. Eisenberg, 'The "Human" Nature of Human Nature' in

A.L. Caplan (ed.) *The Sociobiology Debate* (NY: Harper and Row, 1978), p. 167.

Lorenz, K. (1966) *On Aggression* (NY: Harcourt, Brace and World; London: Methuen).

Lorenz, K. (1971) 'Part and Parcel in Animal and Human Societies' in L. Stevenson (ed.) (1981) *The Study of Human Nature: Readings* (Oxford: Oxford University Press).

Lorenz, K. (1973) *Civilised Man's Eight Deadly Sins* (London: Methuen).

Luker, K. and Orr, J. (eds.) (1985) *Health Visiting* (Oxford: Blackwell Scientific Publications).

Lukes, S. (1967) 'Alienation and Anomie' in P. Laslett and W.G. Runciman (eds.) *Philosophy, Politics and Society* (Oxford: Blackwell), pp. 134–56.

Lumsden, C.J. and Wilson, E.O. (1981) *Genes, Mind and Culture: The Coevolutionary Process* (Cambridge, Mass: Harvard University Press).

MacCormack, C. (1980) 'Nature, Culture and Gender: A Critique' in C. MacCormack and M. Strathern (eds.) *Nature, Culture and Gender* (Cambridge, NY: Cambridge University Press).

MacCormack, C. and Strathern, M. (eds.) (1980) *Nature, Culture and Gender* (Cambridge; NY: Cambridge University Press).

Macey, M. (1992) 'Racism in Europe: Trends and Comparisons' paper presented to *Social Work and Social Rights: European Perspectives* conference, University of Bradford, 17–19 September.

MacIntyre, A. (1966) *A Short History of Ethics* (NY; Oxford: Oxford University Press).

MacIntyre, A. (1981)*After Virtue: A Study in Moral Theory* (London: Duckworth).

Maclean, M. and Groves, D. (eds.) (1991) *Women's Issues in Social Policy* (London: Routledge).

Macpherson, C.B. (1962) *The Political Theory of Possessive Individualism* (Oxford: Oxford University Press).

Magill, K. (1991) 'Conservatism Analysed: Review of T. Honderich, "Conservatism" ' in *Radical Philosophy*, 59, autumn.

Mairet, P. (1948) 'Introduction' to J-P. Sartre, *Existentialism and Humanism* (London: Methuen).

Marcuse, H. (1955) *Eros and Civilization* (Boston: Beacon Press; London: Allen Lane Press, 1964).

Marcuse, H. (1964) *One Dimensional Man* (Boston: Beacon Press).

Marcuse, H. (1968) *Negations: Essays in Critical Theory* (Boston: Beacon Press).

Marcuse, H. (1972) *Studies in Critical Philosophy* (London: New Left Books).

Marx, K. (1844) *Economic and Philosophical Manuscripts* in T. Bottomore (ed.) *Karl Marx: Early Writings* (NY: McGraw-Hill, 1968).

Marx, K. and Engels, F. (1868–94) *Capital* – Collected Works (Moscow: Progress Publishers; London: Lawrence and Wishart; NY: International Publishers).

Marx, K. and Engels, F. (1947) *German Ideology* (ed.) R. Pascall (NY: International Publishers).

Maslow, A. (1968) *Towards a Psychology of Being* 2nd edn. (London: Van Nostrand).

Maslow, A. (1972) *The Farther Reaches of Human Nature* (NY: The Viking Press).

Masson, J. (1984) *The Assault on Truth: Freud and Child Sexual Abuse* (NY: Farrar, Straus and Giroux; London: Fontana, 1992).

Masson, J. (1988) *Against Therapy* (NY: Atheneum; London: Fontana, 1990).

May, R. (1953) *Man's Search For Himself* (NY: Norton; Harmondsworth: Penguin).

May, R. (1992) *The Art of Counselling* revd edn. (London: Souvenir Books; NY: Gardener Press, 1989).

McCaugherty, D. (1992) 'Theoretical Shift' in *Nursing Times*, 7 October, vol. 88, no. 41, p. 66.

McFague, S. (1982) *Metaphorical Theology* (London: SCM Press).

McLuhan, M. (1964) *Understanding Media: The Extensions of Man* (London: RKP).

McMillan, C. (1982) *Women, Reason and Nature* (Oxford: Blackwell).

Mead, G.H. (1934; 1962) *Mind, Self and Society: From the Standpoint of a Social Behaviourist* (Chicago; London: University of Chicago Press).

Mead, M. (1928) *Coming of Age in Samoa* (Harmondsworth: Penguin, 1963).

Mercer, K. (1986) 'Racism and Transcultural Psychiatry' in P. Miller and N. Rose (eds.) *The Power of Psychiatry* (Oxford: Blackwell), pp. 112–42.

Merton, R. (1957) *Social Theory and Social Structure* revd ed. (Glencoe: The Free Press).

Mestrovic, S.G. (1991) *The Coming Fin de Siecle: An Application of Durkheim's Sociology to Modernity and Post-Modernism* (London: Routledge).

Midgley, M. (1978) *Beast and Man* (Hassocks, Sussex: Harvester Press).

Miles, A. (1991) *Women, Health and Medicine* (Milton Keynes: Open University Press).

Miles, I. (1979) 'Social Forecasting: Predicting the Future or Making History?' in J. Irvine, I. Miles and J. Evans (eds.) *Demystifying Social Statistics* (London: Pluto Press).

Miles, R. (1989) *Racism* (London: Routledge).

Milgram, S. (1974) *Obedience to Authority: An Experimental View* (NY: Harper and Row; London: Tavistock, 1976).

Millett, K. (1970) *Sexual Politics* (NY: Doubleday; London: Abacus, 1972).

Mitchell, J. (1974) *Psychoanalysis and Feminism* (NY: Vintage; London: Penguin).

Mommsen, W. (1974) *The Age of Bureaucracy: Perspectives on the Political Sociology of Max Weber* (Oxford: Blackwell).

Mommsen, W. (1987) 'Personal Conduct and Societal Change: Towards a Reconstruction of Max Weber's Concept of History' in S. Whimster and S. Lash (eds.) *Max Weber, Rationality and Modernity* (London: Allen and Unwin).

Montagu, A. (ed.) (1968) *Man and Aggression* (NY; London: Oxford University Press, 2nd edn. 1972).

Moore, B. (1978) *Injustice: The Social Bases of Obedience and Revolt* (London: Macmillan).

Morris, B. (1991) *Western Conceptions of the Individual* (Oxford: Berg).

Morris, D. (1968) *The Naked Ape* (London: Corgi).

Morris, D. (1971) *The Human Zoo* (London: Corgi).

Morris, D. and Marsh, P. (1988) *Tribes* (London: Pyramid Books).

Morris, P. (1991) 'Freeing The Spirit of Enterprise: The Genesis and Development of the Concept of Enterprise Culture' in R. Keat and N. Abercrombie (eds.) (1991) *Enterprise Culture* (London: Routledge).

Mosse, G.L. (1978) *Toward the Final Solution: A History of European Racism* (London: Dent).

Munn (1986) *The Fame of Gawa: A Symbolic Study of Value Transformation in a Massim (Papua New Guinea) Society* (Cambridge: Cambridge University Press) cited in M. Strathern (1992) *After Nature: English Kinship in the Late Twentieth Century* (Cambridge: Cambridge University Press).

Naidoo, J. (1986) 'Limits to Individualism' in S. Rodmell and A. Watt (eds.) *The Politics of Health Education: Raising the Issues* (London: RKP), pp. 17–37.

Nash, P. (1968) *Models of Man* (NY: Wiley).

Neuman, B. (1982) *The Neuman Systems Model* (NY: Appleton Century Croft).

Noble, D. (1993) 'Unravelling the Meaning of Life' *Observer*, 1 August, p. 56.

Nye, R. (1992) *Three Psychologies: Perspectives from Freud, Skinner, and Rogers* 4th edn. (Belmont, Calif: Brooks Cole).

O'Brien, M. (1989) *Reproducing the World: Essays in Feminist Theory* (Boulder: Westview Press).

Oakley, A. (1972) *Sex, Gender and Society* (London: Temple Smith).

Okin, S.M. (1980) *Women in Western Political Thought* (London: Virago).

Okin, S.M. (1991) 'On Plato' in M.L. Shanley and C. Pateman (eds.) *Feminist Interpretation and Political Theory* (Oxford: Polity Press).

Ortner, S. (1974) 'Is Female to Male as Nature is to Culture?' in M. Rosaldo and L. Lamphere (eds.) *Women, Culture and Society* (Stanford: Stanford University Press), pp. 67–87.

Owen, R. (1813) *A New View of Society* and *Report to the County of Lanark*, V.A.C. Gatrell (ed.) (1970 edn.) (1813/4) (Harmondsworth: Penguin).

Parker, I. (1989) *The Crisis in Social Psychology: And How To End It* (London: Routledge).

Pavlov, I.P. (1927) *Conditioned Reflexes* (Oxford: Oxford University Press).

Payne, M. (1991) *Modern Social Work Theory: A Critical Introduction* (London: Macmillan).

Peacocke, A. (1986) *God and the New Biology* (London: Dent).

Pearson, A. and Vaughan B. (1986) *Nursing Models For Practice* (Oxford: Heinemann).

Pearson, G., Treseder, J. and Yelloly, M. (eds.) (1988) *Social Work and the Legacy of Freud: Psychoanalysis and its Uses* (London: Macmillan).

Pearson, M. (1986) 'Racist Notions of Ethnicity and Culture in Health Education' in S. Rodmell and A. Watt (eds.) *The Politics of Health Education: Raising The Issues* (London: RKP), pp. 38–56.

Phillipson, C. (1982) *Capitalism and the Construction of Old Age* (London: Macmillan).

Philp, M. (1985) 'Michel Foucault' in Q. Skinner (ed.) *The Return of Grand Theory in the Human Sciences* (Cambridge: Cambridge University Press).

Philpot, T. (1986) *Social Work: A Christian Perspective* (London: Lion).

Piaget, J. (1971) *Structuralism* (London: RKP).

Pilgrim, J. (1992) 'Change or Acceptance: Human Nature and the Sociological Perspective' in *The Raven: Anarchist Quarterly*, 19, vol. 5, no. 3, July–September, pp. 41–8.

Plant, R. (1974) *Community and Ideology: An Essay in Applied Social Philosophy* (London: RKP).

Plant, R. (1992) 'Enterprise in Its Place: The Moral Limits of Markets' in P. Heelas and P. Morris (eds.) (1992) *The Values of the Enterprise Culture* (London: Routledge), pp. 85–99.

Platt, A. (1989) 'The Child Savers: The Invention of Delinquency' in E. Rubington and W.S. Weinberg (eds.) *The Study of Social*

Problems: Six Perspectives 4th edn. (Oxford: Oxford University Press).

Plumwood, V. (1988) 'Woman, Humanity and Nature' *Radical Philosophy*, 48, spring.

Plumwood, V. (1989) 'Do We Need a Sex/Gender Distinction?' *Radical Philosophy*, 51, spring.

Rabinow, P. (ed.) (1984) *The Foucault Reader: An Introduction to Foucault's Thought* (Harmondsworth: Penguin; NY: Random House).

Rack, P. (1982) *Race, Culture and Mental Disorder* (London: Tavistock).

Radford, T. (1993) 'Your Mother Should Know' *Guardian*, 17 July, p. 23.

Reich, W. (1942) *The Function of the Orgasm* (NY: Noonday Press; London: Panther Press, 1970).

Reuther, R. (1975) *New Woman/New Earth* (NY: Seabury Press).

Reynolds, V. (1973) 'Man Also Behaves' in J. Benthall (ed.) *The Limits of Human Nature* (London: Allen Lane Press), pp. 143–57.

Reynolds, V. (1976) *The Biology of Human Action* 2nd edn. 1980 (Oxford: W.H. Freeman).

Rich, A. (1976) *Of Woman Born: Motherhood as Experience and Institution* (NY: W.W. Norton).

Richardson, K. and Spears, D. (eds.) (1972) *Race, Culture and Intelligence* (Harmondsworth: Penguin).

Robertson, J. (1983) *The Sane Alternative : A Choice of Futures* 2nd edn. (London; Oxfordshire: James Robertson).

Rocheron, Y. (1991) 'The Asian Mother and Baby Campaign: The Construction of Ethnic Minorities' Health Needs' in M. Loney et al. (eds.) *The State or the Market* 2nd edn. (London: Sage).

Rodmell, S. and Watt, A. (eds.) (1986) *The Politics of Health Education: Raising The Issues* (London: RKP).

Rogers, C. (1961) *On Becoming a Person: A Therapist's View of Psychotherapy* (London: Constable).

Rorty, R. (1982) *The Consequences of Pragmatism* (Minneapolis: University of Minnesota Press).

Rose, N. (1992) 'Governing the Enterprising Self' in P. Heelas and P. Morris (eds.) (1992) *The Values of the Enterprise Culture* (London: Routledge), pp. 141–64.

Rose, S., Hambley, J. and Haywood, J. (1973) 'Science, Racism and Ideology' in R. Miliband and J. Saville (eds.) *The Socialist Register* (London: Merlin Press), pp. 235–60.

Rose, S., Lewontin, R.C. and Kamin, L.J. (1984) *Not in Our Genes: Biology, Ideology and Human Nature* (Harmondsworth: Penguin).

Rose, S. and Rose, H. (1986) 'Less than Human Nature: Biology and the New Right' *Race and Class*, vol. XXVII, no. 3.

Rosenau, P.M. (1992) *Post-Modernism and the Social Sciences: Insights, Inroads, and Intrusions* (NJ: Princeton University Press).

Royce, J.R. and Mos, L.P. (eds.) (1981) *Humanistic Psychology: Concepts and Criticisms* (NY; London: Plenum Press).

Royle, J.A. and Walsh, M. (eds.) (1992) *Watson's Medical-Surgical Nursing and Related Physiology* 4th edn. (London: Bailliere-Tindall).

Rubington, E. and Weinberg, M.S. (eds.) (1989) *The Study of Social Problems: Six Perspectives* 4th edn. (NY; Oxford: Oxford University Press).

Ruddock, R. (ed.) (1972) *Six Approaches to the Person* (London: RKP).

Runciman (ed.) *Philosophy, Politics and Society* 3rd series (Oxford: Blackwell).

Ruse, M. (1985) *Sociobiology: Sense or Nonsense?* 2nd edn. (Dordrecht: D. Reidel Publishing Co.).

Ryan, J. and Thomas, F. (1987) *The Politics of Mental Handicap* 2nd edn. (London: Free Association Books).

Sahlins, M. (1976) *The Use and Abuse of Biology* (Ann Arbor: University of Michigan Press).

Sandel, M. (1982) *Liberalism and the Limits of Justice* (Cambridge: Cambridge University Press).

Sartre, J-P. (1943) *Being and Nothingness* trans. H.E. Barnes (London: Methuen, 1969).

Sartre, J-P. (1948) *Anti-Semite and Jew* trans. G.J. Becker (NY: Schocken Books).

Sartre, J-P. (1950) *Baudelaire* (London: Tavistock).

Sartre, J-P. (1963) *Saint Genet: Actor and Martyr* trans. B. Frechtman (NY: Braziller).

Sartre, J-P. (1976) *Critique of Dialectical Reason* trans. A. Sheridan-Smith (London: New Left Books).

Sarup, M. (1993) *An Introductory Guide to Post-Structuralism and Post-Modernism* 2nd edn. (Hemel Hempstead: Harvester Press).

Sashidharan, S. (1989) 'Schizophrenia – or Just Black?' in *Community Care*, no. 783, pp. 14–15.

Sattaur, O. (1988) 'The New Genetics' *New Scientist*, 3 December, reprinted in Richard Fifield (ed.) *The New Scientist: Inside Science: The Guide to Science Today* (Harmondsworth: Penguin, 1992), pp. 249–62.

Saxenhouse, A. (1991) 'On Aristotle' in M.L. Shanley and C. Pateman (eds.) *Feminist Interpretations and Political Theory* (Oxford: Polity Press).

Sayers, J. (1982) *Biological Politics: Feminist and Anti-feminist Perspectives* (London; NY: Tavistock).

Sayers, J. (1988) 'Feminism, Social Work and Psychoanalysis' in

G. Pearson et al. (eds.) (1988) *Social Work and the Legacy of Freud: Psychoanalysis and its Uses* (London: Macmillan), pp. 97–113.

Sayers, S. (1992) 'The Human Impact of the Market' in P. Heelas and P. Morris (eds.) (1992) *The Values of the Enterprise Culture* (London: Routledge), pp. 120–38.

Scheff, T.J. (1966) *Being Mentally Ill: A Sociological Theory* (Chicago: Aldine Press).

Scruton, R. (1984) *The Meaning of Conservatism* (London: Macmillan, cited in Gordon and Klug, 1986, p. 14).

Sedgwick, P. (1982) *Psychopolitics* (London: Pluto Press).

Seidel, G. (1986) *The Holocaust Denial: Antisemitism, Racism and the New Right* (Leeds: Beyond The Pale Collective).

Seidel, G. (1988a) 'Right-wing Discourse and Power: Exclusions and Resistance' in G. Seidel (ed.) *The Nature of the Right: A Feminist Analysis of Order Patterns* (Amsterdam and Philadelphia: John Benjaminus).

Seidel, G. (ed.) (1988b) *The Nature of the Right* (Amsterdam and Philadelphia: John Benjaminus).

Shanley, M. and Pateman, C. (eds.) (1991) *Feminist Interpretation and Political Theory* (Oxford: Polity Press).

Shaw, J.W. (1972) 'The Personal Imperative: A Study of the Evidence for Self-actualisation' in R. Ruddock (ed.) *Six Approaches to the Person* (London: RKP).

Sheldon, B. (1982) *Behaviour Modification* (London: Tavistock).

Shotter, J. (1974) *Images of Man in Psychological Research* (London: Methuen).

Sivandan, A. (1992) 'The Hydra-Headed Monster of Germany' *New Statesman and Society*, 4 December.

Skellington, R. and Morris, P. (1992) *'Race' in Britain Today* (London: Sage).

Skinner, B.F. (1948) *Walden Two* (London; NY: Macmillan).

Skinner, B.F. (1953) *Science and Human Behaviour* (NY: Macmillan).

Skinner, B.F. (1957) *Verbal Behaviour* (NY: Appleton-Century).

Skinner, B.F. (1971) *Beyond Freedom and Dignity* (NY: Bantam; London: Penguin, 1973).

Small, J. (1989) 'Towards a Black Perspective in Social Work: A Transcultural Exploration' in M. Langan and P. Lee (eds.) *Radical Social Work Today* (London: Unwin Hyman).

Smith, D. (1988) *The Chicago School: A Liberal Critique of Capitalism* (London: Macmillan)

Smithies, B. and Fiddick, P. (1969) *Enoch Powell on Immigration* (London: Sphere Books).

Sociobiology Study Group of Science for the People (1978) 'Sociobiology – Another Biological Determinism' in A. Caplan (ed.) *The Sociobiology Debate* (New York: Harper and Row), pp. 280–90.

Solomos, J. (1989) *Race and Racism in Contemporary Britain* (London: Macmillan; 2nd edn., 1993).

Soper, K. (1981) *On Human Needs* (Brighton: Harvester Press).

Spelman, E.V. (1991) 'Simone de Beauvoir and Women: Just Who Does She Think "We" Is?' in M. Shanley and C. Pateman (eds.) *Feminist Interpretation and Political Theory* (Oxford: Polity Press).

Stanton Rogers, W. (1971) *Explaining Health and Illness* (Hemel Hempstead: Harvester Wheatsheaf).

Starhawk (1979) *The Spiral Dance: A Rebirth of the Ancient Religion of the Great Goddess* (San Francisco: Harper and Row).

Staub, E. (1989) *The Roots of Evil: The Origins of Genocide and Other Group Violence* (Cambridge: Cambridge University Press).

Stefano, C.D. (1991) 'Masculine Marx' in M.L. Shanley and C. Pateman (eds.) *Feminist Interpretations and Political Theory* (Oxford: Polity Press).

Steiner, G. (1967) *Language and Silence* (London: Faber and Faber).

Steiner, G. (1971) *In Bluebeard's Castle* (London: Faber).

Stent, G.S. (1978) *Paradoxes of Progress* (San Francisco: W.H. Freeman).

Stevens, R. (1990) 'Evolutionary Origins of Identity' in J. Anderson and M. Ricci (eds.) *Society and Social Science: A Reader* (Milton Keynes: Open University Press), pp. 150–61.

Stevenson, L. (ed.) (1981) *The Study of Human Nature: Readings* (Oxford: Oxford University Press).

Stevenson, L. (1987) *Seven Theories of Human Nature* 2nd edn. (NY: Oxford University Press).

Stoesz, D. and Midgley, J. (1991) 'The Radical Right and the Welfare State' in H. Glennester and J. Midgley (eds.) *The Radical Right and the Welfare State* (Hemel Hempstead: Harvester Wheatsheaf), pp. 24–42.

Strathern, M. (1992) *After Nature: English Kinship in the Late Twentieth Century* (Cambridge: Cambridge University Press).

Sullivan, M. (1992) *The Politics of Social Policy* (Hemel Hempstead: Harvester Wheatsheaf).

Sutton, C. (1979) *Psychology for Social Workers and Counsellors: An Introduction* (Routledge and Kegan Paul).

Swingewood, A. (1991) *A History of Sociological Thought* 2nd edn. (London: Macmillan).

Sydie, R. (1987) *Natural Women: Cultured Men: A Feminist Perspective on Sociological Theory* (Milton Keynes: Open University Press; Ontario: Methuen).

Szasz, T. (1967) 'The Myth of Mental Illness' in T.J. Scheff (ed.) *Mental Illness and Social Processes* (NY, London: Harper and Row), pp. 242–53.

Szasz, T. (1970) *Ideology and Insanity: Essays on the Psychiatric Dehumanization of Man* (Harmondsworth: Penguin, 1974).

Taylor, C. (1969) 'Neutrality in Political Science' in P. Laslett and W. Runciman (eds.) *Philosophy, Politics and Society*, second series (Oxford: Blackwell), pp. 25–57.

Taylor, C. (1985a) *Human Agency and Language: Philosophical Papers 1* (Cambridge: Cambridge University Press).

Taylor, C. (1985b) *Philosophy and the Human Sciences: Philosophical Papers 2* (Cambridge: Cambridge University Press).

Taylor, C. (1989) *Sources of the Self: The Making of the Modern Identity* (Cambridge: Cambridge University Press).

Taylor, C. (1992) *The Ethics of Authenticity* (Cambridge, Mass; London: Harvard University Press).

Taylor, M. (1990) 'Fantasy or Reality? The Problem with Psychoanalytic Interpretation in Psychotherapy with Women' in E. Burman (ed.) *Feminists and Psychological Practice* (London: Sage).

Thomson, G. (1987) *Needs* (London: RKP).

Thorndike, E.L. (1911) *The Fundamentals of Learning* (NY: College Bureau of Publications).

Todorov, T. (1993) *On Human Diversity: Nationalism, Racism, and Exoticism in French Thought* trans. C. Porter (Cambridge, Mass; London: Harvard University Press).

Toffler, A. (1970) *Future Shock* (NY: Random House).

Tomlinson, J. (1990) *Hayek and the Market* (London: Pluto Press).

Tong, R. (1989) *Feminist Thought* (London: Routledge).

Touraine, A. (1988) *Return of the Actor: A Social Theory in Postindustrial Society* (Minneapolis: University of Minnesota Press).

Trigg, R. (1982) *The Shaping of Man: Philosophical Aspects of Sociobiology* (Oxford: Blackwell).

Trigg, R. (1985) *Understanding Social Science* (Oxford: Blackwell).

Trigg, R. (1988) *Ideas of Human Nature* (Oxford: Basil Blackwell).

Turner, B. (1991) 'Recent Developments in the Theory of the Body' in M. Featherstone, M. Hepworth and B.S. Turner (eds.) *The Body: Social Processes and Cultural Theory* (London: Sage).

Turner, B.S. (1987) *Medical Power and Social Knowledge* (London: Sage).

Tyne, A. (1991) 'Normalisation: From Theory to Practice' in H. Brown and H. Smith (eds.) *Normalisation: A Reader For The Nineties* (London: Routledge), pp. 100–11.

Vygotsky, L.S. (1962) *Thought and Language* (Cambridge, Mass: MIT Press).

Watson, J. (1930) 'Behaviorism' in R.W. Marks (ed.) *Great Ideas in Psychology* (London; NY: Bantam Matrix, 1966), pp. 416, 419.

Watson, J. (1930) *Behaviorism* 2nd edn. (NY: Norton).

Weber, M. (1958; 1920) *The Protestant Ethic and the Spirit of Capitalism,* trans. T. Parsons (NY: Scribner).

Weber, M. (1947) *The Theory of Social and Economic Organisation* trans. A.M. Henderson and T. Parsons (eds.) (NY: The Free Press; London: Collier-Macmillan, 1964).

Weeks, J. (1991) *Against Nature: Essays on History, Sexuality and Identity* (London: Rivers Oram Press).

Weiner, A. (1976) *Women of Value, Men of Renown: New Perspectives in Trobriand Exchange* (Austin: University of Texas Press), cited in M. Strathern (1992) *After Nature: English Kinship in the Late Twentieth Century* (Cambridge: Cambridge University Press).

Weldon, F. (1992) Lecture: Psychoanalysis and Literature, *Cheltenham Festival of Literature* (Cheltenham).

Westergaard, J. (1992) 'About and Beyond the "Underclass": Some Notes on Influences of Social Climate on British Sociology Today: BSA Presidential Address' *Sociology,* vol. 26, no. 4, November.

WHO (1946) *Constitution* (Geneva: World Health Organisation).

Wicks, M. (1991) 'Family Matters and Public Policy' in M. Loney et al. (eds.) (1991) *The State or the Market: Politics and Welfare in Contemporary Britain* 2nd edn. (London: Sage), pp. 169–83.

Williams, F. (1989) *Social Policy: A Critical Introduction* (Cambridge: Polity Press).

Williams, J.G. (1991) *The Bible, Violence, and the Sacred: Liberation from the Myth of Sanctioned Violence* (London: Harper).

Williams, R. (1974) 'Social Darwinism' in J. Benthall (ed.) *The Limits of Human Nature* (London: Allen Lane).

Wilson, E. (1977) *Women and the Welfare State* (London: Tavistock).

Wilson, E. (1983) 'Feminism and Social Policy' in M. Loney et al. (eds.) *Social Policy and Social Welfare* (Milton Keynes: Open University Press).

Wilson, E.O. (1975) *Sociobiology: The New Synthesis* (Cambridge, Mass: Harvard University Press).

Wilson, E.O. (1978) *Human Nature* (Cambridge, Mass: Harvard University Press).

Wilson, E.O. (1980) *Sociobiology* abridged edn. (Cambridge, Mass: Harvard University Press).

Winnicott, D. (1988) *Human Nature* (London: Free Association Books).

Wittig, M. (1979) 'One is Not Born a Woman' *Proceedings of the Second Sex Conference* (NY: New York Institute for the Humanities).

Wolfensberger, W. (1972) *The Principle of Normalisation in Human Services* (Toronto: National Institute on Mental Retardation).

Wolfensberger, W. (1980) 'The Definition of Normalisation: Update, Problems, Disagreements and Misunderstandings' in R.J. Flynn and K.E. Nitsch (eds.) *Normalisation, Social Integration and Community Service* (Baltimore: University Park Press).

Wolff, K.H. (ed.) (1964) *Emile Durkheim: Essays in Sociology and Philosophy* (NY: Harper and Row).

Wootton, B. (1959) *Social Science and Social Pathology* (London: Allen and Unwin, 2nd edn. 1963).

Index